The True Story of the Empress Dowager

An Insider's Account

Princess Der Ling

Originally published as
"Old Buddha"

Copyright 2015, Soul Care Publishing. All rights reserved. This book may not be reproduced or transmitted in any manner whatsoever, transmitted electronically, or distributed by any means without the written permission of the publisher.

Library and Archives Canada Cataloguing in Publication

Der Ling, Princess, author
 The true story of the Empress Dowager : an insider's account / Princess Der Ling.

Reprint. Originally published under title: Old Buddha: New York : Dodd, Mead & Co., 1929.
Issued in print and electronic formats.

1. Cixi, Empress dowager of China, 1835-1908. 2. Empresses-- China-- Biography. 3. China--History--Guangxu, 1875-1908. 4. China--Court and courtiers. I. Der Ling, Princess. Old Buddha. II. Title.

DS764.23.T93D37 2015   951.035092
                         C2015-903590-2
                         C2015-903591-0

Published by Soul Care Publishing, Vancouver, Canada

DEDICATED
TO THE MEMORY OF
HER MAJESTY
TZU HSI
THE OLD BUDDHA
WHO LOVED ME AND WHOM
I LOVED

Table of Contents

A WORD OF EXPLANATION i
PRINCESS DER LING iii
I. IN A MANCHU GARDEN.. 1
II. THE HUMBLE COBBLER.. 10
III. HSIEN FENG TAKES A SECONDARY WIFE 17
IV. THE EMPEROR COMMANDS 25
V. THE LITTLE EUNUCH.. 32
V. TINY FINGERS 37
VII. LADY MEI.. 45
VIII. TWO WOMEN 51
IX. ALL HONOR TO THE HEIR 57
X. THE IMPERIAL BANQUET 62
XI. JEHOL 69
XII. THE MARCH OF THE DEAD.. 80
XIII. OUT OF THE DARKNESS 84
XIV. THE WAY OF THE TRAITOR 92
XV. SUCCESSOR TO SU SHUN.. 100
XVI. THE MARRIAGE 105
XVII. TUNG CHIH 110
XVIII. THE STAGE OE EMPERORS.................................... 115
XIX. THE JOURNEY OF AN TEH HAI................................ 120
XX. THE NEW CHIEF EUNUCH.. 133
XXI. THE DEATH OF TUNG CHIH 139
XXII. THE CORONATION 143
XXIII. THE ILL-FATED WEDDING 149
XXIV. THE RETIREMENT OF OLD BUDDHA 152
XXV. THE HAIRLESS MAN.. 157

XXVI. THE STRATEGY OF KWANG HSU 163
XXVII. THE COUP D'ETAT 174
XXVIII. THE PRISONER OF YING TAI 179
XXIX. THE PEARL CONCUBINE 184
XXX. THE HATRED OF OLD BUDDHA 187
XXXI. THE CROWN PRINCE 195
XXXII. EVOLUTION OF THE BEAST 198
XXXIII. THE SNARLING OF THE BEAST 203
XXXIV. OMINOUS WHISPERS 211
XXXV. LOOSING OF THE DRAGON 215
XXXVI. THE FLIGHT OF OLD BUDDHA 222
XXXVII. A CITY IN FLAMES 229
XXXVIII. MARCHING FEET 233
XXXIX. OLD BUDDHA'S RETURN 238
XL. A CHILD IS BORN 247
XLI. TZU HSI IS PREOCCUPIED 250
XLII. THREE YEARS OF RESPITE 254
XLIII. THE DEATH OF KUANG HSU 258
XLIV. THE OMINOUS PARALLEL 264
XLV. VIA DOLOROSA 267
XLVI. THE CORONATION—AND
THE FATEFUL WORDS 271
XLVII THE PASSING OF TZU HSI 274
XLVIII. THE COURT OF UNHAPPINESS 278
XLIX. PU YI PASSES 285
L. CONCLUSION 287

A WORD OF EXPLANATION

Most of the stories which have been woven around the life of Her Majesty, Tzu Hsi, known to the world as the Old Buddha and the Empress Dowager Cixi, emanate from tea houses in Peking and other cities, where folk who knew nothing whatever about her gathered and gossiped. I am very much afraid that many writers of works which pass as history, that part of China's history dealing with the regime of Old Buddha, went to people such as these as authority for the preposterous stories which have been told as truth.

For almost three years I was a favorite of Her Majesty, and I say this without egotism, in an attempt to show my own right to tell the story I have told here. Old Buddha made me her confidante on many occasions, and this hook is based upon what she herself told me. I have merely tried to put it together, a fairly connected whole.

Scandalmongers have said that neither An Teh Hai nor Li Lien Ying was a eunuch, that Old Buddha was mistress to each in turn, that she bore a son to the former. I merely content myself by saying that it was impossible for a false eunuch to escape detection at court, because every eunuch was required to pass an entrance examination which made fraud impossible. I knew the reputed "son" of An Teh Hai and Old Buddha.

Even folk at court, unless admitted to the inner sanctum of Old Buddha's confidence, knew little or nothing about her. The gossip at court was as unreliable as the gossip of the tea houses. China has always been a prolific creator of fanciful stories, especially concerning those who were highly placed.

I knew and talked with most of the characters I have mentioned in this story. I knew Kang Yu-Wei, Li Lien Ying, Yung Lu, Yuan Shih Kai, Kwang Hsu, the Young Empress (called Lung Yu after the death of Old Buddha), Prince Tuan, the four concubines of Tung Chih (whom I visited in that part of the Forbidden City allotted them until they died), Pu Yi as a child, the sister of the Pearl Concubine, Chang Teh, Prince Kung—and Her Majesty, the Old Buddha. I knew every important member of the court who was alive in 1903-5. I knew and liked Kwang Hsu immensely. Had I

i

been less a child, I might have been able to influence Old Buddha to many needed reforms, for she was always willing to listen to me.

That I was able to do so little is one of the chief regrets of my life.

I am not unmindful that, while other writers have been too far removed from Old Buddha to do her justice, even to tell the truth about her, I myself may have been too close—though I have tried to keep personal bias from entering too obviously into this story.

In the hope of creating what I wish to have regarded as more or less of a personal narrative, a connected story based upon reminiscences—hearsay if you will—I have deliberately used as few dates as possible, and have tried to make my story clear without the use of footnotes.

When Tung Chih is referred to by that name, it is to be understood that Tung Chih is the name of his reign, rather than his personal or family name. The same applies to Kwang Hsu. Hsuan Tung is the reign of Pu Yi. Pu Yi never actually reigned as Emperor, the Young Empress being Empress Dowager from the time of his coronation to the downfall of the Dynasty.

In telling of the love of Yung Lu for Old Buddha I have adhered strictly to the truth, striving only to make a human, readable narrative.

I sincerely hope I have succeeded.

LING.

LOS Angeles, California, March 1, 1928.

PRINCESS DER LING

Princess Der Ling needs no introduction to the reading public. The continued success of her Two Years in the Forbidden City, first published in 1911, assures me that this is so.

I am honored in the acquaintanceship and, I sincerely hope, the friendship of Princess Der Ling, whom I first met in Tientsin, China, September 11, 1927.

I have read the manuscript of Old Buddha. I liked it.

But oddly enough, after the reading, it is not of "Old Buddha" I think, as I seek for words to express my appreciation of this latest work of Princess Der Ling.

Instead, I close my eyes, and my fancy goes back to an unforgettable afternoon when, with Princess Der Ling and a small party of friends, I paid a visit to the Summer Palace, toward the Western Hills. On the following day I was to accompany her through the Forbidden City, that portion of the sacred place of the Manchus which even today is unknown to the foreigner; but though I enjoyed the visit to the Forbidden City, realizing myself especially privileged, that visit does not stand out in memory as does the visit to the Summer Palace, Old Buddha's favorite abiding place.

A far-flung palace of many buildings, almost covering an artificial hill at the edge of an artificial lake, a lake which Old Buddha loved, the Summer Palace is one of the beauty spots of the Orient. Once, before making the acquaintance of Princess Der Ling, I visited this famous palace, and came away with my thoughts in such a whirl that I could scarcely remember a thing I had seen. There was too much of the place and, besides, it was empty, like a mausoleum from which ghouls have stolen the dead.

But how different on this second visit!

Every building in the Summer Palace, every courtyard. Every winding pathway, every cobblestone, almost had a story to tell to the Princess, and each of the stories she told to me. For me she peopled the Summer Palace with living, breathing human beings, instead of ghosts without substance or shadow. As she talked Old Buddha became very real person. I half expected to come upon her, laughter of court ladies, the voices, high-pitched and womanish, of eunuchs; rubbed my eyes to make sure that I hadn't, after all, seen those ladies-in-waiting, in their gorgeous robes of great richness.

"Here," said the Princess, "is the audience hall, where the Old Buddha received her ministers, who kowtowed fearfully, before her–"

The Princess described the audience so skillfully that I could see the ministers there, bowing and bending like worshipers before a shrine.

"These marks on the cobblestones of this walk were made by the wheels on the guns of foreign soldiers, in 1900-"

I listened then, and distinctly heard the rumbling of those same guns, the shouts and the oaths of the gunners This building referred to, as we passed hurriedly, was filled with coolies in soldier garb! Coolies slept on the floors which had known the footsteps of royalty.

"This is Peony Hill—"

In ruins now, because China no longer cares!

"This is the famous Colonnade! Once, when terribly homesick, I sat down, exactly here, and wept. I was such a baby, I suppose, and wasn't at all sure that I liked the life at court."

I could see her there, plainly, a mere child as she had said. I never knew that child, but realized that this very modern woman beside me must be very like her.

At the end of the Colonnade, before passing through a door to the famous Marble Boat, the Princess stopped suddenly, and laughed. It was not a happy laugh. It was the laughter of one who has been deeply wounded, but who does not wish to show the hurt to strangers. There was a huge piece of brown paper tacked to the woodwork beside the door, and on the paper were many Chinese characters, which meant nothing to me.

But they meant something to the Princess!

"It is an advertisement," she explained, "extolling the virtues of the beer, sandwiches and tea which may be purchased next door!"

Right above this sacrilegious placard, covered with cobwebs, was the Imperial Seal of Old Buddha! If Old Buddha could only come back for a moment, and see! Verily, I believe, would alien heads adorn the cobblestones of the palace!

Tea on the Marble Boat.

Then the boathouse, which tourists seldom visit, where pigeons coo endlessly under the eaves, where one of Old Buddha's unwieldy pleasure boats rocks at anchor, as it has rocked for twenty years, where another has almost sunk from sight, its decks perpetually awash. A tomb filled with dead hopes.

Der Ling, in the long ago, had ridden out upon the lake in these same boats.

The aged keeper of the keys to the boathouse knew her, and we were permitted to roam the boathouse as we willed.

It was not a happy place. It typified China, I thought..

Pigeons cooing endlessly under the eaves—

Then back to Peking, modern Peking, Peking of the Republic, where Princess Der Ling was to be guest of honor at a lavish dinner in a famous hotel.

The personality of this little lady, who for an afternoon had been the lady-in-waiting she once had been, who now became a very modern woman whom all Peking was glad to honor, filled the great hotel. Chinese and foreigners in full dress rose to do her honor.

It was a triumphal affair, highly flattering. Der Ling was leaving China for America, and that soon.

But I didn't enjoy that dinner, especially.

I was thinking of a little lady of the long ago, of Old Buddha's time—of a little lady-in-waiting, who had sat in the shadows under the famous Colonnade, and wept because she was lonely!

Recalling all this, remembering how she peopled for me the Forbidden City and the Summer Palace, it is perhaps not strange that I believe her peculiarly fitted for the task which she has here just completed.

ARTHUR J. BURKS.
Los Angeles, California,
April, 1928.

I. IN A MANCHU GARDEN

The home of Lan Kuei, "The Orchid," was a haven of peace and contentment. Her father, long since retired from his country's service, with the rank, title and emoluments of a General, sat the hours away lazily. His pipe was seldom absent from his lips, save when he slept and his relaxing lips allowed it to fall down across his ample bosom to lie in the folds of his robe. At these moments his bell-shaped cap might go slightly askew on his head, the red button pointing off at nothingness at a rakish angle. His wife, who loved to sew, because there was inborn artistry in her fingertips, would gaze at this man who had been beside her down the endless avenues of the years, and smile a little. No worries expressed themselves in the calm face of either, for life had been good to them. Life had given them four children, two boys and two girls. Even now the two girls, in the little room behind the canopies which separated it from the sitting room, were busily engaged in study of the classics. Their teacher, lovable old soul, obese and short of breath, sat in there with them, and if at times they shirked their studies the teacher did not mind especially, unless he wakened without warning and surprised the girls in idleness.

Lan Kuei, The Orchid, was ambitious. She was a dreamer, and her dreams were so vast that they sometimes even frightened her, so that she told them to no one, nestling them close against her heart, poring over them in secret, longing for knowledge whereby to make her dreams come true, longing for a distant some time when she might be able to break down the dictates of custom and have a peep at the world which lay beyond her doors, and further still, beyond the walls which surrounded the quiet garden where the old gardener puttered the hours away, loving hands slowly and gently busy with his beloved flowers and plants.

The father sat smoking, a bit lazily, half asleep. The mother was industriously sewing. The teacher, in the other room, was nodding. The sisters pored over then- books, and it is rather doubtful whether either really saw the Characters which sprawled across the pages like shapeless dragons out of some infant's nightmare.

It was spring, and the peonies, azaleas, and magnolias were blooming in the walled garden beyond the doors.

Lan Kuei placed a pensive finger to her lips and peered through the window. Outside in the garden bees were droning a sleepy lullaby. No wonder the teacher nodded, and the father dozed! For it was spring. Across the square of garden visible to the dreaming eyes of Lan Kuei strode the figure of a servant, an amah to Lan Kuei, whose name was Shou Chu, "Little Bamboo." The servant, noiselessly striding across the somnolent square, looked up and met the eyes of The Orchid. She placed a secretive finger to her lips, looked right and left apprehensively, nodded her head, turned squarely about and vanished from the view of Lan Kuei, striding into the garden whence she had come.

How well The Orchid knew that signal! She had seen it countless times before.

"He has just entered the garden, through the moon door!" the signal said.

Lan Kuei looked at her sister. Her sister, though she smiled slightly, was perturbed. She looked anxiously at the nodding teacher, leaned forward to peer in at the parents. She almost shook her head in negation. And then she didn't, for she loved this daring sister of hers. And Lan Kuei was daring, for a little lady of a high Manchu family. Quietly, slowly, watching her teacher with almost frightened eyes, The Orchid rose from her place and slipped to the hanging canopies, through which she passed, making scarcely a sound. She did not waken her father, whose pipe had now fallen to lie upon the ample folds of his robe, and her mother looked up but did not question. It was usual for Lan Kuei to take a brief walk in the garden at this time, and there could be no harm, especially since Little Bamboo had just appeared at the door to accompany her lovely little mistress. So The Orchid passed into the garden.

It was a huge garden, riotous with flowers. There were peonies, pink as the inside of a baby's mouth, azaleas white and pink, as though their little faces blushed with very shyness, magnolias white as the faces of Christian nuns. Prom flower to flower, sipping their cloying sweetness, droned the bees in little armies, armies without formation, their winged soldiers darting here and there as fancy drew them, humming to themselves their vast enjoyment of the scents of spring. Trees of many different kinds ranged along the walls of the garden, trees and shrubs bordered the pathway. Trees spread their mantles of cool shadow over the marble benches and tables which were never missing from a Chinese garden of the better class. Dapplings of sunlight and shadow danced upon the tiled roof of the little summerhouse in the garden's most remote corner. The limbs of trees which made the shadows seemed to be beckoning, signaling with their leafy arms, telling all who might see that here could be found quiet peacefulness, where one might escape for an hour or two from the world of workaday things. And off to the side of the summerhouse, where it nestled against the wall, was the moon door, which was now closed and locked.

Fancied security! Lan Kuei smiled softly to herself, as her feet, marching straight and without faltering, with never a step taken in indecision, carried her toward the summerhouse. That door was closed and locked, but there was a secret in the lock, a secret which was shared by three people. One was Little Bamboo, who had a key and loved her little mistress as she might never love any other living thing, not even a child of her own body. The second was Lan Kuei, The Orchid, whose feet now led her so straight to the third person who knew the secret of the lock on the moon door. Of course there might have been a fourth who knew the secret, or guessed it; but this possible fourth, the aged gardener, was very old, and very deaf, and almost blind, who, moreover, loved Lan Kuei, too. He would never speak, this old gardener, unless Lan Kuei herself gave permission.

Straight to the summerhouse—with the faithful amah, Little Bamboo, treading in her very footsteps a little way behind, respectfully as became a maid who served the highborn—moved Lan Kuei on her tiny unbound feet. Straight to the summerhouse, up the steps through the doors, which she closed behind her soundlessly. Little Bamboo did not enter the summerhouse. Little Bamboo was very wise. Moreover, she loved Lan Kuei as she loved no other living thing. She went to the marble bench near the summerhouse, where she seated herself, facing an area which was masked from the dwelling place of Lan Kuei by the summerhouse itself, so that if anyone looked forth from the house, seeing her there, that one would know that Lan Kuei was beyond the summerhouse, and think no more about the matter.

Very wise and clever was Little Bamboo, in whom Lan Kuei had the utmost faith.

Lan Kuei entered the summerhouse, closed the doors behind her.

From a bench before a long table, a table on which reposed several books, some opened, some closed, rose a young Manchu in all the glory of young manhood. His eyes were alight as Lan Kuei came in and he saw her, noted anew the rare beauty of her, the fragile hands, the black eyebrows, like the wings of tiny blackbirds, the shapely feet which just peeped out below the hem of her pale lavender gown. A beautiful picture, Lan Kuei, in her gown that just matched the atmosphere which possessed the garden and the summerhouse. Gold braid trimmed the bottom of the gown. Shining buttons, like a string of precious stones, hung about her neck, fit frame for the cameo-like loveliness of her face. A high forehead was hers. Red silk strings held in confinement the hair which came down to make a square black line along the center of her finely chiseled brow. Her cheeks just now were flushed as, closing the doors behind her, she stood, erect as a little soldier, to face the admiration of the Manchu young gentleman who rose to receive her.

"Yung Lu," she murmured his name. "I have come again."

He took her little hands in his. A picture these two made; Lan Kuei in pale lavender, Yung Lu the somewhat gaudy uniform which became him in spite of its gaudiness, of a Manchu Guard Commander. A regal pair. He held her hands, looking into her eyes, noting her flushed cheeks, in which he read the story he most desired to read, and Lan Kuei did not deny him. They were alone. It was against all the dictates of custom. No Manchu maid may meet, without a chaperon, a Manchu gentleman. Least of all might she go to him secretly, so that he hold her hands, smile into her eyes with eyes that danced and told their age-old story. Yet Lan Kuei had come, and Yung Lu, straight, tall and proud, held her hands, gripping them firmly—yet not too firmly, because they were so fragile, like petals of a gorgeous flower—and looked into her eyes, black pools in whose depths all the feminine wisdom of the world was mirrored.

Their hands clung. Thus far they had not disobeyed the dictates of custom. A Manchu man and a Manchu maid might clasp hands to show affection. They might do no more. But Lan Kuei had already come to a secret meeting. Her punishment would be as great as though she had allowed herself to show more openly the affection she felt for this handsome guardsman. So, when he drew her to him, still smiling, a smile that was gentle, a lover's smile, she did not resist him. She could not resist Yung Lu, because he was so gentle, because he always disarmed her opposition with his smile.

He held her at the full length of his arms, which were strong to hold her captive.

"You are beautiful, Lan Kuei," he almost whispered it. "I love you as I could love no other, were that other my sister or my mother. There was never another like you in the world. You could be a queen if you desired, and the great men of the world would lay the wealth of the world at your little feet, and would fight among themselves for the merest glance of approbation from those black eyes of yours. How beautiful you are! How much I love you! I wonder if you know!"

Lan Kuei held silent for a long moment, searching the eyes, reading the smiling lips of this man who had come to her secretly in her own garden, daring the fury of her parents, flouting the ancient traditions; and her own bps almost parted in a tremulous smile.

"I know," she said softly at last, "because I love you, too."

They sought each other's arms again, and the world stood still.

There came a slight sound from outside the summerhouse. Lan Kuei stepped back from Yung Lu.

"Little Bamboo gives the signal," she whispered, "and I must go. Tomorrow, Yung Lu?"

He nodded, releasing her with vast reluctance.

"I am calling on your parents in a few moments," he said with that quiet smile of his. "This time I shall not come through the moon door. I have news of import for your father. You may listen from beyond the canopies of your study. I do not tell you now, because our moments together are so few that there seems nothing important to tell you save that I love, shall love you always, Lan Kuei, and shall be faithful to you to the grave."

She brushed his lips lightly with her fingertips. A daring gesture, since no Manchu maiden of reserve might offer a caress unasked. But then, you see, Yung Lu had said he loved her. She was gone, out of the summerhouse, and Yung Lu watched her through a window, until the corner of her father's house hid her from view. He saw the servant, Little Bamboo, come back after a time, toward the moon door. The door swung open. Yung Lu quitted the summerhouse swiftly, without a glance to right or left, knowing that Little Bamboo would not unlock the door if there were danger of detection, and passed from the garden, through the wall, leaving his life's most precious gift behind him.

Then he circled the wall, approached the dwelling place of the general, was announced by a servant, entered as an honored guest. Lan Kuei's father wakened at his entrance, hurriedly retrieved his pipe from the ample folds of his robe. The mother rested her sewing on her knees. In the room beyond the canopies, where Yung Lu could see the bowed heads of Lan Kuei and her sister as they poured studiously over their books, the teacher snapped awake with a start; and an ejaculation that was wordless, sounding like a snort of impatience, came from his fat lips. He harked something at the girls in mandarin, and the bowed heads bent lower. Yung Lu smiled, and seemed not to see what transpired in the room beyond the canopies.

He seated himself on the *kong*, a shelf-like bed, against the wall opposite the door by which he had entered, and servants brought tea and cakes. Lan Kuei's father would never fail in hospitality, especially if the visitor were Yung Lu. He loved Yung Lu as a son, and back in the depths of his mind the thought was hidden that Yung Lu might one day be his son indeed. No one knew this thought, save only Lan Kuei's father. Her mother had a thought that was very like it, but she said nothing, either, since always the father rules the household, and arranges the marriages of the children. But the mother could wait in patience, and hope for happiness for Lan Kuei. Yung Lu must certainly have smiled had he been able to read the thoughts of the two old people, parents of the girl whom he loved, who loved him. But he did not know.

In A Manchu Garden

So there were five people who had secrets in the house of Lan Kuei. Little Bamboo, who shared with Lan Kuei the secret of the trysting place. Lan Kuei's sister, who guessed more than she really knew—because this calm sister was somewhat of an enigma to her; she was always dreaming, ofttimes spoke of great ambitions, far beyond attainment for ladies highly born, who might never go forth into the world to seek the pot of gold at the foot of the rainbow of their fancy. Lan Kuei's father had his secret. The mother had a secret, too.

But it was Yung Lu himself, all unknowing, who caused the most secret of these secrets to remain secrets forever.

He was a Guard Commander, entrusted with command of a detachment which watched at the gates of the Forbidden City, safeguarding the lives and property of the Imperial Clan, and because such responsibility was his he often had news of what transpired beyond the walls of the Forbidden City. This news he always brought to the father of Lan Kuei, because the father, being very old, still interested in the armed service where he could no longer command, liked the feel of gossip on his tongue.

It was after the usual civilities, the traditional circumlocutions which masked the real purpose of his visit, that Yung Lu told his story.

"The Empress has failed to bear a son to Hsien Feng," he said tentatively.

The old man said nothing. He merely allowed a trickle of smoke to pass his bps. But his eyes were very bright. Yung Lu would tell him, after a while. Yung Lu seemed deeply interested in the tea the servants had placed before him, and the cakes. He knew how to secure the most from a dramatic announcement.

"There is no heir to the throne of the Middle Kingdom," said Yung Lu a moment later.

And then the news came out with a rush. Yung Lu had noticed the impatient tossing of the head beyond the canopies, the head of Lan Kuei, who listened when she seemed to be studiously immersed in her classics.

"So," he said, "Hsien Feng has decreed that he will take a Secondary Wife. She must come, of course, from a family of high degree. Seventeen young Manchu women, whose names are borne on the registry of titled births, have been named in the decree. They are to go to the Forbidden City on a date which will be decreed later, in order that Hsien Feng, the Emperor, may make his choice from among them. Her Majesty, the Empress, they tell me, is furious. But there is really nothing she can do. The Emperor is all-powerful. There will shortly be a Secondary Wife at the court of the Manchus. His Majesty hopes thus to repair the royal fortunes and beget an heir to the throne of China!"

Lan Kuei then did a remarkable thing. She ignored her teacher. She paid no heed to the horrified frown of her sister. She rose from her place, failing even to close the book she had been pretending to read, and entered the room.

"My name is among the seventeen!" she said, her voice high-pitched with excitement. "I know it is! Something tells me *here*!"

She pressed her fragile hand to her heart.

Yung Lu's heart became cold within his breast. There was something, something cold, heavy and depressing, like the hand of a person drowned, which pressed heavily upon the heart of him. His face was stony as he met the gaze of Lan Kuei. He looked at Lan Kuei's father. The father looked aghast at Lan Kuei, his mouth gaping open as he sought for words.

And then a servant announced the royal messenger.

It was a messenger, a eunuch in official robes, who entered importantly, as became a herald for Hsien Feng, and tendered to Lan Kuei's father a hit of yellow paper, stamped with many seals.

An Imperial Decree! A mere piece of yellow paper, China's color for royalty!

Yet it was destined to change the whole life of Yung Lu, of Lan Kuei, and to write whole chapters in the ponderous history of the Middle Kingdom.

Lan Kuei's father read it, stiffly performed the kowtows decreed by custom, and looked up at Yung Lu.

But the door had already closed behind the Guard Commander. He had guessed, perhaps, or perhaps his heart had told him, what message the eunuch brought to this dwelling place of his beloved, and long before the aged general had finished reading, Yung Lu had passed for a second time that day, this time unseeing, from the garden which sheltered the summerhouse where he had dared to dream and hope for his dream's fulfillment.

II. THE HUMBLE COBBLER

Dense crowds milled incessantly before *Tung Wha Men*, the East Gate, along the length and breadth of *Nan Chi Tzu*, the street which passes close to the gates of the far-flung Forbidden City. There were coolies bearing market produce, coolies bearing sedan chairs, whose occupants were hidden from view by the silken canopies which sheltered them. A barber plied his trade in an eddy in the crowd, and a host of idlers watched him with the utmost interest as he performed cleaning operations upon the huge ears of a coolie who had just now saved the price to pay for tonsorial attention. A milling flood of unwashed humanity, going nowhere with great speed, returning mysteriously with their missions, whatever they may have been, accomplished to their satisfaction. The air was vibrant with shouted words in a dozen different dialects. Men and women jostled one another good humoredly, or swore roundly in the vile oaths of cooliedom, according to their natures. It was a primitive crowd, engaged upon the great business of pandering to its own stomach, seeking futile amusements— milling, jostling, with nowhere to go and with all eternity in which to reach their destinations.

In another eddy in the crowd, a youthful cobbler sat upon the chest of drawers which held the tools of his trade. He wasn't happy, this cobbler, for he was ambitious, and a cobbler does not stand high in the social scale. But he comforted himself with the knowledge that, low as he was in the scale, he had climbed the social ladder from a rung far lower in China's scheme of classifying her people. Just at the moment he was idle. Moodily, his eyes narrowed, his lower lip sagging petulantly, he stared at the high walls which surrounded the Forbidden City, at the yellow tiles of the forest of roofs beyond, where all the splendor of the Manchu holy of holies so emphasized his own poverty. Thoughtfully he munched away on a turnip, for turnips were cheap, could be purchased with one copper cash, and there was no need of fire to prepare them. There was no salt, no seasoning, and the cobbler ate his turnip peeling and all, unwilling to lose any of the food value of his repast. He was very poor; but he had been poorer by far, and knew that food, food of any kind, was not to be scorned. People

The Humble Cobbler

jostled him as he passed, and he snarled impartially at them all. Not that he nurtured enmity against the people themselves, but because the world had used him ill, and he hated her in all her myriad manifestations.

He sighed, after a while; his eyes swerved from their steadfast consideration of the Forbidden City, and, ignoring the crowd which swirled, an endless stream, about him, he fell to examining the folds of the worn, ragged, patched, padded gown which protected his unwashed body from the rigors of winter, and the cold of Peking nights. His pigtail, which he never found it necessary to comb, next claimed his attention. Ever and anon he snarled again, crushing between his sharp nails the tiny occupants of his gown, and of his pigtail; but his snarls as he rid himself of crawling pests were snarls of satisfaction, because he joyed in vengeance. A surly boy, this youthful cobbler.

His name was Li Lien Ying. He was indescribably dirty, his face needed washing, had needed washing for years. He was under sixteen, though large for his years. A more unprepossessing person could scarcely have been found on a search the length and breadth of the Middle Kingdom. Yet he was worthy of notice, though there was none in all the crowd could know that. Li Lien Ying himself did not know it.

But it was written in the stars that this humble cobbler, with a temper that bordered on insanity, with a lust for vengeance against the world that might never be satisfied, was destined to write his name large in the history of China. Just now he gazed enviously at the closed gates of the Forbidden City, and cursed the inmates of the city under his breath, or aloud if he felt that no informers could overhear. He would have given his soul for a glimpse into the holy of holies. But the Forbidden City was not for the class to which Li Lien Ying belonged.

There was a story behind Li Lien Ying. No so long ago he had been a farmer in the north. A farmer who tilled the fields, slept on dirty rags if rags were procurable, ate corn or millet, or went hungry if no corn or millet were available, and did his daily, back-breaking stint in the parched and tortured fields—fields annually called upon to produce food for the stomachs of more people than could be reasonably fed. There had been beatings of the bamboo at the hands of a harassed father. There had been days and years when Li Lien Ying had not known what it was to enjoy a full meal. His waking hours were filled with thoughts of food, because his stomach was perpetually empty. He dreamed of food, and while he slept he rubbed his stomach in anticipation, and woke to snarl anew at the world because his dreams lacked substance and did not satisfy his cravings.

He had run away from the harsh fields of his ancestors. Peking, the melting pot of China, where one may hear the dialects of all the provinces, of all the Oriental and Occidental countries under the sun, had claimed him. The life was harsh and terrible, but the fields where his back had almost become permanently bowed from perpetual toil were definitely behind him, relegated to the limbo of the past and gone. Yet Li Lien Ying was not satisfied. Li Lien Ying never would be satisfied. He had been deprived of so much in his youth, if he might be said ever to have had a period of youth, that no matter how much the world might lay at his feet in the end, he would go to his grave with his major cravings—especially craving for food—unsatisfied, and with a snarl of hatred at the world he was leaving.

He had served his apprenticeship as a coolie, bearing twin baskets on his shoulders—twin baskets whose dirty interiors received bits of coal, cigarette butts cast aside by the affluent, all the odds and ends which clog the gutters of any city of size. He retrieved these usable oddments fastidiously, with a long stick provided with pincers at the end, so that his hands, already grimy, since he could not recall when they had been washed, might not be further contaminated by contact with refuse from the gutters. Fastidious, after a fashion, was Li Lien Ying. He never washed his face or his body, or combed his queue, and crawling things found refuge in his garments, but Li Lien Ying boasted pride of a sort.

He was proud of Li Lien Ying. He took pride in the fact that, low as was his station in life, it was far above that which he had forever put behind him,

He toyed with his cobbler's knife, a two-handled, razor-like knife in the shape of a half circle, and thought of the past, and wondered what the future held in store for him. He had come this far, from farmer-slave to cobbler. How much further might he go,

The Humble Cobbler

if he diligently applied himself? His gift for saving was prodigious. A turnip, for example, cost a copper cash, yet he purchased this raw food but rarely, because, through skill and courage, turnips could so easily be stolen.

He raised his head, noting that a lull had settled over the crowd. The crowd was still there. It was always there. But it had fallen suddenly silent. Noises, Li Lien Ying did not mind; for Peking was full, ever and always full, of noises—and of smells. But when there was no noise, he noticed, as did all the others in that vast crowd which had milled and eddied along the length and breadth of Nan Chi Tzu.

Li Lien Ying noticed, as I have said, and raised his head to see what had silenced the vast concourse of the lowly.

A mounted cavalcade was passing along the center of Nan Chi Tzu. Men in gorgeous gowns of the finest silk. They were mounted on curveting, lively Mongolian ponies. The ponies were grey or pure white, with long flowing manes, decked in all the glory of royal stables. Leading the cavalcade was an obese man, astride a dancing grey. Behind this man rode the most striking man in the group. A great man, one knew at once by the look of him. He held his head high, and proudly, as became a man of noble birth. The others in the cavalcade wore caps bedight with gleaming pearls, but none wore so many pearls, or wore them so grandly, as this second man. Behind this second man were sixteen others, all mounted, outriders for the second in line. Some carried whips, and as the cavalcade passed gloriously along, its members ignoring the riffraff which eddied and swirled through *Nan Chi Tzu*, those who carried whips laid them lustily upon the backs, the legs, arms, and even faces of those who did not swiftly enough make way for the prancing ponies of the mighty, the highly placed. A regal procession of Mongolian ponies, proud of their burdens.

Li Lien Ying's mouth fell open in amazement. This was his first visit to *Nan Chi Tzu*. He did not know the habits of this crowded street, or the great folk who deigned to pass along its odorous length.

Li Lien Ying plucked at the sleeve of a man who stood before him, almost masking his view of the approaching cavalcade.

"Get out of my way, turtle!" he snarled at this one. The man made haste to oblige. He even smiled at the vehemence of the young cobbler, who thawed enough to ask another question.

"Who is that? Who are these mighty ones who lay the lash upon the common folk as though they were dogs in the gutter?"

The man addressed looked at Li Lien Ying in surprise.

"Surely you must be new in Peking, not to know them?"

"Enough!" snapped Li Lien Ying, who had no patience with the circumlocutions so necessary to Chinese conversation. "Answer my question!"

"That," began the man—and then hesitated, joying in anticipation of a dramatic announcement,—"is An Teh Hai, Chief Eunuch to His Imperial Majesty, Hsien Feng, the Emperor! The others with him are eunuchs, too, but lesser eunuchs, who are honored at being chosen as outriders to so great a man as An Teh Hai! They have just left the Forbidden City for a ride about the streets which border the Forbidden City, where they live, and enjoy the bounty of the Imperial tables!"

"What," asked Li Lien Ying, "is a eunuch?"

And then he snarled when the man burst into laughter. "You must be ignorant indeed, fellow, if you do not know that eunuchs are the chosen fortunates of the Middle Kingdom! They—But don't you know?"

Li Lien Ying replied again that he did not know.

The man laughed once more, and offered detailed explanations.

"They are very rich, the eunuchs," he added. "They receive more money than they can spend. They feed on the best. Look! An Teh Hai has the stomach of a sow that is ready for the knife of the butcher, and yet I'll wager he's always hungry, always ready to gorge himself on food such as folk like us never even see, save when the scraps are thrown from the gates of the Forbidden City during some rare mood of His Majesty the Emperor."

"How," said Li Lien Ying, quietly, "does one become a eunuch?"

"It is not difficult," replied his gossipy informant. "All one needs is courage—and a knife. That cobbler's knife of yours, for example—"

The Humble Cobbler

Li Lien Ying gazed at the knife in question, gripped its handles more tightly in his two hands. He pressed the man for further details which the latter gave freely, since it cost him nothing, and he could talk and watch the passing cavalcade simultaneously.

Then An Teh Hai rode past where Li Lien Ying sat. Li's informant bowed and stepped aside to avoid the lashes of the outriders. Li Lien Ying did not stand up.

He stared boldly at the members of the cavalcade. Its leader, in advance of the great man, looked down at him.

"Stand up!" he whined, in a high voice that was oddly like that of a hysterical woman.

But Li Lien Ying did not stand. He merely ignored the speaker, and devoted himself to a fresh turnip; and the press of eunuchs in rear forced forward the eunuch who might otherwise have stopped to deal out punishment to the man who had failed to do honor to the Chief Eunuch of His Majesty.

"An Teh Hai!" muttered Li Lien Ying to himself. "An Teh Hai!"

The name, somehow, had a familiar sound to him. It was easy to trace ancestry in China. He'd remember the name of the Chief Eunuch, and make inquiries. Long after the cavalcade had passed, Li Lien Ying sat bowed in thought. Once he raised his eyes to the walls of the Forbidden City, and the yellow tiles of the forest of roofs beyond. Now his face, however, was not hate-filled as it had been when first he had gazed upon the holy of holies of the Manchus. It was very thoughtful. Li Lien Ying was a man of intelligence, for all that he had never spent one day of his life in school, or learned to read the classics, or make the sprawling characters which every educated Chinese must master.

When night had fallen Li Lien Ying wended his way to an obscure section of Peking, where among others of his kind he might seek additional information and find it. He asked much about eunuchs, what one did to gain entry to the Forbidden City after all requirements had been fulfilled—and he asked many questions about An Teh Hai.

It was a very old man, a professional story-teller, who gave him the clue he sought. It was rather astounding, when one considered the matter; but the fact remained that Li Lien Ying, the scrofulous, smallpox-marked cobbler, was a distant relative of the Chief Eunuch to His Imperial Majesty, Hsien Feng the Emperor!

Li Lien Ying was a man of intelligence. He made a momentous decision, once satisfied with his myriad investigations. He went forth into the highways and byways, stealing wherever he went, gathering food against the time when he would not be able to go out and seek it. Then, first taking a grimy restaurant-keeper into his confidence, he found a place where he would not be disturbed during the period of waiting, and laid his plans. They were deep plans, concerning which he told no one. Close mouthed all his days was Li Lien Ying. It was his very secretiveness which was to prove his greatest ally in the years to come.

In his plans, however, figured a certain implement out of the trade he was leaving behind him, casting it into the past as he had flung off, like an outworn garment, the life of a farmer—and that implement was the cobbler's knife which his informant in Nan CM Tzu had called most forcibly to his attention.

Li Lien Ying became a eunuch by his own hand; and, when the dreadful period of his convalescence had passed, a white-faced neuter presented himself at the gates of the Forbidden City.

It was Li Lien Ying, who had put behind him forever the life of a humble cobbler.

III. HSIEN FENG TAKES A SECONDARY WIFE

This was a memorable day for China.

It was also a memorable day for seventeen little Manchu ladies who were daughters of men of the first rank, men who were authorized to wear the red coral button. For it was the day when Hsien Feng had decreed that they appear in court, together, and at a certain hour. It was known the length and breadth of Peking that Hsien Feng was taking a Secondary Wife. .The seventeen little ladies, and their parents, were in a very fever of excitement. This meant honor for the daughter, were she chosen. It meant power, prestige, for the father of the fortunate girl. It meant happiness—perhaps—for the girl herself. So seventeen girls whose names were borne on the decree were wildly excited as the date drew near. Each girl wondered whether or not she would be chosen.

Only Lan Kuei did not wonder. She knew. Deep in her heart she had always known. She told the reason for her knowledge to her father. Then she told no other person, not until many years later, when time had fled for scores of years down its endless corridors.

A devout Buddhist, she had prayed that good fortune attend her, as soon as she found that her name was borne on the first decree. She had burned incense before her shrine, in a corner of her father's garden, had knelt and asked the gods of her race to prosper her, to feed her ambitions—ambitions in which Yung Lu did not figure, though she loved him, and Had told him that she loved him.

And this was the story she had told her father:

"I burned incense before the shrine, father. The smoke which rose from the burner eddied, swayed, and took the form of a man's face. I had never seen the face. But in my heart I knew who it was! It was an omen, Father! I shall become the Secondary Wife of the Emperor!"

Her father had been skeptical. He had never really understood this child of his. She was a dreamer, and the father did not understand dreamers. He was phlegmatic himself, open, as easily readable as the faces of the many clocks which cluttered up the corners of his dwelling-place.

Lan Kuei, on one of her meetings with Yung Lu, who met her several times after he learned that her name had been borne on the

Emperor's first decree, had stood on the rockery beyond the summerhouse, where they could look over and into the noisy street which passed the wall about the home of Lan Kuei. A cavalcade had passed by, and the face of one of the riders had attracted the gaze of Lan Kuei. She turned to Yung Lu.

"Who is that man?" she asked.

Yung Lu was bitter. His lip curled slightly, but he made answer.

"That is His Imperial Majesty, Hsien Feng the Emperor," he said.

Lan Kuei's eyes narrowed thoughtfully. The great man and his cavalcade passed without anyone who accompanied the Emperor taking note of the two who stood on the rockery beyond the wall. Lan Kuei whispered to herself.

"The face is the same," she told herself. "It is the face I saw in the smoke from the incense burner!"

An omen! An omen of good or evil fortune. Only the years could tell.

But from that moment, Lan Kuei discouraged the lover-like overtures of Yung Lu, who loved her more as the days passed, loved her more and more madly as she receded from him, drawing into her dream-house, which was a place of ambitions that had no end.

So the great day drew near.

And seventeen little ladies of high Manchu families journeyed to the Forbidden City for the private audience with Their Majesties, Hsien Feng the Emperor, and his Empress, Tzu An.

Seventeen excited little ladies, hobbling into the City on their Manchu shoes of the terribly high heels, each one eager to become Secondary Wife to Hsien Feng. The clacking of their high-heeled shoes, their excited chattering with the others who went—since the decree insisted that they all arrive together. They were dressed in many colors, the best that money could buy. All wore the high black headdresses of the unmarried, with the lotus designs, the pink flowers in the center, the seed pearls here and there, and various designs dear to the hearts of the several seventeen. There were dabs of rouge on the trembling lower bps. Eyes were bright and shining with anticipation. It was a great honor to be concubine to the Emperor of the Middle Kingdom!

Hsien Feng Takes A Secondary Wife

Lan Kuei, The Orchid, was a trifle late to the audience. This may have been intentional. It may have been accident. It was never wise to be late to audience with His Majesty, nevertheless, Lan Kuei was late, and it may be that the moment or two she was late changed the whole history of China.

Yung Lu was at the gate through which Lan Kuei entered the Forbidden City. He was very straight, very proud, in his uniform of the Manchu Guardsman. His face was expressive of hope, and of hopelessness, a veritable battleground of emotions. He was proud of Lan Kuei, because he loved her. He wished her to be chosen, because all honor would be hers; but if she were chosen, he would lose her forever. If she were not chosen she would be unhappy all her days, and if she were chosen she might also be unhappy. All these things Yung Lu knew. Yet he stood very proud, and very straight, as Lan Kuei, on her entrance to the Forbidden City, saw him on duty at the gate.

His eyes looked straight into Lan Kuei's eyes, and his stiff lips, which strove to keep from trembling, shaped the words:

"You are glorious today, Lan Kuei!"

She smiled a little. She read the face of Yung Lu; but she was ambitious. She comforted herself for failing Yung Lu with the knowledge that her name had been written in that first decree, and that she would have been compelled to come to the Forbidden City in spite of any reluctance she might have entertained. But she had prepared herself for this audience. She wore her best, and she would not have been a woman had she not known that she was "glorious," as Yung Lu had said. She wore her favorite color, lavender. She was "glorious" indeed. She could not hide from herself, nor from Yung Lu, that she would be very unhappy indeed if she were not chosen. The question of loving, or of being loved, entered into the matter not at all.

She passed Yung Lu without a backward glance, putting love from her.

The sixteen had already entered the place of the private audience when Lan Kuei, The Orchid, arrived. The sixteen were a laughing lot. They were excited, expectant —for one of them would be chosen as Secondary Wife. The room in which the sixteen were was a double room, with a partition, a partition which was pierced by many shelves, shelves which groaned under their burdens of priceless treasures. Under the windows wide benches, high as tables, lined the walls; and the tables, too, were heavily laden with treasures—works of art in jade, porcelain, cloisonné, gold, and precious stones. Scrolls upon the wall, signed by great artists who had long since passed to whatever rewards were theirs, testified to the tastes of the Emperor and the Empress. There were landscapes and seascapes by the greatest Chinese artists, living and dead; there were scrolls which set forth the merits of Emperors dead and gone these many years. The brick floor sounded and resounded to the clacking of high-heeled Manchu shoes, as little Manchu ladies exhibited their graces, and their plumage, before Hsien Feng the Emperor. They passed freely here and there, looking at the priceless treasures, the like of which they had never seen before, and as they walked, always the provocative glances, glances intended to be alluring, at Hsien Feng.

There were eunuchs, servants, ladies-in-waiting. The audience hall was a busy place. As the young ladies passed in review Hsien Feng, seated, on the right of his Empress—who, by the way, was almost frowning in high displeasure—glanced casually from youthful face to youthful face. Almost bored was Hsien Feng.

Then entered Lan Kuei, The Orchid, sweetheart of Yung Lu.

The Orchid made no pretense of trying to please. As Lan Kuei, no more no less, she had left her father's house. As Lan Kuei, no more no less, she entered into the presence of the two greatest people in all China. Natural, was Lan Kuei, exhibiting no graces that were not naturally hers. She sent no provocative glances at Hsien Feng. She did not strive to please. She seemed as bored as Hsien Feng himself. She was easily the most beautiful of the seventeen, and the other sixteen recognized that fact at once. Hostile glances, envious glances, were cast at Lan Kuei, but she paid no heed to any.

Then in a droning voice the Chief Eunuch, An Teh Hai, began to intone the names and ages of the seventeen.

"Pou Yu" (Precious Jade).

"Lan Kuei" (The Orchid).

On down the list, sing-song of voice, read An Teh Hai, the Chief Eunuch.

Hsien Feng Takes A Secondary Wife

The Empress had a voice in the choosing of a Secondary Wife. Often, as the names were read, after all the seventeen had kowtowed together, Hsien Feng would turn to his Empress, with a question on his lips.

"What do you think of this one?"

The little lady in question would be called before the Empress, who would take her hands and examine them.

"She will not do! Her hands are not the hands of the high-born! They are too coarse!"

This in the court language, which the seventeen could not understand.

"And what of this one?"

"She will not do, either. She tries to walk with decorum, but does not know how."

"Which of the seventeen do you believe suitable?" "My choice would be her who is named Pou Yu!"

The Emperor almost smiled, almost forgot his Imperial dignity, for Pou Yu was not fortunate in the matter of beauty. She was marred by a few smallpox scars, and her eyes were crossed. Moreover she walked awkwardly. She was very anxious to be chosen, for she looked very often toward the Emperor, and tried to be alluring; and because of her crossed eyes she only succeeded in appearing ludicrous. So the Emperor, at mention of Pou Yu, only shook his head slightly.

"I like the girl Lan Kuei," he said finally, "she has all the graces. She makes no pretense of being other than she is, and she is very beautiful."

"I do not feel she is suitable, for the very reason you name! She is too beautiful to be good!"

Once more Hsien Feng shook his head, but for a different reason. Lan Kuei missed nothing, though she appeared bored with the whole proceeding. Very wise, and clever, was Lan Kuei, for she noted that the eyes of His Majesty came back to her again and again. No thought of Yung Lu entered her mind during the audience. She willed that the man on the *kong*, beside the Empress—whom Lan Kuei recognized immediately as an implacable enemy—desire her from all the seventeen. She studied his face when opportunity offered, when he was not looking at her, and remembered the omen of the spiraling smoke from the incense burner; how that smoke had taken the form of a man's face—and the man in the smoke was the man on the Imperial *kong* before her at this moment, up there beside the Empress whom Lan Kuei recognized as an enemy.

Lan Kuei's heart beat high with excitement, though she gave no sign, seemed not to notice when the other sixteen, who, being women after all, missed nothing, looted at her with hostile glances, sensing that the Emperor preferred her to them all. Still, though the sixteen knew the Emperor had already made his choice, they strove to attract his attention, giggled often, strode here and there with exaggerated dignity, kowtowed, laughing, before an imaginary Emperor when the real Emperor seemed not to notice—because his eyes were other where—seeking to compel Hsien Feng to alter the choice he had already made within his mind.

Tea was served, so that the Empress and the Emperor might observe the ladies closer, know something of the training that had been theirs. The girls giggled often still, looked into one another's eyes, smiling—save that when any of the sixteen looked at Lan Kuei, that one did not smile at all. The Empress and the Emperor, long before the audience was over—despite the fact that the decree had given the period of the audience, at the end of which the little ladies must leave whether they willed or no—were plainly bored. Proof, their boredom, that Hsien Feng had already made his choice, and that it was really not necessary for them to wait.

Lan Kuei did not look again at Hsien Feng the Emperor. She already knew all she cared to know.

The end of the audience was near. The Emperor shifted in his seat upon the *kong*. His eyes, for the merest fraction of a second, swerved again to rest upon Lan Kuei, easily the most beautiful of the seventeen.

After a while the Chief Eunuch, glancing at one of the many ornate clocks which ornamented the hall of the audience, made pronouncement.

"The audience is ended. You may all go."

Had none been chosen? No, that was not the answer. Sixteen had not been chosen. One had been chosen. All were dismissed, though, in order that the fortune of the one would not make

Hsien Feng Takes A Secondary Wife

envious the other sixteen, or cause the less fortunate to "lose face." Of the seventeen who were leaving, one would return later, in obedience to another Imperial decree.

Seventeen beautiful Manchu little ladies, one of whom, Pou Yu, was only less beautiful than all the others, kowtowed gracefully to their Emperor and his Empress, and withdrew.

Lan Kuei glanced at Yung Lu as she passed out through the gate, to where her sedan chair was waiting; but she scarcely saw him. She was thinking that soon there would be another Imperial decree, ordering one of the seventeen back to court, which she might never leave again.

Seventeen little ladies, the oldest scarcely seventeen, the youngest scarcely fourteen, passed out of the Forbidden City. Sixteen of them would return no more. Yet one would return; and Lan Kuei, sure in her heart that she had been fortunate, scarcely saw Yung Lu, or the misery in his face, as she passed out of the Forbidden City, took her place in her sedan chair, and was borne into the heart of Peking.

Was she sure she had been selected?

Long years later she said:

"I was leaving with the others; but I knew I would return, and that soon!"

She stopped to make a trivial purchase at one of the many little shops along Hattamen Street, and the keeper of the shop, because perhaps business had been dull for days, was very much lacking in civility to Lan Kuei.

Lan Kuei resented his incivility. She allowed the shopkeeper to know of her resentment.

"When I am Secondary Wife to His Majesty, Hsien Feng, I shall have you decapitated!" she told him.

The shopkeeper laughed scornfully.

But he was to remember her words, as she herself remembered them, and laughed over the memory, as she related the story in the years that then were still ahead.

If she ever had tender thoughts of Yung Lu thereafter, she told them to no one—unless it were Yung Lu himself—but if she did, Yung Lu, faithful to her until death, never told.

So Lan Kuei returned to the house of her father, and waited—but during the wait she quietly prepared the elaborate headdress of the married Manchu lady.

IV. THE EMPEROR COMMANDS

A little lady, Lan Kuei, waited in her father's house .for the summons. She knew it would come. All her life she had known something marvelous would happen to her. She had always been ambitious, had always dreamed great dreams. Though this was to go beyond her wildest hopes, to her it was not unexpected, because she dared to dream.

So she sat in her father's house and waited.

How different this time the demeanor of the messengers who came with the tidings! On the first visit the eunuch who had brought the decree had been arrogant, supercilious, with the air of one who bestows largess, or casts pearls before swine. This time there were many eunuchs who came; eunuchs who carried priceless presents for the father and the mother of Lan Kuei, The Orchid; eunuchs bearing an empty sedan chair of great richness.

Lan Kuei, expecting the summons, had expected to be wildly excited. Yet when the great moment came, when she saw the eunuchs, a great crowd of them dressed in the robes of office, approaching her house, she was very calm, took it all as a matter of course. She had expected greatness, and greatness had been thrust upon her, all because of the fact that she had been born beautiful.

The father and mother were in ecstasies over the presents, worth many thousands of *taels*, they were overjoyed at the good fortune of their daughter Lan Kuei. They took the presents, after the eunuchs had been announced and had politely entered the dwelling place, and gave Lan Kuei into their keeping. Regally, as one to the manner born, Lan Kuei left the house of her father, where she had enjoyed those ambitious dreams of hers; while two eunuchs preceded her, and others walked behind, as though she were already wife to His Majesty, Hsien Feng. Lan Kuei entered the sedan chair, which was hoisted to the sturdy shoulders of eunuchs, and quitted the garden whose very atmosphere suggested Yung Lu, and passed through the wall, by way of the moon door, to obey the summons of Hsien Feng.

Long afterward, having been borne slowly and carefully, as though she had been a fragile flower of great price, along the road which led from her father's house to the gates of the Forbidden

City, she entered the latter place, and the ponderous doors swung shut behind her.

There was excitement in the Forbidden City. This was a great date in the life of Hsien Feng. Instinctively the folk who lived inside the holy of holies knew this, and there was wild rejoicing.

Lan Kuei was borne to the palace where Hsien Feng, masking his impatience behind a fine air of boredom, awaited her coming. He recalled, as he waited, every line of her features, for they had been impressed most forcibly upon his memory. Of the seventeen who had attended that first fateful audience, he remembered the faces and names of not one, save that of Lan Kuei, The Orchid. Regal of bearing, calmly disdainful of inessentials, a beautiful little lady, born to turn the heads of men—to be given into the bored keeping of Hsien Feng, to become his plaything, to be cast aside when he tired, if that should be his whim.

Lan Kuei reached the palace of this second audience, the audience which must finally and completely change the whole course of her life, shut her off forever from contact with Yung Lu, and the eunuchs lowered her sedan chair almost reverently to the ground. Lan Kuei, still with her head held high, was assisted from the chair.

It may have been accident, it may have been design, but the first person upon whom her eyes fell, ere they lifted to the moon door, another moon door, beyond which the Emperor waited, was Yung Lu, who had told her he loved her, who had heard from her own lips the words which told him his love was returned. Yung Lu's face was grey as ashes. The fateful summons, then, had been received. Lan Kuei was forever lost to Yung Lu. Henceforth he might only look at her from afar, as a humble man may look at a Queen from among the crowd which wait with craned necks to watch her passing. For many moments Lan Kuei hesitated, looking into the eyes of Yung Lu. Perhaps her lips trembled slightly, but if they did she conquered the trembling, lifted her head higher with pride. Yung Lu's lips trembled, too, but there was nothing he could do or say. He could only look into her eyes, his heart creeping into his own, so that Lan Kuei must have seen the wild and sorrowed beating of it— like invisible, imprisoned wings, behind his eyes.

The Emperor Commands

THE FIRST COURTYARD OF THE FORBIDDEN CITY, WITH THE INNER BOW-SHAPED MOAT

Then Lan Kuei, noting how Yung Lu straightened, strove to disguise the story she must have seen in his eyes, looked away from her erstwhile sweetheart, to whom she had been sweetheart since childhood, and, urged forward by impatient eunuchs, moved steadily to the moon door. It was opened for her by eunuchs, who pushed her forward. Just as she entered she turned for a fleeting, maybe triumphant, glance back over her shoulder at Yung Lu. He was still standing there, but his eyes were not upon her. They were looking away, blankly, at an empty world, and as though he sensed her turning, without seeing, Yung Lu faced smartly about, strode away.

The moon door was open. The eunuchs urged Lan Kuei forward. Inside the palace, on a *kong* or shelf against the wall opposite the door—a shelf that was like a great commodious bed—sat Hsien Feng, the Emperor. The officious eunuchs made haste to place a cushion for Lan Kuei, so that she might perform the necessary kowtows, do honor to her lord and master, who was also lord and master to all the hosts of China's people. She walked steadily to the cushion they had placed for her, unfaltering, and dropped upon it to her knees, her head bowed forward, her eyes downcast, her breasts rising and falling rapidly.

Hsien Feng, for perhaps the first time since he had become Emperor, broke the rules of the court.

Lan Kuei appealed to him, as no woman whom he had ever known had appealed. Usually he was bored in the presence of women, usually he regarded the most beautiful of his concubines with impatience. But here—well, here was Lan Kuei, whom he had chosen from among the seventeen, and she was beautiful to look upon, beyond power of words to describe.

So Hsien Feng broke the rules.

He waved the eunuchs from his presence with an imperious gesture. They went, striving to mask the polite surprise which persisted in showing itself in their eyes, and closed the moon door behind them. Hsien Feng stepped down from the *kong*, moving toward the girl who still knelt humbly on the cushion the eunuchs had placed for her, and raised her to her feet.

Never in his time had he done this for any woman!

He raised her to her feet—

The Emperor Commands

"You are very beautiful, Lan Kuei!"

His voice was not very steady as he spoke the words. Lan Kuei did not make answer. She held her peace. But her breasts rose and fell more rapidly. She was trembling. Lan Kuei, so calm usually, so proud and regal, was trembling in the presence of Hsien Feng. Hsien Feng retained her fragile little hand, and golden lights leaped into his bored eyes when he felt the trembling of the hand within his own.

"You are very beautiful, Lan Kuei!" he repeated, and his voice was harsh, a trifle more husky than when he had first spoken.

Lan Kuei trembled more, and strove with all her force of will to stay the trembling. Her limbs almost refused her, would have refused her had not the hand of the Emperor held her stoutly, though even then she swayed a little on her high-heeled shoes.

"Lan Kuei, I love thee!" said His Majesty. "In all my court there is never another as beautiful as thee!"

Then, slowly, as though all her will were being expended in the effort, Lan Kuei raised her eyes to meet the eyes of the Emperor, and in the moment of that meeting, both were lost. Ambition had suddenly made a wanton of Lan Kuei, so that she desired this man above all others, because of what he could give her, because of the high place to which his love, or his lust, could raise her. Personable, was Hsien Feng. Lan Kuei might have loved him. That she desired him there can be no doubt, because Hsien Feng was the Emperor. So she met his eyes, and in her own was all the age-old coquetry which is the heritage of women. The fire in her eyes made answer to the desire which shone naked from the eyes of

Hsien Feng, eyes in which golden lights, like golden motes of sunshine, glowed and flickered. Slowly the arm of Hsien Feng passed around the wasp-like waist of Lan Kuei, The Orchid. The thumb and forefinger of his right hand were raised, to pinch playfully the blush-dyed cheeks of the new Secondary Wife, a Manchu gesture denoting affection. Lan Kuei trembled. Involuntarily her eyes turned for a fleeting moment toward the moon door. But the moon door was closed.

In that fleeting moment of turning, did Lan Kuei think of Yung Lu? Perhaps. She never told, in the years that followed, for Lan Kuei was proudest of the proud. But perhaps she turned to see that the moon door was really closed, to^ assure herself that no moon-faced eunuchs, snickers visible behind their motionless lips, were standing just inside, devouring the scene with the eyes of bored wisdom.

The moon door was closed. No eunuchs watched from beside it, and the windows which gave on the courtyard masked the interior of the palace. The eyes of Lan Kuei went back to the eyes of Hsien Feng, and in them His Majesty read the tale of abject surrender. Perhaps he would have been less vain, less proud of his conquest, had he been able to read the thoughts behind the cold austerity of Lan Kuei's broad, intellectual brow. But perhaps not. The fact that she indicated surrender, telling the story with her eyes, was sufficient for Hsien Feng who was not analytical in inessential things.

Softly, though there still was huskiness in his voice, Hsien Feng spoke into the upturned face of Lan Kuei!

"You are very beautiful, Lan Kuei," it was almost a whisper. "I shall love thee, and cherish thee always t"

His arm tightened on her wasp-like waist.

His eyes looked deeply, ever more deeply, into the eyes of Lan Kuei.

His fingers caressed her cheeks, pinched them until she blushed again, blushed somewhat furiously, not sure how to conduct herself, because she lacked experience. But instinct is woman's oldest preceptor. What she does not know at once, the ages whisper into her ears, which are ever wide to listen. Instinct then, in words that whispered silently, in the heart of Lan Kuei, prompted The Orchid. She smiled, a smile that was tremulous, that carried a luring suggestion of fear and something of the courtesan's oldest blandishments; and the lips of Hsien Feng, trembling just a little too, smiled back at her.

Silence, deep, purposeful, settled over the palace of the second, and most fateful, audience.

Outside, at the gates of the Forbidden City, Yung Lu clinched his hands until the long nails bit into the palms, and blood dyed them. The blood was the blood of his palms, really, but his heart was bleeding, too, for something precious had been forcibly torn from it, and down the years there must be a wound beyond all healing, a heart that must ever be empty.

V. THE LITTLE EUNUCH

There were some three thousand eunuchs in the court of Hsien Feng. There were small eunuchs, large eunuchs, fat eunuchs, slim eunuchs-and the least of them all was Li Lien Ying, who had been a farmer, a cobbler, and had become a eunuch by his own hand. Unloved was Li Lien Ying. He was ugly, did not strive to please, seemed to care little whether or not he prospered, if only he were given opportunity to fill his stomach, which always clamored for food. The small eunuch's lot was not nice in the best of circumstances. But most of the small eunuchs, ambitious to a certain extent, strove to please, thus bettering their condition. Li Lien Ying did not try. He entered the court nursing a hatred toward all mankind. That hatred never left him. He fought with the other small eunuchs-a "small eunuch" being a eunuch serving his apprenticeship, doing odd jobs, etc., -beat them and bullied them and was himself in turn beaten and bullied by the larger eunuchs who instinctively disliked him because of his beastly temper.

But Li Lien Ying, despite the fact that he had no friends, despite the fact that all his days and years at court were friendless, still nurtured selfish ambitions. His duties were many, various and arduous, and as he performed them his bold eyes missed nothing that transpired within range of them. He studied the habits of An Teh Hai, and lesser eunuchs, taught himself to emulate them. to learn duties above his own station, so that when his opportunity came he would be ready for it. He watched An Teh Hai, as I have said, because deep in his heart he nurtured the ambition to some time supplant the famous eunuch as Chief Eunuch to Hsien Feng.

There was little that went on that was missed by Li Lien Ying.

He was at the court, a broom-boy whose duty it was to see that the courtyards remained free of refuse, when Lan Kuei became Secondary Wife to Hsien Feng; and as he studied the habits of An Teh Hai, Li Lien Ying studied the habits, the likes and dislikes, of Lan Kuei, The Orchid.

Wise eunuch! Great and wise eunuch, Li Lien Ying. He could see farther into the future than most, could this beastly tempered neuter. He studied Lan Kuei, saw that she found favor in the eyes of Hsien Feng—a fact that was no secret after the first day of her

The Little Eunuch

arrival, since Hsien Feng neglected his duties for The Orchid, passed all the bounds of imperial dignity in ministering to her, pleasing her, and. striving to keep smiles upon her cameo-like cheeks—and planned against the time when he, too, should please Lan Kuei. Just now she did not notice Li Lien Ying. He was only a small eunuch, after all, a boy with a short broom, on his knees on the cobblestones because the broom had no handle; and Lan Kuei, on the rare occasions when she walked in the open away from the palace, held her head so high that she saw no one—no one, that is, who swept cobblestones, and was down on his knees to perform his labors.

But Li Lien Ying, when he thought no one would see him, dared to raise his eyes to Lan Kuei. He knew every line of her features, the curve of her eyebrows, the sound of her little feet on the cobblestones, the cadences of her voice. He knew when she was pleased and when she was displeased. She soon knew the great power that was hers, since she had become the favorite of Hsien Feng, and there were many eunuchs, and folk who were higher placed than any eunuch, who felt the weight of Lan Kuei's displeasure. Imperious she was, and regal, though but a Secondary Wife with, theoretically, no standing at court. However, standing was hers, for Hsien Feng wished her to be pleased always, and made sure that no one caused her to frown; for when she did frown, and the word went to Hsien Feng, there was endless trouble, and much of punishment. Hsien Feng's power was that of life and death, and that same power was Lan Kuei's power, because Hsien Feng denied her nothing.

Just where was the Empress?

Ah, Li Lien Ying could have told that, too. The Empress had been wise to oppose the choice of Lan Kuei, for after the arrival at court of The Orchid, Hsien Feng never again waited upon his Empress, to do her honor, to shower her with his favors, or give to her of his love. There is little wonder that the Empress hated Lan Kuei.

Li Lien Ying listened to all the gossip at the court, and there was always gossip. If a eunuch loved a serving maid, the other three thousand eunuchs knew about it, talked about it among themselves, laughed at the futility of such a love and Li Lien Ying listened, gathered bits of information which he might one day need, and put them away in his storehouse of memories. Many years later he was to make strange and terrible use of his knowledge. But if those who, in those first terrible years of Li's life at court noticed the ugly little, evil tempered eunuch at all, none guessed that, while now he danced to the fiddle while someone else wielded the bow, the day would come when those who had played would pay the piper, and Li himself would wield the bow.

Down in his heart, however, Li Lien Ying knew.

Now there was one thing that Li could do, and he did it well, according to China's standards. He could sing. He had the high falsetto of all eunuchs, and could sing better than most; though most eunuchs at court were actors and singers of one kind or another, because of the imperial theatres—where none might act save eunuchs, in plays written by members of the royal household, usually by Hsien Feng, the Empress, or someone highly placed whose efforts Hsien Feng desired to favor.

Li could sing.

For days and weeks he studied Lan Kuei, whenever opportunity offered.

"With a face so beautiful, and manners so grand," he told himself, "this favorite of His Majesty must take delight in music."

So Li, though never happy, pretended to be, and sang as he worked—though when he sang the observing must have seen that Lan Kuei herself was always within hearing distance. If she deigned to notice the ugly eunuch, however, none observed it. Her entire interest reposed in Hsien Feng, and his in her. In all the world there were only these two.

But Li Lien Ying sang, watched his opportunities, and waited with patience that knew no bounds.

"Cease that noise!"

That would be An Teh Hai—striding majestically here and there through the Forbidden City, seeking things about which to find fault, administering punishment at the hands of his underlings—commanding Li Lien Ying, the little eunuch, to cease from his singing. Perhaps the lash would fall across the shoulders of the wan-faced little neuter, just to remind him that An Teh Hai's words must be obeyed. And then, after An Teh Hai had passed, the other eunuchs, who had witnessed the incident would take cue from the words of An Teh Hai, and any who heard the singing of Li Lien Ying would bid him cease his noise, and lash him across the shoulders, or across the face. Li's life at court, those first few years, was not happy.

But Li's day was coming. None knew it save Li Lien Ying. He did not know for a surety, save that he had the utmost faith in Li Lien Ying. He hated all the world, all the eunuchs, everybody, and vengeance, he promised himself, would be his if he lived.

So he ceased his singing when An Teh Hai, or any of the greater eunuchs, were near, and bowed his head over his menial tasks.

"Someday, An Teh Hai," he would whisper to himself, "I shall kill you, though you are my kinsman!"

An Teh Hai, however, did not know, and would have laughed until his great paunch squirmed like jelly, had anyone told him of the thoughts in the mind of Li Lien Ying—and would, perhaps, have handed the name of Li Lien Ying to the royal executioner. An Teh Hai had power of life and death—as long as he did not use it too openly.

"Someday, An Teh Hai—"

It became a sort of litany, this threat against the life of An Teh Hai, a hymn of hate that sang aloud day after day, night after night, waking and dreaming, in the vengeful heart of Li Lien Ying.

Li Lien Ying cleaned the cobblestones. He was chore-boy for many of the greater eunuchs. But each new duty assigned him was a step, though ever so short, up the ladder he had reared for himself, and when the step came next under his feet, he was always ready to mount, because he was intelligent, and prepared against the future.

"Someday, An Teh Hai—"

Kicks and cuffs, beatings with the bamboo, quarrels with serving-maids who could not understand a eunuch in whose eyes they found no favor, featured the daily life of Li Lien Ying.

Verily do some great men mount to places of vast importance from the smallest of beginnings.

There is a lesson in the life of Li Lien Ying, evil as he was, from which folk far more fortunately endowed may profit, if they will.

He had no friends. He never forgot his enemies.
He believed in himself.

V. TINY FINGERS

For weeks and months all the court waited in a fever of excitement, in hope that bordered on despair. The Empress of Hsien Feng, nor all his concubines, had borne the Great Man an heir. So the court waited, excited and hopeful, from the moment the doctors made the marvelous discovery that Lan Kuei was to bear a child.

Would the child be a girl? Would it be a girl, to fill the heart of Lan Kuei with disappointment, because she had failed her lord and master, who so much desired a son to succeed him? The Empress was excited, too. If Lan Kuei gave birth to a girl, she would rejoice, for she hated Lan Kuei, who had stolen from her the love of the Emperor—if that love had ever been hers to lose.

Would it be a boy? Would Lan Kuei bring forth a man-child, to do honor to Hsien Feng? To become heir to the throne of China?

The court waited, spoke almost in whispers when doubts were voiced; but the court made ready, just the same, to do honor to a son. All China received the word that Lan Kuei was to bear a child, and all China waited, excited, to hear the glad tidings that a son had been born.

The fruit of the womb of Lan Kuei was discussed the length and breadth of China.

Lan Kuei herself waited in fear and trembling, and then she ceased to fear. Fate had been good to her thus far. She was the favorite of the Emperor. He loved her, had neglected court routine, the Empress, and all the other concubines, for Lan Kuei. Fate could not now be so cruel to her as to deny her a son.

And the time passed.

Every day the doctors dosed Lan Kuei with strange and terrible medicines, well knowing that they would lose their heads if the child came prematurely and did not live. Lan Kuei was the most precious treasure in the Forbidden City, with the Summer Palace and the Winter Palace combined. She knew it, too, and waited for the fateful day which should justify her. It would be a son, she told herself.

And it was!

The True Story of the Empress Dowager

There was wild excitement all over China when the word went forth that Lan Kuei had borne a son, and that his name was called Tung Chih.

The sacrifice, founded on legendry, was made ready. No one knows, perhaps, the full significance of the sacrifice, save perhaps the Royal Clan. Perhaps Hsien Feng knew, for of all the great ones, only he might make this sacrifice.

A table was set in the courtyard. Eunuchs, ladies-in-waiting, princes, the Empress—glowering in high displeasure and striving to hide the fact—were present; though none might touch the sacrifice save the Emperor.

On the table were three offerings. In the center a golden dish on which a live fish, just caught for the purpose from the nearest lotus pond, was fastened securely with red ribbons. He struggled there, against his fragile bonds, which held him securely while the sacrifice, or offering, was made to the God of Heaven by the sacred hand of His Majesty the Emperor. On the right of the live fish was the head of a pig, parboiled white, steaming hot. On the left of the fish was a rooster, also parboiled, denuded of feathers save for the tufts on the neck and a tuft on the tail. No one knows, as I have said, the exact significance of the three offerings, save that one must make it to assure good fortune to the newborn child, and that it must be made by the hand of the Emperor. Be-' sides the three offerings there were three cups of wine, wine in three cups, each having three legs, made of silver throughout, which must also be offered up.

The Emperor burned incense, set off firecrackers, and was very proud and very happy in the birth of a son to succeed him, and to worship at his grave. The offering was left on the table, and none might touch it. Yet it was not left too long, else the fish might die—for the ceremony provided that the fish must be returned living to the lake whence it had been taken. If it died, bad luck would attend the heir; if it lived, good fortune would be his, all his days. On this occasion, when the fish returned to the lake where it had been captured, it leaped from the water many times, seemed wildly happy to return to its element, and all the court was happy in the knowledge that good fortune would attend the life of Tung Chih.

Tiny Fingers

Later, after the fish had been returned, the wine from the three cups must be poured, as an offering to the God of Earth, upon the cobblestones of the courtyard, while the pig's head and the rooster must remain for a day upon the table.

When making this offering the Emperor would kowtow to the only Being in all the Universe, above the earth or below it, to whom he must bend the knee. And when the offering was removed, he must kowtow, too, and pour the wine upon the cobblestones. For a child had been born, and the child was a son, and all the court, all China, rejoiced and was glad.

And the following prevailed throughout China, with the birth of Tung Chih:

All the prisons opened wide their doors, and all the prisoners, of whatever crime condemned, were allowed to go free.

No animals might be slain for three days, and none in China might eat of meat.

All stores must be closed, and no business transacted.

Every cage which contained birds must be opened, the length and breadth of China, so that the feathered songsters might go free.

Fish which had been captured and kept in tubs or vats, awaiting the market, must be returned to the waters whence they came.

Banished officials, whatever the crime for which they had been banished, were granted leave to return, and reinvested with the rank and title which they had relinquished with their banishment.

All this because of baby fingers, tiny fingers, which had already wrapped themselves about the great composite heart of a nation—in theory. Tiny fingers, which held so much of power! Criminals who wore the cangue, prisoners condemned to die, to be shot or beheaded, were freed when they expected to pay for their crimes, all because of those tiny fingers, and a tiny form, fruit of the womb of Lan Kuei, The Orchid. Birds of many colors, which sang songs in all the tones that beauty knows, were released from bondage, because a cooing babe had been born, and rested in the swaddling clothes of custom, in the arms of an amah who had never hoped to be so greatly honored. Animals awaiting the slaughter had a new lease on life, however hopeless it might be; stores closed down for a holiday, and silence held sway over China, as though all China prayed, reverently, with bowed heads.

And banished officials, some of them grown grey in exile, lost long since to hope of return to the homeland, were called back, to receive their rank upon return, to be received once more into the bosoms of families who had waited.

Immense power, this, in the hands of a child.

Tung Chih, a little Emperor, born to glorify the pathway of Lan Kuei, to feed her vast ambitions, to make her great before the eyes of the world.

Yes, a very important little personage was Tung Chih, son of Lan Kuei, The Orchid!

Then came night. The baby slept in his swaddling clothes, the swaddling clothes of age-old custom.

And the dignified celebration began within the heart of the Forbidden City.

There were paper lanterns of many colors, carried by proud eunuchs; there were skyrockets of many shades, to make snaky pathways across the sky of night. Streamers and flags flew from every building, not only in the Forbidden City, but all over the Middle Kingdom—for a child had been born, and he was the most important child in all the broad land.

There was feasting throughout the Forbidden City, and throughout China. The eunuchs, in that part of the Forbidden City set aside for them, prepared feasts for themselves. Good fortune must attend the court, now that a child had been born.

An Teh Hai, fat, contented, jovial, presided over the feast of the neuters, discoursing at great length on the honor which Lan Kuei had conferred upon the court.

The tables groaned with food, and the eunuchs, a gluttonous lot, stuffed themselves to repletion.

There was one among them who stuffed even more than the others, who snarled over his food, warningly, like an evil tempered cur—Li Lien Ying, who had been a farmer, a cobbler, and who envied An Teh Hai. A lowly "little eunuch," who dreamed great dreams.

All over China people feasted, paid their debts, and fired off firecrackers, shot fireworks.

Inside the Forbidden City none was allowed to forget that it had been The Orchid who had borne the Emperor an heir.

Tiny Fingers

Fireworks had already been prepared, because the court hoped for a son, against the great occasion. There were rockets, in many colors and strange, which burst above the walls and, descending in their own flames, took the forms of warriors on horseback, of lotus blossoms, of Peking carts with drivers—

But prominent among all the many sorts, kinds and sizes of fireworks, there was one design that caused great comment. It was a firework which, bursting at the height of its skyward flight, fell earthward, expanding, in the shape of a glorious flaming orchid. Glorification of Lan Kuei, the Orchid!

What a change now in the court, since Lan Kuei had born Hsien Feng an heir! To begin with, Hsien Feng changed her name to Tzu Hsi, which means "Holy Mother," and Holy Mother was her name the rest of her days. It is as Tzu Hsi that she is still remembered, and will be remembered as long as there is a written history of China. There were other changes, too. The Empress, Tzu An, who had lived in hope that Lan Kuei, now Tzu Hsi, should be confounded in the birth of a daughter, was filled with a seething hatred for the Secondary Wife that was destined never to leave her. She went to the bedside of Tzu Hsi, to ask after the health of the erstwhile Orchid, smiled upon her—and the Orchid read behind her spurious smile the hatred which Tzu An felt for the little lady who had supplanted her, and had confounded Tier by bearing a son.

Li Lien Ying, who knew his singing had attracted the attention of the Secondary Wife, felt a glow of hopefulness in his heart, for though it might be years in coming, his day would come, he knew, and in the birth to Tzu Hsi of a son he saw vast possibilities for Tzu Hsi—and for Li Lien Ying if he played his part well.

The court had been more or less in the background since the advent of Lan Kuei. There were few of its members who stood out, who held any great place in the book of life at court. For Lan Kuei had usurped it all, had stolen the limelight, as it were, from those who otherwise would have basked in its glow. Lan Kuei was the court, because she was the favorite of Hsien Feng, and since she had borne him an heir to the throne, the others receded more and more into the background.

The hatred of the Empress for Tzu Hsi grew daily more unbearable. She hated Tzu Hsi with a hatred that death would not conquer, yet there was nothing she could do, because of Hsien Feng.

Then there were Su Shun and Prince Yi. Su Shun was Grand Councillor. Prince Yi was nephew of Hsien Feng, and his duties at court were to enjoy life without laboring, a mission which he prosecuted with great success.

These two early developed a hatred for Tzu Hsi which was only less virulent than that of the Empress, Tzu An. But Tzu Hsi, her heart beating high because she realized the vast possibilities that now were open before her, like an endless road, paid no heed to the hatred of Tzu An, though she recognized it, as I have said, and knew nothing of the hatred and jealousy of Su Shun and Prince Yi—which made that hatred, and that jealousy, all the more dangerous.

The path of little Tung Chih was to be beset by thorns.

But in Tzu Hsi, Tung Chih had a mother who would fight for him as a tigress fights for the threatened cub.

And in Yung Lu, though he was yet but a humble Commander of the Guard, Tzu Hsi had a friend, a slave if you will, who was to serve her faithfully, all the years of his life.

At the court there was yet another man who was to play an important part in shaping the destiny of Tzu Hsi and her son Tung Chih. That one was Prince Kung, own brother to His Majesty, Hsien Feng.

He made a remark to a member of the Imperial Clan, immediately he learned that Lan Kuei, the Orchid, had been selected to be Secondary Wife to Hsien Feng.

"She is too clever! She is too beautiful! She will either bring good fortune, great good fortune, to the Middle Kingdom, or she will wreck it beyond all power of restoration P*

Fateful words, yet in those far-off days there was none who knew how fateful.

Hsien Feng thought of nothing but Tzu Hsi, and of Tung Chih. He was the happiest of mortals.

To show his people his happiness he caused the crumbs from the tables inside the Forbidden City to be thrown out the gates, so that the populace might fight for the leavings, and be happy, too. The crumbs were cast forth, load after load of them, by the supercilious eunuchs, who had the air, as they performed the rite, of casting pearls before swine.

What was going on in China when this great happiness was hovering, like an angel showering blessings, over the Forbidden City?

In the interior, whither the word of the birth went as though on the wings of morning, coolies labored endlessly in the fields. Their backs were bowed over their labors. Their knees were bare and bony, their flesh exposed to biting chill because their clothing was inadequate to cover their nakedness. The harsh fields were forced to give of their bounty, which was meager enough. Here a farmer labored in the muck and slime of a garden fertilized by evil residue, striving to close his nostrils to keep out the pestilential odors. There another farmer toiled at the single handle of an aged plow, a plow drawn by another coolie and a mule, striving to open the hard heart of the soil and make it bring forth food for the mouths of his little ones. Farms that were barren as the heart of an aged spinster.

There was happiness, and plenty, inside the Forbidden City and the Palaces, while in the interior humble folk were starving. These humble folk might have wondered if the wondrous birth would not in some small measure make more bearable their lot; but perhaps they wondered not at all. Ages of slavery to the soil had taught them that slavery was their only portion, and that no matter what wonders came to bless the court, they themselves must labor on, to the end of their days, unloved, unloving, slaves to the soil which produced food of the poorest kind, and that only at expense of unbelievably arduous toil.

It is little wonder then, that those who fought for the morsels of food cast from the gates of the Forbidden City by the minions of Hsien Feng, did not thank His Majesty, even in their hearts, for his generosity. They only fought like beasts for their several shares, and slipped away with them, to munch the bits in solitude, snarling.

So there was happiness all over China when Tung Chih was born, and there was sorrow, too, sorrow which might inspire deep and awful tragedies.

Verily, the little hands of Tzu Hsi, though she could not know it then, were soon to be forced to grasp and hold vast responsibilities.

Tzu An, Her Majesty the Empress, held her peace, nurtured her hatred of Tzu Hsi, and waited.

Su Shun and Prince Yi waited, too.

Hsien Feng thought of nothing save his good fortune, and his happiness.

Prince Kung, a great man though little known to history, waited to ascertain the accuracy of his prophecy.

Li Lien Ying bided his time, looking into the future. He snarled as always at those who spoke to him, his overseers, his masters the greater eunuchs, and raised his eyes, above his sagging lower lip, looking forth from his face, all hideously marked with smallpox scars, to the high place now occupied by the Chief Eunuch, An Teh Hai.

And An Teh Hai?

He pandered to his stomach, already fat with overfeeding, and honored the birth of Tung Chih by adding succulent morsels to a table filled to overflowing—his own.

The populace of Peking gathered outside the gates of the Forbidden City, that first evening, and the lights which rose and fell, as fireworks spluttered and sparkled from behind the walls, drawing their weird pictures in the sky, drew weird pictures of their faces, too. Faces, dead-white, drawn with hunger; faces marked with many scars; faces dirty and grimy from years without washing; faces alight with hope; faces in which might have been caught a faint echo of the happiness which reigned inside the Forbidden City—the faces of a Chinese multitude, a silent multitude that milled restlessly, watching the fireworks.

Faces, as the lights rose and burst, seemed to move forward out of the darkness, in bold relief, marked with lights and shadows, as though they were the very pulse- beat of life. They were the essence of all futility.

Yet none among them more futile, perhaps, than the puppets who sat upon the throne of China, striving to shape its destiny—to their own selfish ends.

VII. LADY MEI

Sixteen or seventeen, sweet, petite and clever. That was Lady Mei, the daughter of Su Shun. For her the Secondary Wife of Hsien Feng entertained the greatest affection. She loved Lady Mei, of all the court ladies, the best. She had her brought to the court, where she kept her, taught her to read, had her tutored in the graces.

Su Shun was Grand Councillor. His lust was the lust for money and power. He was pleased that Lady Mei had been taken into court, because in some small way it added to his own prestige. Lady Mei sat close to the throne, because Tzu Hsi sat close to the throne. Tzu Hsi was the favorite of the Emperor. Lady Mei was the favorite of Tzu Hsi.

Delicate and fragile was Lady Mei, a tiny little thing with great eyes that were always wide with amazement because there were so many wonderful things in the world in which she found herself. She did not love her father, knowing him for what he was, a grasping seeker after wealth and power. She did not know why she did not love him. She only knew that she did not, and the knowledge sometimes made her unhappy. But she forgot that unhappiness because she was happy in the presence of Tzu Hsi, and Tzu Hsi had said she would never allow her to leave the court, as long as she herself remained the favorite of Hsien Feng. That she would remain his favorite she knew, because hers were the wiles and the blandishments of the courtesan, the woman who seeks with all her coquetry to hold the affections of a man, a man, moreover, who was vain of his accomplishments with women.

So Tzu Hsi taught Lady Mei to read the classics, to make the sprawling characters without the knowledge of which no Manchu was considered educated, and praised her always for her cleverness.

This writer was in the confidence of Tzu Hsi, who told her much of Lady Mei, whom Tzu Hsi missed after circumstances robbed Tzu Hsi of her favorite's companionship.

Lady Mei had the freedom of the court. She went where she willed, whether the court were in the Forbidden City, the Summer Palace, the Winter Palace, or far Jehol. She was seen of many. Great men visited the court, great men who saw Lady Mei and desired her, for her beauty, and because she was so obviously clever. But she would have none of any of them.

The reason was not difficult to find. Lady Mei had allowed her eyes to rest upon the stalwart figure, the handsome face, of a Commander of the Manchu Guard. That commander's name was Yung Lu, erstwhile sweetheart of Lan Kuei!

But for Yung Lu there was never another than Lan Kuei.

Lady Mei first took notice of Yung Lu on that fateful day when Lan Kuei bore an heir to Hsien Feng. A Commander of the guard who was not happy, made no pretense of being happy, when all the court was delirious with joy, because Lan Kuei had borne a child to Hsien Feng a child, moreover, who was a man-child, and might one day sit as Emperor upon the throne of China. Yung Lu found no pleasure in the excitement which possessed the Manchu court. Quite the contrary. It was no pleasure to him to realize, as this celebration made him realize, how far Lan Kuei had gone from him. Hitherto, she had been the favorite, the plaything, of an Emperor. That might have been against her will (though Yung Lu suspected otherwise) for Hsien Feng had issued a decree, a decree that might not he disobeyed, and any little Manchu lady of high family could have been named on that decree, for the Emperor was all-powerful. Lan Kuei had been named. She had gone. She had been chosen, and a dark cloud had ever afterward obscured the sun of Yung Lu's life.

Then she had built still higher the wall that separated them, by hearing a son to her lord and master.

And Yung Lu, of all those who knew the innermost secrets of the court, was not happy.

He stood, morose, sullen, downcast, at the gates of the Forbidden City. A great light, in the birth of Tung Chih, had descended upon China, yet none of that light shed itself upon Yung Lu. For Lan Kuei now was irrevocably lost to him. So, ever and anon, he looked toward the place where the sick mother rested beside her first-born, and sorrow and heartache possessed his very soul.

It was thus that Lady Mei found him. He found favor in her eyes at once, though he was but a humble Commander of the

Lady Mei

Guard, she the daughter of the Grand Councillor. She went to him, when she saw him.

"You are not happy, Yung Lu?" she asked, diffidently.

Yung Lu faced her, bowed deeply.

"Of course," he said. "Is not all China happy in the fact that His Majesty Hsien Feng has fathered an heir to the throne of the Middle Kingdom?"

"All China is happy, Yung Lu," replied Lady Mei, "all China, save Yung Lu, who does not seem to be happy. Tell me, Yung Lu, why are you so downcast?"

Yung Lu made no answer. He strove to control the twitching of his face, the slight trembling of his lips. He did not succeed. Orientals have excellent control of their features, save when they love madly, wildly, and their love is not returned. Their blood is warm, and they may even be dangerous when their love is, for some reason, thwarted.

Lady Mei, realizing that she stood in the presence of something beyond her knowledge, something almost cataclysmic, studied the face of Yung Lu for many moments. She thought, perhaps, that Yung Lu was not in sympathy with the court, and may have been minded to make report of the fact to Lan Kuei, now Tzu Hsi, for she loved Tzu Hsi with a love that was boundless, and would never permit anything to mar the happiness of her favorite. But then, again, there was nothing a humble Commander of the Guard could do. And he looked so sad, so entirely heartbroken, that Lady Mei pitied him. At least she thought she pitied him, not understanding that what she felt for him was something far deeper, something else that was outside her experience hitherto, something that might lead to happiness, yet was destined to set her feet in a pathway that would lead to eternal despair.

She loved Yung Lu at once, did Lady Mei, and did not understand the meaning of love. She knew, after that first meeting, that she missed the face and form of Yung Lu when he was absent, that she took pleasure in his companionship, aloof as it always was, when he was with her, or when she so far forgot maidenly modesty as to seek him out.

But on this occasion she studied the face of Yung Lu, noted how various expressions, mirrors of his heart, came and went

The True Story of the Empress Dowager

across his handsome face. She noted how straight he stood, how personable he was in his guardsman's uniform, and knew that she took pleasure from his masculinity. But she could not read the reason for his lack of pleasure in the celebration of the birth of Tung Chih.

"Why are you so downcast, Yung Lu?" she asked again.

Yung Lu then turned upon her savagely.

"You court ladies," he began savagely, "who fawn before the Emperor like paid courtesans, ready to submit yourselves to him if only he will deign to reward you with a single supercilious glance! Ready to flagellate yourselves to be near a man who cares nothing for your souls, if souls you have! but only for your bodies, which you deck in glorious finery, sweeten with alluring perfumes, striving to attract his glances, to call to his attention the fact that you are females, with femininity's age- old commodity, which is his for the merest asking! You have no pride, you ladies of the court. You have no real desire for this puppet who sits upon the throne of China, but lust after the things he can give you—power, wealth, prestige, and the lustful *glory* of his imperial *kong* after nightfall. The woman who is chosen to be his plaything is envied of all the others. Why? Because, while he is different from no other man, save that satiety has jaded his appetites, he is China's Emperor, and it is a great thing for a woman to be honored at the bed of his Imperial Majesty! My sister, if I had one, and the family were of sufficient rank to allow that my sister be thus honored, would likely be as eager to be the plaything of the Emperor as any courtesan-at-heart who has already been thus honored—like The Imperial Mistress, for example, and all the Emperor's concubines! Is it any wonder that a humble man quails before this knowledge of the depravity of women from China's very highest families?" "It is The Imperial Mistress then, Yung Lu?"

"No, it is not The Imperial Mistress!" denied Yung Lu savagely. "What is she? The concubine of an Emperor! Who is she? Nobody, until she became mother to Hsien Feng's son!"

Yung Lu, like any man who is hurt, struck out savagely and because he so vehemently denied the implication in the question of Lady Mei, he affirmed her words more surely than had he uttered affirmation in words direct and to the point.

"I know," said Lady Mei softly. "It is The Imperial Mistress—whom you may never have! Do you not realize, Yung Lu, that Lan Kuei, or Tzu Hsi, as the Emperor now calls her 'Holy Mother'—may one day be Empress Dowager of China, if her son is named to succeed The Emperor, and The Emperor dies?"

For many moments Yung Lu hesitated, and was totally lost. If Lady Mei had only guessed before, she knew the whole truth now. When Yung Lu finally faced her he knew that she had penetrated his secret, and suddenly the desire possessed him to confide in her.

"Yes," he said softly, miserably, "it is Lan Kuei. I may never have her, as you say; but," and Yung Lu raised his head proudly, standing very straight in his uniform, "I can serve her always! I can be faithful to her until death, and afterward. I can be her loyal servant, her most abject slave, and thus shall I serve her, as long as she shall have need of me—and in the court of China, where there are continually plots and counterplots, there may be many times when she will need me."

Lady Mei said nothing for a moment. Since no one seemed to be noticing them, she so far flouted custom as to approach closer to the person of Yung Lu, and to take his hand.

Savagely he flung her hand away. He hated sympathy, or tried to make himself believe he did. Like all men, Yung Lu was a child at heart. Subconsciously he knew it, and the knowledge angered him. So when Lady Mei, recognizing his need, realizing that he required a woman's sympathy, took his hand and offered hers, Yung Lu flung her fragile hand aside with an ejaculation of impatience, and wondered why a little smile, a hurt smile, with just a hint of triumph in its depths, rippled across her lips that were so red, so gloriously shaped for the kisses of a man who loved her.

"We do not all strive to lure His Majesty, Yung Lu," she said. "There are some of us who do not offer our bodies to the Emperor. There are many of us who would bitterly oppose him, were he to demand it of us."

"You are all the same, where the Emperor is concerned," replied Yung Lu.

He turned his back upon Lady Mei. Before she left him, smiling a little mysterious smile, she touched his hand, a touch that was like a caress; but he did not seem to notice.

Court eunuchs, who came upon the scene just as Lady Mei was leaving, moving like a little queen upon her high- heeled shoes, talked about this latest thing among themselves.

"What a wonderful couple!" was the gist of their gossipy comment. "So much alike. Wonderful mates they would make for each other—she so beautiful, Yung Lu so straight and handsome!"

But, noting the black forbidding scowl upon his face, the eunuchs took great pains to assure themselves that Yung Lu did not hear their words.

Then, after a time, Yung Lu looked away again toward the closely guarded door of the place where a child had been born, who now rested in his swaddling clothes, in the arms of an amah, or beside his mother on an imperial *kong*, and the merest of smiles displaced his scowl.

After all, he loved the little lady who had been Lan Kuei, and when he had said that his dearest hope was to serve her always, as faithful retainer, humble slave if she required it of him, he had meant just that—and his words had come from the very depths of the loyal heart of him.

Yung Lu did not perhaps realize that what he had said to Lady Mei concerning the Secondary Wife of the Emperor, might have been used as evidence leading to his decapitation, for no man, no woman, may say anything against the Chinese sovereign, nor may they even mention his name.

VIII. TWO WOMEN

Playing important parts in the babyhood of Tung Chih were two women. One was Tzu An, the Empress; the other was Tzu Hsi, the mother of the heir. None knew better than Tzu Hsi that her son might one day he sole ruler of the Middle Kingdom—none, that is, save Tzu An who, being somewhat stupid, slower by far of wits than Tzu Hsi, was insanely jealous of the Secondary Wife. So Tzu Hsi, being wise, clever, and loving her son as she never loved another living creature, decided to secure the friendship, at least the toleration, of Tzu An.

To begin with, the jealousy of Tzu An, who had not borne a son, was so all-encompassing that she refused to visit the chamber of Tung Chih, which the young heir might not leave, even in the arms of an amah, for one month after birth, or until the time came for the ceremony of shaving the head—reasons for which ceremony may not be entered into on the printed page. But Tzu An was clever, as the stupid are sometimes clever to save themselves from the righteous anger of those set above them. Tzu An knew that the Emperor would be furious if he realized the jealousy, the downright hatred, which Tzu An felt for Tzu Hsi. This Tzu An knew fully. So, to cover the failure to visit Tung Chih, Tzu An made the statement that her month of birth was inimical to the birth month of Tung Chih and that for her to approach him would bring evil fortune to the heir.

This requires a bit of explanation.

Each month of the Chinese year is symbolized by an animal—snake, rat, rooster and so forth. The rat is inimical to the serpent, and a man or woman born in the month of the rat, may not mate with a man or woman born in the month of the snake. Such a mating is doomed to evil fortune, according to the Chinese belief. There was justice, superstitious justice, in Tzu An's claim, and little was thought of the matter, therefore, when Tzu An refused to visit the Young Emperor in his own chamber.

But Tzu Hsi knew the real truth. Tzu An was jealous, insanely jealous, and it was not beyond the bounds of possibility that Tzu An might do something to injure, or even kill, the Young Emperor, despite the fact that, according to the custom, the child of a concubine belonged to the Empress as much as or even more than to the concubine.

On her part, Tzu Hsi, loving Tung Chih, with perhaps now a modicum of love for the child's father, believing in the efficacy of the old superstitions, called to her aid all her own knowledge of those same superstitions, in order to safeguard her son. In China, when a son is born, the fear that he may die while yet a baby is inborn. Many safeguards are used to prevent this. Tzu Hsi fastened a chain about the neck of Tung Chih, a chain whose ends were secured by a padlock, in order that Tung Chih might be bound to the earth, and not escape it by dying. Another custom, in the case of children born to commoners, was for friends of the parents to adopt the child, in order that the child have so many parents, all of them desirous that the child live and prosper, that their combined wills might defeat the wills of the Ancestral Spirits, and so keep the child alive. This belief is very complicated, very difficult to make plain to the westerner, to whom Orientals as a whole are closed books—mysterious, with no keys by which the westerner may unlock the secret doors.

Since Tzu Hsi could not, of course, have others adopt Tung Chih, because in all China there was no family of sufficient rank, no family in which ran the blood of royalty, save in the Imperial Clan, whose influence would be with Tung Chih in any case, she did what she believed would be as efficacious as the multiple adoption. She secured one hundred of the finest pieces of silk obtainable, from one hundred heads of the highest families in the Middle Kingdom, and from the hundred pieces of silk she had a cloak made for Tung Chih, in the belief that the hands from which the bits of silk had come would serve to hold back from death the boy Tung Chih. The Little Emperor wore his cloak of many colors, and Tzu Hsi was satisfied that she had done the best she knew for her son—save one thing.

This one thing she also essayed to do, as soon as she was able to leave the room where Tung Chih was born. She needed the friendship of Tzu An, for though Tzu An herself had been a concubine, she had been raised to the rights and powers of Empress with the death of the real Empress, and no law could change her right as Empress —in whom was vested a proprietary right in Tung Chih.

Tzu Hsi, stung to the quick because Tzu An had failed to visit her son, and reading in that failure something ominous to the future of Tung Chih, visited the Empress.

The eunuchs and court-ladies listened with wide-open eyes, and in utter silence, when Tzu Hsi came to speak to Tzu An about the boy Tung Chih. It was a fateful meeting, and all the court knew it. Tzu Hsi, knowing her power, knowing what greater power might be hers when her son finally assumed the throne of China, strode proudly into the presence of the Empress Tzu An. She spoke with hut few preliminaries.

"I would have your friendship," she said. "Your rights to Tung Chih are greater than mine! You are the Empress, I a secondary wife. Though I am the child's mother, you are more than his mother. I wish your friendship, Tzu An, no matter where the destiny of Tung Chih may lead us."

Tzu An listened in silence. The eunuchs heard the words, and the court ladies. Her words would be whispered in every nook and cranny of the Forbidden City in a matter of hours—and the words of Tzu An's reply. It behooved Tzu An to answer thoughtfully, in order that good report should reach the ears of His Majesty, the Emperor.

"My friendship?" she asked.

Her lips smiled, though Tzu Hsi could see into her eyes, that they were deep wells of hate and jealousy.

"My friendship?" she repeated. "And why should you not have it always? You are the mother of Tung Chih, whose father is my consort, the Emperor!"

Tzu An half raised her hand. Tzu Hsi, moving close to her, reached forth her own and grasped the right hand of Tzu An.

Tzu An went even further, though her lips were parted in a set smile that was like a grinning mask, without mirth.

Have you not been told that His Majesty, the Emperor, has decreed that we are just the same as sisters? And there is more between sisters than mere friendship?"

"I understand you—Sister!" replied Tzu Hsi, who understood her perfectly, who pronounced the epithet of relationship with an emphasis that was weighted with meaning for those who heard.

Tzu Hsi pressed strongly the fragile hand of Tzu An, her own hand as fragile, seemingly, though strong because of her love for Tung Chih. Tzu An, though she tried to mask the expression, could not prevent sudden excruciating pain from showing on her fine features.

The eunuchs and court-ladies, discussing the meeting later, and it was often to be discussed in the days, weeks and months, and years which followed, said that after Tzu Hsi had released the hand of Tzu An, there were red weals (weals from which they would have seen the blood welling had not Tzu An straightway hidden her hand) on the hand of the Empress, where the sharp fingernails of the Secondary Wife had scored the fragile hand of Tzu An.

They also said that they had seen abject fear in the eyes of Tzu An, before the iron control, which was hers of necessity, forced her to mask the expression almost as soon as it was born.

Later Tzu Hsi bore Tung Chih to the Empress. Again eunuchs and court-ladies were present. Tzu Hsi was politeness itself to Tzu An. She tried with all her artistry to seem friendly to the Empress, spoke to her kindly, called her "Sister," and seemed to be all to Tzu An that even the Emperor could have desired.

Yet the eunuchs and the court-ladies could not forbear noticing that though the Empress seemed to miss nothing with those expressive eyes of hers, they never once rested on the helpless bundle in the awkward swaddling clothes, which was Tung Chih, the Little Emperor.

Whispers went the length and breadth of the Forbidden City, the Summer Palace and the Winter Palace; the whole court, save perhaps His Majesty, Hsien Feng, knew that there was a silent, implacable feud between the Empress and the Secondary Wife, a feud based upon jealousy that all the years to follow would not erase.

Yung Lu heard the whispers, and remembered that he had sworn within his heart to be faithful to Tzu Hsi. It seemed that the time might come when she would have need of him, and his loyalty.

Two Women

Prince Yi heard—but Prince Yi was a weakling, a parasite who lived for pleasure, and he did not pay heed to the whispers until another brought their purport to him so forcibly that he could not fail to heed.

That one was Su Shun, the Grand Councillor, the grasping miser who desired gold, and more gold, power and prestige, for himself. Su Shun knew of the feud, and wondered how he could turn it to his own advantage. He thought of Prince Yi, nephew of the Emperor, and began cannily to play upon the vanity of the parasite.

Li Lien Ying heard the whispers, and looked anew, and more covetously, upon the throne of importance occupied by the portly form of An Teh Hai, the Chief Eunuch.

An Teh Hai heard the whispers, but he could not trace their source, since everyone whispered, repeating whispers they themselves had heard—but An Teh Hai was devoted from the first to Tzu Hsi, and fairly adored the Little Emperor. Had he been father to Tung Chih, he could not have loved him more. An Teh Hai was a powerful friend.

But if Hsien Feng, who was most interested after Tung

Chih and Tzu Hsi, heard the ominous whispers, he gave no sign.

The Empress nursed her hand, marked by the fingernails of Tzu Hsi, and nursed her hatred as she nursed her hand. Too powerful by far was Tzu Hsi, and Tzu An knew that the road before her would be dotted thickly with stumbling blocks. She began to cast about her for means by which to reduce the fortress, invisible yet none the less tangible, in which Tzu Hsi had taken refuge— that fortress being the love and adoration of Hsien Feng, whose death, which comes some time to all living, would alter the whole course of the life at court, would fill it with intrigue and dark deeds and thoughts, would make the life of the Empress a life of horror and despair, would make the life of Tzu Hsi a life that she could scarce call her own, since she never could tell when someone might rise up to take it from her.

There were ominous whispers, whispers whose echoes were to ring down the corridors of the years which lay ahead, behind the misty horizon which masks the future.

But Tzu Hsi dressed her firstborn in the cloak of the hundred pieces, and kept her faith in the efficacy of signs and portents.

But most of all she kept her indomitable faith in herself.

Iron willed was Tzu Hsi, destined to be molded by harsh circumstances into a creature ruled by her loves and her hates, a woman whom all China would remember forever.

With the birth of Tung Chih, she came into her own, though then she knew it not. On that fateful day when she had left her chamber to converse with Tzu An, she had thrown down the gauntlet to the Empress, and the Empress had almost seen the iron hand which was clinched inside the glove, while Tzu Hsi's own hand, less harsh perhaps, had emphasized the hurling of the gauntlet in the red marks she had left on the back of the right hand of Tzu An.

Tzu An, nominally, was Empress of the East, higher than Tzu Hsi.

But Tzu An, today, is scarce remembered, save in the dusty annals of China's history, while "Old Buddha," the name by which Tzu Hsi is best remembered, the name which she herself liked best, has left her ineradicable impress upon the Middle Kingdom.

IX. ALL HONOR TO THE HEIR

They came as givers, bearing gifts. From all the provinces and the towns, came the secretaries and lesser officials, representing Provincial Governors and Viceroys, bringing the gifts of their masters. There were many groups of coolies, bearing the gifts. Trays heaped high with showy baubles worth thousands, sometimes millions, of *taels*. Coolies bearing carefully and reverently vari-hued vases from foreign countries, vases whose purchasers were perhaps Chinese Ministers who had seen the priceless creations and had straightway thought of their sovereign. Sweating coolies, barefoot, with scarce enough rags to cover their nakedness, their stomachs gaunt with lack of food, their eyes hopeless, bearing priceless gifts. The loss of a single one, the breaking of a vase, might have meant the beheading of a coolie who had no idea what it all signified.

Hour after hour came the gifts, the trays, the bundles, to the gates of the Forbidden City—the gates of the Summer and Winter Palaces. Priceless gifts, which would have ransomed the coolies who bore them from a score of generations of slavery to exacting toil.

Gifts to commemorate the birthday of the Emperor, of his Empress; gifts for the New Year; gifts to do honor to the birth of Tung Chih.

Those who bore gifts on this particular day, and the days that followed—the gifts kept coming in because many came from far distances, and time was consumed in journeys that seemed endless—brought those gifts to do honor to the heir to China's throne.

Came a procession of trays to the gates of the Forbidden City. Trays heaped high with gifts sent hither by one of China's most powerful Viceroys. Jewels, marvelous clocks of foreign make, deep blue vases as high as the shoulders of a large man.

They came to the gates of the Forbidden City and were halted. Two eunuchs stood watch and ward there, over this holy of holies of the Manchus, and any who entered there must first satisfy the eunuchs that they were worthy. Their worthiness, usually, almost always, was measured by other gifts they brought, gifts with which to feed the rapacious appetites of the eunuchs themselves.

No man might enter the city if those two eunuchs denied him entrance.

So the representatives of the high officials brought other gifts, as I have said.

"Here," said one, "are four hundred *taels*. A small gift with which to buy yourselves a small supply of tea."

That the eunuchs had more tea than they could ever use, given them by merchants in Peking for certain favors, was well known to the officials, as to the eunuchs. There was nothing in the rules that said the eunuchs must buy tea with the four hundred *taels*. What they did with the four hundred *taels* concerned none save the eunuchs; and the givers, if the four hundred *taels* were considered enough, were allowed to pass through the first of the gates, into the first courtyard.

Only to find there were other gates, with other guardians, who must also be passed ere the gifts could reach the greatest gift-receiver of them all, who must pass on the suitability of the gifts—An Teh Hai.

The procession entered the gates of the Forbidden City. It entered the secondary gates, after suitable gifts had been made other eunuchs; entered other gates after yet other eunuchs' rapacity had been satisfied.

Then the inner courtyard, where the procession halted, and word was taken to An Teh Hai.

With the word went the official accompanying the gifts, bearing also a list of them all, with the name of the giver, on a huge piece of yellow paper, in whose center, large and important, were the characters denoting the person for whom the gifts were intended.

An Teh Hai, lordly An Teh Hai, in whom was vested responsibility, vast responsibility too, for deciding upon the suitability of gifts, was a man whose friendship was valuable at court. Oh, quite valuable! Gifts which did not please the Imperial Person for whom intended caused that person to lose appreciation for the sender, for which reason it was a disgrace for presents to be

All Honor To The Heir

turned back at the gate, or to be refused of presentation by An Teh Hai.

The Chief Eunuch would go out to view the gifts, the whole procession of them.

"Argil!" he would snort. "They are not suitable! They are no good!"

"Ah," the official would reply, "I almost forgot! The Viceroy wishes to be remembered to his good friend, An Teh Hai, and has sent along a small, insignificant present, in the shape of money with which to buy tea! He does not send the tea, realizing his inability, because of lack of taste, to choose the tea most pleasing to the palate of An Teh Hai. So he has sent the money in order that An Teh Hai may make the purchase himself or, disdaining to thus demean himself with barter, may send forth the money by some lowly servant to make the necessary purchase."

Since the purchase price amounted to twenty thousand *taels*—in silver ingots shaped like little shoes, each shoe worth fifty *taels*, the whole amounting to about fourteen thousand dollars in American money—it is little wonder that An Teh Hai found the gifts suitable.

An Teh Hai would then take the gifts to the person for whom designated, the Empress, the Emperor, or the Imperial Mistress, who might even turn up his or her nose at the gifts as being entirely unsuited for presentation to a royal personage. Then, if An Teh Hai had found them suitable, or the retainer large enough—which meant the same thing—he would make reply:

"This isn't suitable, perhaps; but those vases would be suitable for the servants' quarters, that clock would be suitable for placing in the quarters set aside for the guard, and those pearls would look well on the least of the concubines."

Invariably the Empress, the Emperor, or the Imperial Mistress, placing trust in the judgment of An Teh Hai, would agree to this, and the gifts would be accepted— and An Teh Hai could then bank his honorarium. Several banks did business with and for An Teh Hai, and each of the several banks catered to him and his accounts, since he was almost invariably the largest depositor. For gifts came daily to the gates of the Forbidden City. And there were other ways in which money came to the hands of the deserving—who recognized the knuckles of opportunity when she knocked.

But perhaps the honorarium, the "tea-payment," was not large enough.

Perhaps, in this case, the person to receive the gifts found them good.

Then would An Teh Hai speak up.

"This is not suitable, Your Majesty! It is lacking in taste. It cost but little money. It is very evident that the sender does not care for his sovereign, but sends gifts only because he feels he must. I should return them to him by his own bearers!"

The official who had brought the gifts, being thus disgraced by the scorning of his gifts, invariably retired, woebegone and disheartened—usually forgetting to mention the fact that An Teh Hai had deceived his honorarium, which might honorably he demanded of him when the gifts were refused. No, that was usually forgotten; and wise officials made mental note against a future gift-presentation, when An Teh Hai's honorarium should be doubled or trebled.

Perhaps, on the other hand, the gifts never reached An Teh Hai at all. Perhaps they never even entered the Forbidden City—because the two eunuchs drank "tea" that cost more than four hundred *taels*, more in fact, than the givers felt any tea should cost. Disgruntled, showing their displeasure without putting it into words, the eunuchs might pass the gifts; and if, say, one of the pair of beautiful vases should be broken by an accidental fall from coolie hands, who was to say that the fall had not been accidental? And who would dare present one vase to Emperor, Empress, or Imperial Mistress? It just simply wasn't done, and givers returned, wiser, sadder, furious at all eunuchs, yet resolved to bring sufficient *cumsha* on a second journey.

Li Lien Ying, whose labors had taken him bit by bit farther up the ladder he had reared for himself, saw the gifts that were borne to An Teh Hai. His experience as farmer, and as cobbler, had taught him the value of money. He could calculate values in *taels*, dollars, or pounds, and to a nicety. It did not escape Li Lien Ying, the fact that An Teh Hai, because he stood close to the throne, was something of a plutocrat, who received huge sums for his own,

All Honor To The Heir

because his words carried weight when spoken at the foot of the throne.

This only strengthened Li Lien Ying in his desire to take his place where he felt he rightfully belonged, in the huge shoes of An Teh Hai.

Did An Teh Hai suspect the ambitions of Li Lien Ying? Scarcely, else Li Lien Ying had never lived to realize them. Did he see the avaricious light in the eyes of the eunuch when that eunuch saw the money he, An Teh Hai, could produce as though by magic from the money pouches of visiting great men? Perhaps, for he tossed a single "shoe," worth fifty *taels*, to Li Lien Ying, as a beggar tosses a thoroughly gnawed bone to a starving cur. Li Lien Ying snarled, but he took the "shoe" of silver.

And made yet another resolution: if ever he stood in the broad shoes of An Teh Hai, it would cost more than twenty thousand *taels* for viceroys to bring presents to royalty; and the eunuchs at the gate would not require over fifty *taels* each for the purchase of tea!

Li Lien Ying, in the place of An Teh Hai, would require more in the shape of honorarium, and the other eunuchs would require less. If Li Lien Ying added to his own honorarium what he denied the less exalted eunuchs, who would there be to say him nay, if An Teh Hai were eliminated?

So Li Lien Ying took the fifty *tael* "shoe," polished it carefully on a dirty sleeve, snarled in his throat, and hid the shoe away.

It would be a wonderful nucleus on which to build a fortune, moreover, which might well become the envy of great men—even Emperors.

X. THE IMPERIAL BANQUET

Tung Chih was one year of age. Again came the presents, the gifts from great men far and near in the Middle Kingdom, great Chinese and Manchus who were ministers to foreign lands.

Then was held the Imperial Banquet, the like of which had never been known in the Forbidden City. Hsien Feng was proud of this son of his. He worshipped the son as he adored the mother and spared neither pains nor labor—of his henchmen—to make the Imperial Banquet the greatest held in his regime.

To this banquet came the highest of China's ministers. There were scores and hundreds of eunuchs, there to do the slightest bidding of the Imperial Clan and their guests. There were Hsien Feng, Tzu An, and Tzu Hsi, the mother of the heir.

Tzu An, during the year just passed, had allowed her fierce jealousy of Tzu Hsi to utterly possess her. Her jealousy, and the hatred which grew out of that jealousy, ate at her heart like a cancer, souring her whole existence, making life a nightmare—and a waking-and-sleeping nightmare that had no end. She was perpetually rude to Tzu Hsi, who retaliated by being a model of politeness, of all the graces, in the presence of the Empress. Tzu An spoke to her, when she spoke at all, with marked lack of courtesy—lack of courtesy that escaped not even the least intelligent of the eunuchs. Tzu An was even impolite, waspish, to His Majesty, the Emperor, who grew to hate her for her evil disposition. As his hate grew for Tzu An, his love increased for Tzu Hsi; and that love increased the jealousy and hatred of Tzu An for Tzu Hsi.

Then the banquet.

The most magnificent, as I have said, ever held inside the Forbidden City.

One small table was set apart for the three greatest people in the Forbidden City. These three were His Majesty, Hsien Feng, Tzu An and Tzu Hsi. The guests of these three, scores of the highest officials, sat cross-legged on the floor of the Banquet Hall, on soft cushions, and partook of the banquet from little tables perhaps eight inches in height, while eunuchs served them all, so that the place of the banquet was a veritable kaleidoscope of colors.

The Imperial Banquet

Eunuchs moving on swift feet, handling the countless dishes with the skill of long practice. Eunuchs in all sorts of costumes, of many colors, richly embroidered things, costumes which reflected the lights in the Banquet Hall like countless prisms. The three great ones at the table were the most richly dressed of all, because, of them all, these three were greatest. The best tidbits came to this table, where Hsien Feng was master, who was polite to Tzu An, and showed in every act, with every glance, his adoration for Tzu Hsi.

There were lacquer screens; there were screens lacquer-bordered, in whose faces were set rich designs in jade, mother-of-pearl, and even the vari-colored plumage of China's many beautiful birds—all created by the hands of China's masters of this type of artistry.

Above the table of Hsien Feng hung the huge candles, at the ends of swaying ropes bound with yellow cloth, like golden iridescent tassels of superb elegance. For the Banquet was held after nightfall, when mellow moonlight shed its benediction upon the Forbidden City, and peace possessed the world outside. The yellow flames from the gently swaying candles brought out the fantastic scene in strange mixture of color, causing effects no artist, be he ever so great a genius, might ever duplicate. The yellow light shed its radiance, scattering to and fro the glinting beams, upon the almost reverent faces of the Ministers, upon the austere countenance of Hsien Feng, the Emperor. It brought into sharp relief the stolid faces of the eunuchs, schooled by long years at court to masking all emotion; then dropped them into semi-darkness when the light drew back from them because the tassels carried the candles away for a moment; only to bring them back again the next moment, sharper in relief than before. There was the soft sound of soft-soled sandals slithering over the floor that was mirror-smooth.

The lights brought out, in dappling effect of light and shadow, the details of the lacquer screens.

The lights brought out the stolid faces of the many eunuchs, some moving, some immobile as statues.

The lights etched in sharp relief, because he sat directly beneath them, the austere face of Hsien Feng, and his face expressed eternal adoration for Tzu Hsi.

The lights glowed upon the cameo-like face of Tzu Hsi. Her eyes wandered often to the eyes of Hsien Feng, whose eyes were always there, waiting—as though Hsien Feng were breathless with expectancy—to gaze into their depths, which lured him now more even than they had lured him on that day, now many months agone, when Lan Kuei had come to the palace, in obedience to the Imperial Decree, to be chosen Secondary Wife from among seventeen of China's most beautiful ladies of quality. Tzu Hsi was happy, even though she knew, because it enwrapped her like an invisible mantle, like an emanation from some dank tarn, of the hatred and jealousy of Tzu An. She loved Tung Chih. She must have in some measure loved the father of the heir.

The lights glowed on the cameo-like face of Tzu An, who smiled a set smile when, answering some query of Hsien Feng, a smile seemed demanded of her—though that smile was forced, as any who saw it could not help knowing, because she deluded herself with the belief that, because Hsien Feng loved Tzu Hsi, Tzu An no longer loved Hsien Feng.

The lights showed the obese form, the smirking face, of An Teh Hai, who strove always to please Their Majesties, upon whose whims rested the security or the insecurity of his position as Chief Eunuch.

The lights showed the face of Su Shun, and of Prince Yi—Su Shun, the grasping Grand Councillor, Prince Yi, the weakling.

The lights showed the snarling visage of Li Lien Ying, only now, though he may have snarled inwardly, his ugly visage was wreathed in smiles he intended to be ingratiating, for he now waited upon the table where sat the three who were China's greatest. He had traveled a long way since that never-to-be-forgotten day when his unknown informant had told him that all he needed to make himself great in the Forbidden City, were courage and a knife. Ever and anon, he would steal a glance at An Teh Hai. He was very close now to the position held by An Teh Hai, and he strove always to please, to ingratiate himself into the good graces

The Imperial Banquet

of the three greatest, against the time when An Teh Hai might no longer be Chief Eunuch.

The lights showed Lady Mei, most beautiful, most fragile of all the court ladies—Lady Mei, daughter of Su Shun, favorite of Tzu Hsi, because she loved Tzu Hsi, tried to please her, thus winning her love in return. There was another for whom Lady Mei cherished a love that was greater, though she herself did not yet, perhaps, know it, or, knowing it, did not admit it to herself.

And there was one specter at the feast—Yung Lu, onetime sweetheart of Lan Kuei, scarcely noticed by Tzu Hsi, because of custom, the Commander of the Imperial Guard. Yung Lu's rank did not entitle him to a place at this banquet. No one knew, save perhaps Tzu Hsi, how he came to be invited, an Imperial invitation he dared not refuse. But he was there, far subordinate in rank to the least of all nobles present. Tzu Hsi knew he had been asked, for she had inspired Hsien Feng to tender the invitation which, coming from the Emperor, amounted to a command.

Yung Lu, when the opportunity offered, stole surreptitious glances at the beautiful face of Tzu Hsi. But no one seemed to notice save Tzu Hsi herself, who could not seem to notice. If their eyes ever met, they lingered not at all, though Yung Lu trembled in all his being when this miracle happened. Marriage had done great things to Tzu Hsi. It had filled her with wisdom, and her newfound wisdom, for which Yung Lu was not responsible, looked out of her eyes, and its message wrapped about the heart of Yung Lu like the caress of a sweetheart's little fingers, though perhaps Tzu Hsi did not realize that any message had been passed.

But a message had been passed, a fleeting message, true, but a message none the less.

There were several people who caught the message, or a hint of that message's meaning. One was Su Shun, whose eyes became narrow slits as he pondered the matter deeply; one was Prince Yi, a profligate libertine, who read things into the message that he would have read into any message flashed to him by any lady; one was Li Lien Ying, who had always known that something, something sweet and very precious, lay between Tzu Hsi and the humble Guard Commander; one was Tzu An, who frowned as she labored with the thought that here might be a subtle weapon with which she might, sometime in the future, free herself of the presence of Tzu Hsi.

An Teh Hai caught the message—but he loved Tzu Hsi, and worshipped her royal offspring.

Hsien Feng saw nothing.

Lady Mei saw, held her peace because she loved Tzu Hsi., and felt a great weight about her heart, because she did not realize that she herself loved Yung Lu.

The great banquet—with all the many lights, its gorgeous costumes, its vari-colored screens, the scores which came into the light and vanished into the shadows with the swinging of the candles, the bowed figures of the lesser folk who sat on soft cushions and ate from tiny eight-inch tables, the three great ones just beneath the guttering candles—drew on to a close.

"Bring tea for the nobles!"

It was a command. It came from Hsien Feng.

"Bring tea for the nobles!"

An Teh Hai picked the words from the lips of Hsien Feng, and hurled them, burdened with the weight of authority, at the eunuchs charged with serving the tables, and the eunuchs hastened to do the bidding of the Chief Eunuch. There was a stirring in the court. Yung Lu stirred, uneasy. Yung Lu was not a noble. No tea would be brought to him. The fact that none was brought would be noticeable. It might even be cause for hidden, subdued laughter, because he was not a noble, not included in the order to bring tea for the honored guests.

Tea was brought, as An Teh Hai had ordered, and when all had been served, Yung Lu sat in his place, uneasy and mortified, because no tea had been brought him. Agonized, he looked at Tzu Hsi, and swept his eyes away. Mute appeal was in them, but for exactly what he could not say——something, perhaps, to relieve a situation he found to be unbearable. And Tzu Hsi noticed. So did Tzu An.

Defiantly, though she made sure that none noticed what she did, or understood its significance, she prepared a cup of tea herself, dropped into it the petals of a plum blossom, to increase its already wondrous fragrance, and beckoned to Li Lien Ying, who came forward, servile, eager to please, to receive the commands from the

The Imperial Banquet

Imperial Mistress. Into his hands Tzu Hsi pressed the cup she herself had prepared, and instructed the eunuch in a low voice to take the cup to Yung Lu. Li Lien Ying, proud of his responsibility, bore the cup to the humble Guard Commander, who received it and started to rise from his place to kowtow his thanks to the Imperial Mistress for having thus so signally paid him honor. He had been slighted when tea had been served the nobles, and Tzu Hsi, by flouting every rule of court custom, had honored him above all others. But when he half rose to kowtow, Tzu Hsi brought him to pause by an almost imperceptible, yet none the less imperious, shake of her queenly head.

Su Shun noticed, and looked at Prince Yi, slightly smiling.

An Teh Hai noticed, but his smile upon Tzu Hsi was a smile of understanding, because he loved her—in his way.

Li Lien Ying noticed, and his evil heart leaped within him, as his agile thoughts flew, striving to find in this incident wherein his best interests might in some future time be served.

Tzu An noticed, and a triumphant smile, a smile of knowing, flashed from her lips to Hsien Feng. His Majesty, because he had the utmost faith in Tzu Hsi, smiled back at Tzu An, and hurled back at her the challenge she had made him with her triumphant smile.

He turned to An Teh Hai.

"Bring in the present for the Imperial Mistress!"

An Teh Hai, obese An Teh Hai, happy in the knowledge that he was to officiate at a dramatic happening, kowtowed deeply, and issued orders to eunuchs of lesser degree.

And while Hsien Feng returned a smile to Tzu An for the triumphant smile she had tendered him, the present for Tzu Hsi was brought in by the eunuchs, and placed on the table before Tzu Hsi.

The present was a monster peach, golden of skin as a brightly burnished fifty-*tael* "shoe."

It was a manufactured peach, a peach which had been designed in the royal kitchens, fashioned by the hands of culinary artists, as a present from Hsien Feng to the Imperial Mistress. It was a work of magnificence, golden as a summer sunrise. The swaying lights above the table brought out the golden glow of Hsien Feng's gift—

shadow and golden light, golden light and shadow, as the candles swayed to and fro.

Mystified, a little frightened, because she did not understand the meaning of the gift, Tzu Hsi looked down at it. Was it a jest? Had Hsien Feng seen the passage of the fragrant cup of tea, prepared by Tzu Hsi's own hands for Yung Lu, the humble Guard Commander? But of course that was ridiculous. He could not have foreseen that she would thus show preference for a commoner? No, that gift had been prepared before the beginning of the banquet, or during the banquet's endless courses. She looked at Hsien Feng, half-smiling, doubtful.

"Open it," he half-whispered, and the old adoration spoke aloud from his eyes.

Tzu Hsi, realizing that it was no jest, touched her fragile hands to the golden wonder of Hsien Feng's gift, touching it with her fingertips, tenderly, seeking the secret which should unlock the gift and expose the heart of it.

After many moments, during which all the banqueters watched with bated breath, Tzu An watched with a half frown of annoyance, and Hsien Feng with a smile of tender expectation, the peach fell open in the hands of the Imperial Mistress. The peach fell open in the middle, its two halves upon the golden plate upon which it had been tendered to Tzu Hsi, and in the heart of the peach reposed the real gift of Hsien Feng—a creation that was the very essence of beauty, that brought, almost, gasps of admiration from the lips of the spectators; that caused Tzu An, forgetting the courtesy due her lord and master, forgetting the etiquette of the court, to rise from her place and leave the banquet in a towering rage, which she made no attempt to conceal from whosoever cared to notice.

And the gift?

A wondrous pair of shoes, Manchu shoes with high heels, set in the very best of taste, with minute sparkling gems—like the tears of virgins who weep for very happiness!

XI. JEHOL

Jehol...

A palace of magnificence, where the rulers went for vacations from cares of state and. whither, often, they fled when foreign barbarians or civil rebels threatened the safety of the Imperial Clan. Jehol. More beautiful than the Forbidden City, more luxurious. The furniture at Jehol, of precious wood, was inlaid with jade and precious stones; the dragons on the ceiling-panels were of pure gold, while the walls were resplendent in shimmering silk. A quiet summer place, Jehol, where all the most valuable treasures of the Manchus were, and other treasures, too, handed down from dynasty to dynasty by China's rulers.

To Jehol, in spite of the fact that Tzu Hsi tried to dissuade him, fled Hsien Feng, to escape the foreign barbarians as a result of the "Opium War." Tzu Hsi believed that the throne of China should in no case be left vacant. Prince Kung, the brother of the Emperor, believed otherwise, and advised Hsien Feng, who was ill and dying of his dissipations, to go to Jehol, and himself remained in the Forbidden City to negotiate with the foreign diplomats.

Jehol, the beautiful, where Hsien Feng died, where plots and counterplots without end were born. Jehol, a place of bitter-sweet memories to Tzu Hsi.

It was a journey, that flight to Jehol, which Tzu Hsi was to remember always. She went to Jehol afterward, but she never remained long, because for her the place was peopled by ghosts. She would never forget that journey. She never did forget it. There she was shown beyond all possibility of doubting, the faith of Yung Lu, the perfidy of Su Shun and Prince Yi, the moral weakness of Hsien Feng, and the hatred of Tzu An.

Save for a small guard about the Forbidden City, the whole court was removed to Jehol. A three-day journey. Eunuchs by the thousand, ministers and princes, court- ladies and serving maids. An endless concourse of people in rich clothing, the great ones borne in sedan chairs richly decked, on the shoulders of toiling coolies, who must have cursed the great ones under their breath, as they flirted the bitter sweat from their grimy faces. A long procession like a gaudily colored snake, wending its way along a narrow road. The chanting of the chair-bearers who were not too close to the royal chairs, so that their chanting disturb the great ones; the slap and slither of sandaled feet over loose stones; the brassy sun peering down upon all; the wild country; possible pursuit behind —and an Emperor who was going to Jehol to die. Guardsmen on horseback, Mongolian ponies, Mongol tents at night, bonfires in some mountain fastness while the procession, save the guards, slept the tired sleep of the utterly exhausted. The champing of bits, the flashing colors of the guard uniforms. The greatest power of China, on a flight to Jehol, a flight that assumed all the gaudy display of a moving festival.

Ahead of them, save for a mere handful of guards, Jehol, built in the time of His Majesty Chien Lung, slumbered, clean slumber because eunuchs had been sent ahead to make the palaces ready, against the arrival of the court. A great silent place, reflecting from its yellow-tiled roofs the burning light of the sun. Courtyards whose cobblestones gave off no echoes, save perhaps the echoes of ghostly footfalls. Silent halls, with doors closed and barred.

Then the arrival, like an army, of the court and all its attendants. Yung Lu as one of the guard officers, thousands of eunuchs as I have said, all the servants of the court, swept into view of Jehol, increased their tired pace with their goal in sight, reached the great gates, which swung open for them; and instantly Jehol became a place of life, where the slumbering halls, the courtyards and the palaces, wakened to the echo and reecho of human voices, human footfalls. Doors with dust in their jambs swung open to the tune of creaking, rusty locks—and Jehol became a city, a city of importance in China, because it was now the seat of the Emperor, dying though he was.

Hsien Feng took to his bed upon arrival at Jehol.

Tzu An was there, and Tzu Hsi, An Teh Hai, Li Lien Ying, Lady Mei, Prince Yi and Su Shun—all were there. The court in its entirety, save only for Prince Kung, with all its intrigues and dark secrets, came into its own upon arrival at Jehol.

And the very least of the court, the very least of the eunuchs, knew that the Emperor was dying.

THE PALACE WHERE HIS MAJESTY HSIEN FENG DIED, JEHOL, CHINA

Tzu An made her plans. Su Shun, and Prince Yi, the latter forced into the plot by the former, laid yet other plans, and their plans bade fair to succeed. Li Lien Ying, seeing his chance to cement his good standing with Tzu Hsi, kept his ears to the ground, listening, saying nothing, biding his time, awaiting his golden opportunity. Yung Lu listened, too; but he was only a humble Guard

Commander, without power or importance. He could only wait, listen, and hope that he might have an opportunity to prove his loyalty to Tzu Hsi when the time came. Hsien Deng was dying.

Su Shun and Prince Yi bared their fangs. But Prince Yi was a weakling.

"His Majesty is dying," said Su Shun. "We must cause him to sign a decree mating us regents, pending the selection of an Emperor; and regents after the selection, provided the person selected is not of an age to rule. Let us go to him and ask him to make a decree. After he dies, we may then do away with Tzu Hsi and Tung Chih and have China in our hands."

Prince Yi demurred.

"I do not wish to do this thing," he said. "If His Majesty dies, Tung Chih becomes Emperor. If we plot against his life, or that of Tzu Hsi, and are found out, our heads will pay the penalty. I wash my hands of the affair! You may go ahead, and I shall say nothing; but I shall have nothing further to do with it."

"No?" replied Su Shun., "But you have already gone too far. You know too much of my plans. You must go through with it now, else I shall go to the Emperor

Before he dies, tell him that you are planning to dispose of Tzu Hsi and Tung Chih, and he will have you beheaded. He'll believe what I say, for you have no witnesses to prove that what I say is untrue-which, after all, it isn't!"

So Su Shun, who was strong of will, urged Prince Yi, in order that, when Prince Yi should be made regent, he himself should stand behind him, in his shadow as it were, and reap the rewards of his hold over Prince Yi.

Together Prince Yi and Su Shun went to His Majesty, where he lay on his deathbed, rapidly sinking.

"Make us regents," was the gist of their appeal.

The Emperor demurred, shaking his head.

Prince Yi, fearful, vacillating, drew back; but Su Shun urged him on.

"Make us regents," they besought His Majesty.

Neither knew that Li Lien Ying had heard the whispers of their treason to the heir, and to the mother of the heir, and had borne the story of them to Yung Lu, who was in a fever of anxiety.

But Tzu Hsi, while she may not have heard the whispers, knew that in Prince Yi and Su Shun she had two very bitter enemies. There had been too many whispers at court. Su Shun, once upon a time, had said that Tzu Hsi was too beautiful, that she was too clever, to be Secondary Wife of Hsien Feng, with all that might result from the union. Tzu Hsi prepared to fortify her own position against the death of His Majesty, the Emperor.

She went to His Majesty, with Tung Chih, who was now three years of age.

She paused by the bedside of the man through whom she had come into power.

"Is your son to succeed you?" she asked.

Su Shun and Prince Yi, having been advised of the coming of Tzu Hsi, had retired from the presence of Hsien Feng, with their purpose of having themselves named as regents unaccomplished.

But Hsien Feng was pondering the matter.

"Is your son to succeed you?" whispered Tzu Hsi.

Almost imperceptibly, since he was sinking fast, Hsien Feng nodded his head. Tzu Hsi, who believed always in taking time by the forelock, a belief that was of untold value to her in the years that followed, sent for the eunuch-writer, and had the decree prepared for the signature of His Majesty. Mention was made in that decree of regents. There must be a regent, or regents, since Tung Chih was a mere baby. Tzu Hsi and Tzu An were named as regents.

Then came the fatal day when Hsien Feng, in the eleventh year of his reign, passed to his ancestors, and the throne of China became vacant. The body of His Majesty was taken to the Audience Hall, whose high walls almost shut out the sunlight, oddly like a crypt in its construction, and placed in state.

No one might visit the death-chamber of His Majesty. Flickering candles beside a long bier, upon which rested the mortal remains of the Emperor; whispers throughout walled Jehol, whispers of doubt, whispers which hinted at strange happenings to come, whispers of terror, whispers of intrigue. Inside the great hall, silence, the dead form of the Emperor, the flickering candles—and a huge clock ticking dolefully away in one corner, while in other places in the great hall, outside the chamber of death, other clocks ticked dolefully, too, as though they echoed the solemn ticking of the clock beside the bier.

The time had come when word must be sent forth. Hsien Feng had passed away, and all China must go into mourning. The body must be made ready, awaiting an auspicious date for the return to Peking.

Su Shun and Prince Yi came to Tzu Hsi. They did homage to the mother of the heir, but it was mocking homage, their politeness scarcely masking the dislike, even hatred, in which they held the Secondary Wife.

"We are regents to the throne of China," they told her.

"His Majesty, the Emperor, made us regents, by verbal decree, just before he died."

Tzu Hsi looked at Tzu An, who returned her look. There was triumph in the face of Tzu An. She had known nothing of this eventuality, but if it were to cause Tzu Hsi loss of power at court, she was happy. Even with the death of Hsien Feng, her hatred and jealousy of Tzu Hsi had not disappeared. It had increased if that were humanly possible. Tzu Hsi, reading the expression on the face of Tzu An, knew that she could expect no assistance there. She must depend upon herself. She must protect the interests of her son, and must carry out the last wishes of Hsien Feng. She felt that Su Shun and Prince Yi lied; but there was no way in which she could prove that they lied. Hsien Feng might have made a verbal decree, and might have named Su Shun and Prince Yi as regents—because approaching death had perhaps dimmed his mental powers.

She produced, while for a moment her heart almost stopped beating with suspense, the decree which she herself had caused to be prepared and which had been authenticated by the signature of Hsien Feng.

"I have His Majesty's last decree," she managed softly, "naming his son to succeed him! I am his mother! Tzu An is Empress. We are, therefore, regents during the minority of Tung Chih!"

Chagrin showed upon the face of Prince Yi, who might have been the real regent, with Su Shun, as his favorite minister—thus placing Su Shun in the light of a regent, or even, actually making him regent, since Prince Yi was so utterly ineffectual—and he looked to Su Shun for guidance. The producing of this decree seemed to indicate that Tzu Hsi knew of the machinations of Su Shun and Prince Yi, else she had not gone to such lengths to safeguard her own interests, and those of her son. The axe of the executioner for Su Shun, the strangler's noose for Prince Yi hovered close above the heads of the two conspirators, and both knew it. But Su Shun was not yet beaten.

He stared intently at the decree. He half smiled as Tzu Hsi held it up to his gaze, at a safe distance from the man she knew to be a bitter enemy.

"It is not an effective decree, Your Majesty!" he said at last. "It does not bear the Imperial Seal, without which no decree is considered legal!"

Tzu Hsi, who had not known of this eventuality, or had overlooked it, turned the decree and gazed at it. Then she looked in perplexity at Tzu An, in whose face she found no sympathy. She looked back at Prince Yi and Su Shun, on whose faces there was relief—a sort of smile on the face of Su Shun, the dew of perspiration on the face of Prince Yi, who had thus, he believed, narrowly escaped terrible retribution for conspiracy against the throne.

Tzu Hsi, too frightened, too angered to speak, sent Su Shun and Prince Yi from her with a gesture.

AUDIENCE HALL, JEHOL, WHERE HIS MAJESTY HSIEN FENG RESTED IN STATE, AWAITING AN AUSPICIOUS DATE FOR THE RETURN OF THE BODY TO PEKING

Jehol

Immediately then, thereafter, entered Yung Lu without ceremony. It was the closest to Tzu Hsi he had been since she had entered the Forbidden City as Secondary Wife. He had seen Su Shun enter her presence, urging Prince Yi ahead of him. Yung Lu had heard the whispers, knew that Hsien Feng was dead, and was able to put two and two together with accuracy. So he entered the presence of Tzu Hsi, threw himself on his knees at her feet, performed the usual kowtows, and spoke in a trembling voice.

"If there be any way in which I may serve Your Majesty, I shall perform that service gladly!"

Tzu Hsi sent the court-ladies and court eunuchs out of earshot with an imperious gesture, and spoke softly to Yung Lu. She told him where the Imperial Seal might be found, and that none, not even herself, in the present circumstances, dared enter the death-chamber of Hsien Feng. Su Shun and Prince Yi, she told him, knew also the location of the seal, and he must needs hurry if he would serve her well. Yung Lu, kowtowing again, quitted her chamber swiftly.

Ahead of him, moving hurriedly, furtively, Su Shun and Prince Yi were already striding toward the death-chamber and the Seal, in a cabinet there, which was needed to authenticate the claims of Tung Chih.

Since Li Lien Ying had carried the story of the plot to Yung Lu, Yung Lu now called upon the eunuch for yet another service. He sent for him, told him where to find the seal, and bade him go, by a secret passage, to the death-chamber to secure it.

Li Lien Ying, taking with him a "little eunuch" to keep watch at the entrance of the secret passage, entered the passage and strode through the dank darkness, which was poorly relieved by the flickering light of the candle which he carried in his hand, toward the chamber of death.

Meanwhile Su Shun and Prince Yi, knowing themselves in the wrong, were afraid to seek the Seal, afraid to enter the forbidden place where Hsien Feng lay in state. However, necessity, that necessity which bids the sons of men preserve their own lives, forced them on.

But when they reached the death-chamber, and Prince Yi, urged on by Su Shun, as always, opened the cabinet to secure the

Seal, the Seal had vanished! They could not find it, though they sought for it eagerly, frantically, with growing fear gnawing at their hearts.

But their search was of no avail.

Had they seen the ugly face of the eunuch, Li Lien Ying, set in a snarl of satisfaction, hideous in the flickering fight of the single candle which he carried, hurrying back along the secret passageway, they would have been less mystified anent the disappearance of the Imperial Seal.

For Li Lien Ying, hurrying to meet Yung Lu, carried it in his hand!

He had saved the throne for Tung Chih.

Su Shun and Prince Yi, believing themselves undone, hurried from the death-chamber and went into temporary seclusion.

"There is now but one way to save our own fives," said Su Shun. "Tzu Hsi will never forgive us for trying to thwart her. She will have our fives if she loses her own to accomplish her ends!"

"What shall we do?" wailed Prince Yi. "We are undone! It is your fault! I .shall take steps to protect myself."

"Remember," said Su Shun, "that you were with me when I told Tzu Hsi that we had been named regents at the death-bed of His Majesty, the Emperor. There is now no way that we can save ourselves, and we are equally guilty."

"Then what must we do?"

Su Shun whispered into the receptive ear of the weakling.

"We must slay Tzu Hsi and Tung Chih!"

"But how, and where, are we to accomplish this? And how will their death benefit us?"

"We will not do the deed ourselves. We will procure the slaying—and will ourselves be the first to condemn the slayers, and make sure that their mouths do not betray us, by sending them to the executioner."

"But how? How?"

Su Shun paused in thought.

Then he whispered again.

"Soon," he said, deliberately, "the body of His Majesty will be returned to Peking. Tzu Hsi and Tung Chih must arrive in Peking ahead of the funeral cortege, in order to receive the Royal Bier, which means that they must travel by another and shorter route. Surely, my dear Prince Yi, on such a journey there should be ample opportunity for the man, or men, of our choosing to accomplish what we desire. Then, when *Her Majesty* and *His Majesty*, Tung Chih, fail to reach Peking, nothing can be said to us, since we are to accompany the funeral cortege of the late Emperor!"

Perspiration broke out anew on the face of Prince Yi, the weakling, who knew he had advanced too far to dare retreat.

"On the journey to Peking!" he whispered.

And then Su Shun and Prince Yi, with their heads together, began to discuss the details of their plan.

A Captain of the Guard, not Yung Lu, figured largely in those details; and—though he did not know it, could not see into the future—that Captain's head rested most insecurely on his shoulders!

But, meanwhile, the Imperial Seal had been delivered to Tzu Hsi; and the last decree of Hsien Feng, now in a safe place, whose location was well known to Tzu Hsi, had been duly and legally authenticated.

XII. THE MARCH OF THE DEAD

Preparations, slow and solemn preparations, were begun for the return of His Majesty, Hsien Feng, the Emperor, to the Forbidden City. For days he had lain in state in the Audience Hall of the Manchus, at the glorious royal city of Jehol. There had been burning candles, silence funereal, the muted tread of frightened footfalls, the hush which always seems to fall upon the world before the dead is interred. In daytime, motionless eunuchs, waiting for something to happen, with large eyes ever and anon gazing toward the Audience Hall, behind whose darkened windows the closed eyes of the silent, now forever silent, Emperor peered at the pictures of eternity which death had etched behind his lowered, wax-like lids; during darkness, flitting figures, flitting furtively, afraid of shadows, and of shades, because when the dead are unburied the shades of ancestors hover near, and mortals cannot help but fear them, because they are unseen; winking stars, cold as death itself, peer mockingly down upon the transient mortals who so fear the Great Unknown.

Jehol in readiness, awaiting the auspicious day, when His Majesty must return to Peking before the final interment.

Then the day, with additional preparations.

Slow and measured tread. The slow opening of the great doors of the Audience Hall, so that the rays of the sun may penetrate the place of erstwhile silence, dimming the yellowish glow of the flickering candles, now the merest stumps beside the bier. Stumps reposing in their own tallow, dying, soon to be as dead as the mortal beside whose bier they have kept faithful watch and ward. The frightened bearers, their heads bowed, eyes roving fearfully into every shadowed corner, nostrils twitching with the strange and gruesome odors which seem to penetrate the very nooks and crannies in which the dead have slept. The wax-like face, motionless, austere, proud,—with all pain smoothed away amid the silence eternal, where nor care nor worry is—a mummy figure, arms bound at sides, legs bound together, wrappings encasing the whole, beneath the royal funeral cloak which must enshroud the royal dead in order that the dead be not forever restless.

The March Of The Dead

The forming of the guard in the courtyards. The eunuchs in the great white hats, like the shades of old-fashioned lamps, standing in formation, waiting. Mongolian ponies, long of mane and tail, impatiently champing their bits, yet muting the noises somehow, as though they too knew the vast solemnity of this occasion, while their Manchu-guardsmen riders sit like statues, waiting for words of command.

One hundred bearers for the catafalque of an Emperor. Swart-faced eunuchs, slaves to heavy labor, slaves to the dead from the Imperial Clan, bending their necks to the yellow poles, huge and ungainly, upon which rests the huge yellow housing that protects the dead upon this journey-next-to-the-last.

The dead comes forth, swaying with the bodies of the bearers, and is placed within the catafalque. The hundred bearers, stolid of features, sturdy of arm and limb, broad of shoulders, slip under the network of poles, and, at a word of signal, raise the unwieldy creation upon their shoulders and begin the slow solemn march toward Peking, four whole days away because the dead must move so slowly. One hundred bearers, walking close together, with their two hundred legs swinging out of rhythm, like some monster beetle with a multiplicity of limbs.

The Guardsmen, reining in their impatient ponies, ride before and behind the catafalque, straight and erect, immobile of feature, realizing the vast responsibility that is theirs in that they guard the Imperial remains. Guards before and behind, to right and left, the hundred bearers, court attendants, mourners, members of the Imperial Clan whose presence is not required at the Forbidden City gates in advance of the procession—so that the whole procession is like a dragon, whose immense body undulates, serpentine, with the curving of the rough road it must travel to attain Peking. Slow motion, slow and solemn—the rule of an Emperor has ended. The rule of an Emperor has begun.

The last procession, this yellow catafalque, signals the final abdication of an Emperor, the coronation of the next in line.

Afar off, as the cortege moves slowly toward Peking, the humble country-folk take notice of the many membered dragon, come close to peer, then note the imperial yellow which is part and parcel of it all, and fling themselves upon the ground to kowtow to the mighty monarch whose rule is ended; or, recognizing the cortege for what it is, while yet afar off, dash madly hence to hide themselves, because, to them, the Emperor is next to Buddha, perhaps a little higher even, and mortals must not gaze upon the countenance of gods, or look toward the place where Buddha rides in solemn state.

To the living, the passing of the dead is a gruesome reminder that the end for king and commoner is identically the same; it tells them, mutely, how fleeting life is, how swiftly ended, how haphazardly begun, that the knowledge of man crashes into nothingness against the two impenetrable walls—the wall which separates the living from the yet un-born, the wall that separates the living from the dead. 'Tis only the in-between of which men know, and even in the in-between they grope their lives away.

So Hsien Feng, though his cortege was gorgeous, passed the same way that the humble farmer passes; and though the latter have but two bearers, four perhaps, and His Majesty a hundred, each passes through the Final Curtain equal—as far as goes the knowledge of humanity.

Four days, and the funeral cortege was approaching Peking. Peking in mourning, with her shops closed, her streets deserted and silent—while the Secondary Wife, now regent with Tzu An, had started for Peking another way in order to reach the Forbidden City and receive the Imperial Catafalque at the yawning, open gates, through which Hsien Feng, the Emperor, would pass but twice again.

Su Shun and Prince Yi rode with the funeral cortege, and solemn though the occasion was, they thought of a certain guard captain who accompanied the party of Her Majesty, Tzu Hsi, and smiled inwardly, glanced at each other with scarcely masked satisfaction, and rode on toward Peking.

The March Of The Dead

REAR WALL IN THE THRONE ROOM OF JEHOL PALACE, WHERE HER MAJESTY TZU HSI, DURING THE ILLNESS OF THE EMPEROR HSIEN FENG, FIRST HELD THE REINS OF POWER

XIII. OUT OF THE DARKNESS

Yung Lu was detailed to command the small detachment of the guard at Jehol, which would be twice lonely with the return to Peking of the court. Li Lien Ying had whispered into the ear of this faithful lackey of Tzu Hsi, and Yung Lu was terribly afraid, not for himself, but for Tzu Hsi, and Tung Chih, most of all for Tzu Hsi. It was strange, too, his detail to this command. His rightful place was either with the cortege of the Emperor, or the guard which accompanied Their Majesties, Tzu An and Tzu Hsi. He suspected that he had been thus detailed for a reason, and when the procession of the two Empresses left Jehol, he was almost sure that he had surmised correctly.

On the steps of a summerhouse stood Su Shun and Prince Yi, to watch from afar the departure of Tzu An and the Imperial Mistress, who now was Empress Dowager. Toward these two glanced the captain of the guard which was to accompany Tzu Hsi's procession. Toward these two he glanced, as though he watched for a signal. None saw the signal, save perhaps Yung Lu, and Li Lien Ying. It was just a gesture, a flirting of the hand, the right hand of Su Shun, but somehow Yung Lu recognized the gesture for what it was, a gesture that condemned a mortal being to oblivion. The captain nodded, repeated the gesture. Little things, in such a moment, stood out starkly. One of these was to prove the undoing of the captain of the guard.

He wore a ring of strange design upon the thumb of his right hand!

Tzu Hsi, who knew full well that Su Shun and Prince Yi had not by any means acknowledged themselves beaten, also noted that ring—though at any other time she never would have deigned to notice a captain of the guard. But then, perhaps, she might have expected to see Yung Lu in command of her processional guardsmen, and when she did not see him, though she wondered, she dared not ask that he be assigned to guard her, lest her enemies make comment to her detriment, in that a guard commander found importance in her eyes. So, though she Wondered, perhaps, why Yung Lu remained behind, and was not a little disappointed, she

Out Of The Darkness

said nothing; but she noticed the captain who commanded her guard—

And noted, half subconsciously, the ring upon the thumb of his right hand.

A little thing. A little thing of vast importance as it later proved. Upon that notice rested the security of a throne and saved the greatest of China's regents to China's history.

The party of Their Majesties quitted swiftly the palaces of Jehol, moving toward Peking, because they must be at the gates of the Forbidden City to receive the Royal Catafalque of His Majesty, Hsien Feng. With Tzu Hsi rode Lady Mei, who with Tzu Hsi, though Tzu Hsi's glance was fleeting, looked back toward the gates of Jehol, where Yung Lu, straight and proud as always in his uniform of the Imperial Guard, gazed stolidly after the swift-moving procession.

Sedan chairs, mounted men, bearers of camp equipment, for two nights must be spent somewhere along the winding road which led to Peking. The captain of the guard, knowing what duty lay ahead, may perhaps have been a little nervous, but for what he was to do vast wealth, and power had been promised him, and he never thought to question the integrity of the two who had passed their words to make him rich and powerful. That they had merely sentenced him to death, he had no inkling. He rode at the head of the guard, glanced ever and anon at the sedan chairs of Their Majesties, and turned over the details of his dastardly crime in his mind.

It would not be difficult. A sleeping camp. A guard sent on some unimportant errand, who would return to find His Imperial Mistress and the heir gone into the Eternal Silences, and would not dare to shout to any that he had left his post. It would be easy. The captain smiled, and looked ahead. He urged the members of the procession to greater speed, thinking of an ideal spot to spend the night, eager to reach it, and make ready to earn for himself the wealth and power that had been promised him.

They reached the spot, a hollow in the bosom of the eternal hills, and straightway camp was made. Mongolian tents, huge and roomy, for the Empresses. A large one for Tzu Hsi and Tung Chih, set slightly apart from the others, causing no comment because Tzu

Hsi required a certain privacy. A faithful maid for the heir—three people in the tent of Tzu Hsi.

So the captain, in a fever of impatience, made his dispositions, erected his camp, and waited for the utter darkness of far after sunset.

Meanwhile, in far Jehol, a faithful guard commander had deliberately deserted his post. Swayed 'twixt love and duty, Yung Lu was lost to duty, and as the sun went down on that first day of the departure of Tzu Hsi, Yung Lu slipped away from his guard, and from his duty, free of Jehol, mounted his Mongolian pony, which was swift as the wind and as tireless, and started down the trail which Tzu Hsi had taken, bent low over the neck of his shaggy little mount, breathing words of encouragement into a twitching ear. Darkness possessed the land, but the stars were out and soon the moon would appear beyond the horizon's edge, and the going would be less dangerous; though of the danger Yung Lu thought never at all, save that evil fortune to himself might prevent his reaching the side of his beloved in time. He trusted his horse. He bent low over the animal's neck, whispered words of encouragement, and fled like a mad thing, into the night.

At the encampment Tzu Hsi, Tung Chih and the faithful maid had retired. All the camp was sleeping and silence possessed it. A single candle burned in the center of the tent. The maid slept soundly, as did the heir. Tzu Hsi seemed to sleep, though her nostrils twitched, and her eyelids. Not a sound. No movement. Just the interior of a tent whose sides swayed slightly in a mountain breeze, and a single guttering candle to relieve the utter darkness.

Not a bit of warning. No sound. Nothing.

Yet Tzu Hsi awoke as though someone had touched her, as though a cold finger had caressed her cameo-like cheeks. She sat up swiftly, stole a glance at Tung Chih. The maid slept; but Tung Chih, endowed with some of his mother's clairvoyance perhaps, stirred slightly in his sleep, and uttered the merest of sleepy sounds.

What had wakened Tzu Hsi?

She did not know.

Her eyes swerved to the candle in the center of the tent.

Its flame leaned far over, as though it had been thus bent by invisible hands, or as though a vagrant breeze from somewhere had

Out Of The Darkness

breathed against it. Her eyes went back to Tung Chih, to note that his eyes were open, and full of those age-old, unanswerable questions which children mutely ask when slipping out of Dreamland. No movement. Just the asking eyes, which met the mother's eyes. With never a sound, Tzu Hsi caught Tung Chih in her arms, and her eyes went back to the candle, whose flame still leaned far over. She noted the direction of its leaning, and her eyes, startled now, swept to that portion of the tent wall away from which pointed the yellow finger of the candle-flame.

The tent wall had bellied in, ever so slightly. An opening, long and narrow, showed there, like the slit-eyes of a great cat, a feline of the night. Beside the opening, whose edges rippled in the breeze outside, showed the shape of a hand, as though an invisible someone leaned against Tzu Hsi's resting place in the darkness beyond the wall. Tzu Hsi gasped, but her gasp was inaudible. She feared nothing that lived, this great Tzu Hsi, and though she knew a knife had made that narrow slit since she had dropped to sleep, her courage did not desert her in the least. With a flirt of her hand, she extinguished the candle-flame. Instantly, the slit became an eye indeed, an eye through which Tzu Hsi, against the glow of the camp-fires, could get some inkling of what was happening just outside.

She held her breath. Her right hand slipped to the face of the sleeping maid, and moved across it. The maid still slept. Tung Chih trembled slightly in his mother's arms, but made no noise. There was no noise, save the heating of three hearts within the tent—

And the almost inaudible cutting-sound of a knife, as the invisible someone beyond the wall inserted his knife once more to enlarge the opening he already had made. Thought, perhaps, that Tzu Hsi was too badly frightened to cry out. Knew, perhaps, that even though she did cry out, a slash of his knife would so greatly enlarge the slit in the tent-wall that he could slip through, use his murderous weapon, twice or thrice, and slip free again before sleepy guards could reach the tent—and pick up courage to enter the tent of Her Majesty.

Tzu Hsi, fascinated, watched the lengthening of the slit, through which presently a man would step to slay her. No fear. She had no fear of death. She knew, deep in her heart, that such a death as threatened was not for her. Her destiny, she knew, was greater far than this. She had already traveled so far along the pathway to fame, it was unthinkable that Fate would not allow her to proceed, despite a would-be assassin who crept now upon her through the darkness.

The knife was withdrawn. A hand came through the opening, pulling it wide. A profile showed in the great eye for a moment, beside the hand, as though the silent unknown were peering in, testing the meaning of the darkness of the interior with senses which murderous lust had made preternaturally alert. Tzu Hsi, who by now had accustomed her eyes to the darkness, saw the hand.

It bore a ring of quaint and curious design. She searched her memory for a recollection. Only this morning she had seen that ring before. Wise Tzu Hsi! In a flash, she knew where, and upon whose hand, she had seen it. But now she held her breath, and waited, drawing close against her body the warm little body of Tung Chih.

The knife came into play again, slitting slowly, almost without sound. Meanwhile Yung Lu, who had ridden at top speed for what seemed like endless hours, was approaching the encampment. His sturdy little pony was staggering with fatigue, keeping his feet by a miracle, but the distance to the royal encampment, great as it seemed, was diminishing as the moments fled.

How did Yung Lu know which tent sheltered Tzu Hsi, to whom he had sworn himself an oath of eternal faithfulness?

Ask the stars in their courses, ask the Three Old Ladies who Spin the Web of Fate, but, first of all, ask men who have truly loved, and they will tell you that, in crises, a man in love thinks with his heart, and not his head; and that seldom it is his heart betrays him. Yung Lu reached the encampment, swept pass the nodding sentries, made a mental note to discipline them for carelessness when he himself should resume command, and dragged his staggering pony to a halt beside the tent which sheltered his best beloved.

Inside the tent, Tzu Hsi heard the sound of running hoof beats. Did the heart of her tell her who rode into the encampment out of the darkness? Perhaps. Tzu Hsi was very proud. She never told

Out Of The Darkness

how she knew. She only told that she knew. She made no move when the hoof beats ceased. Her eyes held still on the slit in the wall of the tent, where the point of the knife made longer the slit through which a man would step to slay her, if fortune favored his mad intention.

Then the tent shook with the violence of some sudden impact. The knife hung in the slit, then disappeared slowly. Tzu Hsi heard it slip down the tent-wall outside, and strike the ground with a soft thud. No other sound. No cries. Just the shaking of the tent, which presently ceased. All was still. Then when the flaps of her tent began to widen, she knew that someone dared greatly, but dared because that one was faithful, and needs must know the truth of what had happened inside the tent where slept Tzu Hsi and the heir.

Fear, if any she had known, had now left Tzu Hsi. She watched, unafraid, the opening of the tent.

Swiftly she struck a light with flint and tinder, touched flame to the candle again.

A convulsed face—convulsed with horror and doubt—appeared in the doorway. His eyes roved over the interior. Yung Lu forgot that he stood in the presence of an Empress. He thought only of the danger which had passed so closely to Lan Kuei, the Orchid, and as the Orchid he had come to see her, and to assure himself that all was well.

It was Lan Kuei, not Tzu Hsi, who beckoned the guardsman in.

It was to Tzu Hsi, remembering suddenly, and not to Lan Kuei, that the guardsman kowtowed, touching his head to the floor. He could find no words. Before he remembered, his eyes had seen the slit in the wall, had noted that Tung Chih was awake, uninjured—and Tzu Hsi—and the sleeping maid who had known nothing of the near approach of stark tragedy.

He remembered, and kowtowed.

Then Lan Kuei remembered, too, and became Tzu Hsi.

Lan Kuei had put forth her hand to touch the faithful head of the Guard Commander, a sort of caress; but Tzu Hsi withdrew the hand quickly, so that the Guard Commander never knew that a caress had been almost tendered.

"Who was it?" she whispered.

"The Guard Captain, Your Majesty," he replied.

"He shall be beheaded tomorrow morning, Yung Lu! Look to it! It is a command! But question him, learn the whole truth, if the rest of the night is consumed in questioning!"

Yung Lu kowtowed again. He began to withdraw swiftly, to do her bidding.

"Sleep well, and in safety, Lan Kuei!"

Tzu Hsi could not be sure that he said it. Perhaps he didn't. Perhaps it was just a message from his heart to hers; but Tzu Hsi slept soundly, knowing that Yung Lu was now her Guard Commander; that he had come out of the darkness from Jehol, deserting his post, to save her; that the would-be assassin was a prisoner, whose head would fall beneath the axe when morning came.

The captain spoke much that night, hoping against hope that speech would save his neck from the headsman. But it didn't. When morning came, however, he was granted reprieve until the return to Peking—and Yung Lu, who heard every word, took the tale of them to Tzu Hsi, who locked them in her brain, to be brought forth soon, when she should have need of them.

Before the procession had traveled a *li* on that second day's journey, every one of its members knew that Tzu Hsi's, and Tung Chih's, lives had been in danger; that Yung Lu, now in command of the guard, had saved those lives to China.

The names of Su Shun and Prince Yi were mentioned often, for others had heard the words of the captain, as well as Yung Lu, and China's people love gossip and speculation for its own sake.

Lady Mei heard the words in fear and trembling. She knew what they meant to Su Shun, whose daughter she was. Treason! Hideous treason—that was her father's crime. She did not pity Su Shun. She had never loved him, though she had tried. She had never understood why she had no love for her father, but only that she had not. Now she was afraid. When a man is condemned to death for treason, in China of the Empire, his family, from the youngest to the eldest, is condemned with him, in order that this same family may never repeat the offense.

If Su Shun were beheaded, which he surely would be, Lady Mei would go the selfsame way—and life was now too full to relinquish. She loved Yung Lu, and could not bear to die with the knowledge that Yung Lu knew her for a traitor's daughter. And she loved Tzu Hsi, had always loved her, and, found unutterable horror in the fact that the one whom she most loved, next to Yung Lu, must pronounce the words that would bare her own fragile neck to the savage knife of the executioner.

So she trembled, and was afraid, during the rest of the journey to Peking.

XIV. THE WAY OF THE TRAITOR

The Imperial Catafalque swung into *Nan Chi Tzu*, moving slowly and solemnly. In the cortege were Su Shun and Prince Yi, and both were wondering, perhaps, what would happen when there was no Tzu Hsi, and no Tung Chih, to receive the body of His Majesty the Emperor. A dramatic announcement would be forthcoming, and everybody, including Su Shun and Prince Yi, would be properly horrified, properly vengeful, and Su Shun and Prince Yi, because their words would so far outweigh the word of a humble captain of the guard, would then unmask the "traitor," and deliver him up to the royal executioners.

The catafalque swung into *Nan Chi Tzu*, approaching Tung Wha Men, the East Gate of the Forbidden City.

The first courtyard, after the old customs in such matters, was covered over with a mat-shed, the matting all in white, which in China is the color of mourning. Widows wear white for a hundred days, the same clothing, which never leaves their bodies save during sleep, and is never changed during those hundred days. The first courtyard, where the Empress and the Imperial Mistress were expected—by all save Su Shun and Prince Yi—to receive the funeral cortege and the body of the Emperor, was decorated in Imperial yellow, and entirely covered over in yellow, because it is not good to expose the coffin holding a dead body to the open air.

There was a certain tenseness in the air as the cortege approached *Tung Wha Men*. In those days, there was no way of communicating between parties en route from one place to another, and neither Su Shun nor Prince Yi, placing all their trust in the guard captain, knew as yet what had happened at that encampment of Their Majesties in the hills between Jehol and Peking. They believed, however, that the captain, chosen because of his efficiency, and his general lack of conscience, would succeed in the task they had set him.

The catafalque entered *Tung Wha Men*.

Kneeling in the courtyard there, was Tzu An, sorrowful as became a widow, to receive the body of her Royal Consort.

And kneeling beside her was Tzu Hsi! Between Tzu An and Tzu Hsi knelt Tung Chih, the heir!

The Way Of The Traitor

Su Shun looked at Prince Yi. Prince Yi had seen. He refused to look at Su Shun, steadfastly keeping his eyes turned away.

Su Shun's eyes swerved back to Tzu Hsi, to discover that her eyes were upon him. Tzu Hsi, telling of the episode in later years, said that the evil face of Su Shun became pale as ashes—pale almost as the face of Lady Mei, who, with Tzu Hsi, because she was First Lady-in-waiting, waited with her mistress to receive the body of Hsien Feng.

Then the eyes of Su Shun dropped. It is doubtful if any in all the place noted this by-play between Su Shun and Tzu Hsi. There was a ceremony which must be gone through. Su Shun and Prince Yi had parts to play in the solemn ceremony—Su Shun, as Grand Councillor, Prince Yi as a member of the Imperial Clan.

White matting covered the first courtyard; white lanterns hung from the matting. Eunuchs, ladies-in-waiting, the Empresses and Tung Chih were dressed in white. Candles, which ordinarily would have been red, were green, the only spots of color to relieve the dead monotony of the scheme of white.

Kneeling, Tzu Hsi, Tzu An, and Tung Chih received the body of Hsien Feng, after the ancient ritual. A solemn affair. An Emperor, though deposed by Death, was receiving the honor due him, as in life he had received it.

Kneeling, Su Shun spoke to Prince Yi.

"See!" he whispered. "Had you listened to me and killed that woman before we left Jehol, we would not ourselves be in trouble here! We didn't kill her—now she will kill us!"

Prince Yi, the weakling, made no answer.

A certain eunuch, a snarling eunuch, one Li Lien Ying by name, overheard the words of Su Shun; and just as the ceremony ended, he made his way to Tzu Hsi, stood respectfully behind her, and whispered in her ears, repeating to her the words of Su Shun.

"You may all go now," said Tzu Hsi, at last.

Did the hearts of Su Shun and Prince Yi leap within them at this dismissal? Did they think that, after all, they had not been betrayed, that Tzu Hsi did not know of their perfidy, that somehow the Captain of the Guard had failed to make the attempt at all? Did they think this dismissal gave them a new lease on life? Perhaps. It

The True Story of the Empress Dowager

was a reprieve. Hope rising in their hearts, they began to depart from the presence of the Empresses and Tung Chih.

Was this dismissal deliberate on the part of Tzu Hsi, in order that she might later, only a moment later, add to the punishment contemplated, by taking all hope from them immediately afterward? It is difficult to say. Tzu Hsi deserves the title "great," and how may one who is less than great analyze the motives, the emotions, the actions of those whom historians join hands in calling "great"?

"Su Shun! Prince Yi!"

It was the voice of Tzu Hsi.

Instantly Su Shun and Prince Yi, knowing now that there was no hope, turned about and prostrated themselves at the feet of Tzu Hsi, who now stood regally erect, the body of Hsien Feng having been placed in state in the Hall of Audience.

"Su Shun," began Tzu Hsi, "you know the penalty for treason?"

"I do!" replied Su Shun, and his voice did not tremble. Su Shun was not a coward. "I know the penalty! It is decapitation!"

"That is true," said Tzu Hsi. "You are to be decapitated, and all your family with you, after the custom!"

"I deserve it, perhaps," replied Su Shun, "but I am Grand Councillor! I have a right to hear the evidence against me."

There was a thumping sound behind Tzu Hsi. She turned. Lady Mei had swooned and lay unconscious behind the Dowager Empress. Impatiently, Tzu Hsi bade them take her away. She turned back to Su Shun and Prince Yi.

"You shall have the evidence," she said. "Bring in the Captain of the Guard! Before your arrival, I had your house searched, Su Shun, and have your correspondence with Prince Yi, together with certain accounts which show that for years you have been systematically despoiling the government, sufficient in itself to merit decapitation. All your private papers are in my hands! Shall I proceed?"

Su Shun made no reply.

The Captain of the Guard was brought in, and his words of condemnation, with words of extenuation in his own case, tripped over one another as he sought to justify himself and place the burden of blame upon the shoulders of Su Shun and Prince Yi, who, kneeling still, listened motionless to the captain's indictment.

The Way Of The Traitor

THRONE ROOM OF HER MAJESTY TZU HSI IN THE SUMMER PALACE

The True Story of the Empress Dowager

VIEW OF THE FORBIDDEN CITY, PEKING, TAKEN FROM THE WINTER PALACE TOWER

"I did not need this evidence, nor yet the evidence of your own private papers, to prove you guilty of treason," said Tzu Hsi. "Thinking me a woman of no intelligence, you tried to dupe me with a story that you had been named regents at the bedside of His Majesty the Emperor. I knew quite well that such important assignments are not made verbally! Your first error, Su Shun and Prince Yi. Prince Yi, you are a weakling, and your greatest sin lies in the fact that you were so weak as to listen to a greater scoundrel, a scoundrel greater than yourself only because he has the courage you lack."

Prince Yi said nothing. Perhaps a little courage came to him in this terrible moment, for he had ceased his trembling, and something of color came back to his face.

"Prince Yi," said Tzu Hsi, "you know the penalty for treason?"

"I do," he replied strongly. "I confess my fault, freely and entirely. I have no blame to place upon others. I have been wrong, and am willing to atone for my fault. However, I am a member of the Imperial Clan. I ask that my family be spared, in order that the Imperial Clan be not disgraced."

"I shall spare your family, Prince Yi," replied Tzu Hsi.

Tzu An, a quiet spectator, disappointed perhaps in that these two had failed to remove Tzu Hsi from her own path, said nothing. Tzu Hsi dominated the situation, as she dominated every situation in the years that followed.

Tzu Hsi hesitated for a moment, as though she sought for words. Then, rising to her full height, majestically erect, she made a sweeping, condemnatory gesture with her right hand.

"Take them away," she said. "Let Su Shun and the Captain of the Guard be immediately decapitated, and their families with them! Prince Yi, since you are a member of the Imperial Clan, we command you to take your own life, by strangulation!"

The three were taken away.

Tzu Hsi turned to Tzu An. She had been the regal figure at this affair and she knew it; but she tried to pay honor, nevertheless, to Tzu An.

"The Emperor is dead, Sister," she said. "We shall rule together, you and I, and shall do nothing whatever, either of us, without consulting the other."

Tzu An nodded agreement, and departed.

Tzu Hsi retired to her own palace. She was slightly smiling as she took her place on her throne, and glanced at certain papers she had caused to be taken from the home of Su Shun, whose head, by this time, no longer decorated his ugly body.

She spoke to one of her ladies-in-waiting.

"Has Lady Mei recovered?"

The ladies-in-waiting glanced at one another. They knew the law. Lady Mei was the daughter of Su Shun. She too, must bend her neck to the beheading knife. The ladies-in-waiting dared not hesitate in answering, however much they may have desired to delay Lady Mei's punishment.

"She is recovered, Your Majesty," one of them at length replied.

"Bring her here!"

Lady Mei, her face pale as ashes, almost incapable of standing, trembling as she kowtowed to Her Majesty, knew exactly what portended—or thought she did.

Tzu Hsi put to her the same question she had put to Su Shun and to Prince Yi.

"You know the penalty for treason, Lady Mei?"

Lady Mei raised her eyes, wet with tears of sorrow, to Tzu Hsi. How could Her Majesty smile, while she condemned one who loved her to decapitation?

"I know, Your Majesty," replied Lady Mei. "The penalty is decapitation for the traitor and for all his family. I am daughter of Su Shun. But I have been faithful. I have always loved Your Majesty!"

Then Tzu Hsi leaned forward, touched the cheeks of Lady Mei.

"And I have always loved you, Lady Mei! In your father's house were found certain papers, papers which proved many evil deeds of Su Shun—among others that he caused your father to be slain, confiscated his property, and to further cement his claim to the goods and property he had stolen, adopted you himself, and reared you as his daughter! Lady Mei, you are not the daughter of Su Shun! The rule which covers the decapitation of traitors does not apply to you! Steady her, An Teh Hai, else she will swoon again!"

Once more Lady Mei, radiantly happy now, was the favorite lady-in-waiting of Tzu Hsi, and once more the sun was shining.

Tzu Hsi, nominally dividing authority with Tzu An, named regent with her, called "Empress of the East," had taken in her own fragile hands the reins of power.

XV. SUCCESSOR TO SU SHUN

Prince Yi was no more, nor Su Shun.

Su Shun had been Grand Councillor.

Tzu Hsi, therefore, before receiving Yung Lu in special audience, sent for Prince Kung, own brother of Hsien Feng, with whom she discussed the thing she planned. However much she may have loved Yung Lu, Tzu Hsi was ambitious still, wily and clever, and never, in all the years of her power, did one single thing to cause comment, unfavorable comment, that is, regarding herself or her actions, if there were any way at all that it could be avoided. Prince Kung agreed with the plan put forward by Tzu Hsi.

It is said, too, that Tzu Hsi discussed the matter with Tzu An, not that she felt she needed the advice of Tzu An, not that a refusal to countenance the matter would have deterred Tzu Hsi in any case, but because she wished to so conduct the affair that her real motives would not be disclosed—and it was cleverly done.

"Su Shun is dead," began Tzu Hsi, in her audience with Prince Kung, "and the position of Grand Councillor is vacant."

Prince Kung waited.

"Yung Lu saved my life, and that of the Little Emperor, on the journey from Jehol. He should take the place of Su Shun."

Prince Kung was a friend, in a way of speaking, of Yung Lu, in that he held nothing against him.

Yung Lu, at his home, off duty for the moment, received word through his servants that two eunuchs from the court desired to see him. Wondering why they sought him, Yung Lu received the eunuchs who informed him that a decree had been issued, of which decree they themselves now held a copy for Yung Lu's information, appointing him as Grand Councillor to succeed Su Shun.

"We wish to congratulate you, Excellency!" said the eunuchs.

Yung Lu, however, knew eunuchs, especially court eunuchs, that is, eunuchs close enough to the throne to secure the information they brought in the form of a copy of the decree, and understood thoroughly their "congratulations." He paid them, and a stiff sum was required to satisfy their rapacity, and received the copy of the decree. He read it over, marveling. It was true!

Successor to Su Shun

Yung Lu, the humble guard commander, was no longer a guard commander!

Yung Lu was Grand Councillor of the Manchu court!

He needed none to tell him who had done this. Tzu Hsi, once Lan Kuei, The Orchid, who had loved him in a Manchu garden, long years ago now it seemed, had managed this appointment for him. To what the appointment might lead there was no way of guessing. Yung Lu knew full well that Tzu Hsi was not for him, ever. That had been definitely settled long ago, when Lan Kuei had been chosen as Secondary Wife from among the seventeen who had come to court in obedience to another decree issued by Hsien Feng. Yet there was hope in the decree, for all that; Yung Lu, as Grand Councillor, would often see the cameo-like face of his best beloved, and might, perhaps, at times, approach close enough to her person to touch the hem of her robe. Beyond that he dared not hope.

His heart sang within him, as he prepared to follow the dictates of custom.

He spent most of the hours of that first night preparing his full dress, full dress of a Grand Councillor of the Manchu court; for when morning came he must visit the Empresses, to thank them for the appointment in person. He was to see Tzu Hsi again tomorrow, and for many, many tomorrows thereafter. The oath he had sworn himself, to be her slave and vassal always, would now be more easy of fulfillment, since he would be near her, ready at hand in case she should have need of him.

Then morning, and the hour of audience.

Yung Lu, every inch a man in his new full dress, the dress of the Grand Councillor, entered Tung Wha Men, and was escorted by obsequious eunuchs to the palace of audience, where he must enter the presence of the two regents, Tzu An and Tzu Hsi.

He entered, his eyes flashing to the face of his best beloved. She was very beautiful, despite the unrelieved whiteness of her mourning. She met his eyes. There was no smile in them, save perhaps for Yung Lu to see, since Yung Lu knew her as none other knew her, and might have been able to read some message in her eyes. Her face, however, told him nothing; but the face of Tzu An told him much. When Yung Lu came in, Tzu An smiled in a strange fashion upon Tzu Hsi. Yung Lu could read that smile, and knew that it had been Tzu Hsi indeed who was responsible for his appointment. Tzu An did not approve the appointment, and her smile, not at Yung Lu, but at Tzu Hsi, was eloquent of disapproval, and of something else. She said nothing, but her smile told Yung Lu, and Tzu Hsi, that she believed the appointment had been made for another reason. However, Tzu Hsi had fulfilled all the dictates of custom. She had conferred with Prince Kung, and with Tzu An herself, and there was, therefore, no detail in which she might have been criticized; and the fact remained that Yung Lu had been of inestimable service to the crown, because he had saved the lives of Tzu Hsi and Tung Chih. It was a merited appointment, yet Tzu An smiled at Tzu Hsi, a knowing smile.

Yung Lu advanced to the throne, prostrated himself in the ritualistic kowtow, hitting his head smartly on the floor for emphasis, and thanked Their Majesties, in the words of routine, for the honor conferred upon him. It was no small thing to be Grand Councillor. It was a great thing to be promoted from guard commander to Grand Councillor.

So Yung Lu, and one wonders what was in his heart, kowtowed to the woman whose hands his own had once clasped, and thanked her—though he seemed to thank Tzu Hsi and Tzu An impartially—for his appointment.

Since the ceremony had been completed, Tzu An departed immediately, casting that knowing smile back over her shoulder as she swept from the hall of audience. Tzu Hsi read the meaning of that smile. Tzu An believed that Tzu Hsi had inspired this appointment in order to have Yung Lu near her, not as Grand Councillor, but as a lover—so her smile seemed to say.

What would the rest of the court think of the appointment? What thoughts chased one another through the brain of Prince Kung, whom Tzu Hsi had interviewed before making it? Would the world believe in the justice of so great a promotion for a humble guard commander? Would the world condemn Tzu Hsi for showing favoritism? Would the world regard Yung Lu as the lover of Tzu Hsi, because Tzu Hsi had inspired his appointment?

One wonders at the thoughts in the brain of Tzu Hsi when the appointment had become fact. It was impossible for her ever to

Successor to Su Shun

encourage Yung Lu, no matter to what rank she might raise him. There was never a possibility that he might become her husband, and for him to become her lover would have shocked the world. Subterfuge she scorned. She would never accept him as a clandestine lover.

She did, therefore, the best she knew.

Yung Lu became Grand Councillor—and Tzu Hsi tried further to strengthen her position.

"Yung Lu," she said, "it is time you married! I have chosen a wife for you. She is Lady Mei, my first lady-in-waiting!"

Yung Lu was stunned. He could find no words with which to clothe his amazement. He dared not refuse. Tzu Hsi was all-powerful. If she had chosen a wife for him, that wife he must take. He dared not even show that he disliked the idea of marrying Lady Mei.

It was to Lan Kuei that he replied, not to Tzu Hsi. But not in words! It was his face which told her.

"I love but one woman. I may not have her. For me there can be no other, ever! I do not wish to marry Lady Mei!"

Lan Kuei heard the words he had not spoken. Did her heart thrum with gladness when she heard? We may never know, for a surety. But we know that it was not Lan Kuei, but Tzu Hsi, who made reply—and that was not a reply in words.

The Empress Dowager drew herself regally erect, and a frown of displeasure marred the calm beauty of her brow. Yung Lu saw that frown. Did he see the real story behind the frown, the message she would have sent him had she dared? That we may never know, either. We may only draw conclusions from happenings of the years that followed, and words dropped here and there by Tzu Hsi, and Yung Lu—both of whom this writer knew intimately.

It was Yung Lu, the Grand Councillor, who replied to the frown on the face of Tzu Hsi; and his reply was not in words.

He kowtowed his thanks for the honor Tzu Hsi had done him, in selecting for him her own first lady-in-waiting.

Thus could Tzu Hsi keep beside her, as long as life lasted for the three, the two whom she most loved: Yung Lu and Lady Mei.

Her heart was heavy, after her decision; but there was nothing else she could do. Yung Lu could not thus be elevated from a humble position without causing comment. By marrying him to Lady Mei, Tzu Hsi stopped instantly the comment which might point to a clandestine understanding between Yung Lu and herself.

That marriage, then, was to be a marriage of renunciation. It was to cause sorrow and heartache to Lady Mei, to Yung Lu and to Tzu Hsi.

But all three of them, understanding the reason for the union, knowing it were best in this instance, since all life is but a tangle after all, kept their troubles locked in their own brains. Though the years which passed wrote hints of their troubles on their brows, though Tzu Hsi became an old, embittered woman, Yung Lu a grey-haired man who never made his fondest dream come true, and Lady Mei died an unloved wife, at least a part of the dreams of each came true.

Tzu Hsi had Yung Lu always with her, during the day, before the great gates closed, at which time no man was permitted to be inside the Forbidden City, the Summer Palace or the Winter Palace.

Yung Lu was thus enabled to serve faithfully, down the endless years, the woman to whom he had dedicated his entire life.

Lady Mei became wife to the man she loved.

XVI. THE MARRIAGE

Lady Mei had no parents to whom Yung Lu might send the red chair which is the chair of the bride.

Lady Mei could not be married from the court. Rules of the court forbade.

Tzu Hsi, the Empress Dowager, was arranging the marriage. All these things, therefore, were taken into consideration by her. She wished Yung Lu to have as fine a wedding as had ever been held in Peking. So she sent Lady Mei to the private dwelling place of her nephew's wife, Duchess Hui, where were made all arrangements that might otherwise have been made at the home of the parents of the bride.

Yung Lu, from his own home, sent the red sedan chair, borne by eight bearers, to bring Lady Mei. He stood at the gate of his own courtyard, and there was no pleasure in his face, no gladsome expectancy such as an observer, had there been any, might have expected to see in the face of a prospective bridegroom who would soon gaze upon the delectable features of his best beloved. There was that look in his face, perhaps, which one may see on the face of a man who has just witnessed the departure from his home, and out of his life, of the body of one deeply loved. He was procuring a bride, a lady-in-waiting to Tzu Hsi, one of the sweetest and most gracious of God's noblewomen; but he was losing again the woman whose form and features would remain forever, through all vicissitudes, in his heart of hearts.

His heart was leaden, his features replete with sadness, as he watched the trotting coolies bear away the red sedan chair in which, presently, there would be brought to him the wife of Tzu Hsi's choosing.

The chair was taken into the courtyard of the Duchess Hui, the poles detached, and the coolies sent out of the courtyard; for none was allowed to gaze upon the face of the bride. Two elderly women, good friends of Yung Lu's family—women who had sons and daughters, grandsons and granddaughters, and husbands living—accompanied the bride to the red sedan chair, placed her carefully inside, and locked the door. The bride, a beautiful Lady Mei, with flushed cheeks—cheeks ravishingly beautiful because rouged by nature's rouge of excitement and expectancy—dressed in a plain red gown, her hair done up on either side of her tiny forehead, after the manner of young unmarried Manchu women, sat back in the chair. Her dream, at least, was coming true. She was to be bride to Yung Lu, whom she worshiped—worshiped while she knew, in her heart, that Yung Lu did not love her. Wise, as women are always wise, was Lady Mei. He did not love her, but might not her own love, boundless as the sea, win something of love from him after a time, when he realized how much she really loved him? That was her hope, perhaps, and where there is hope, no matter how hopeless, there is a modicum of happiness.

The eight bearers were called back, the poles readjusted in the sedan chair, the chair lifted, and the eight coolies, at a swinging, comfortable trot, began the journey to the home of the bridegroom, where Yung Lu, pacing the floor, wishing that the earth would open up and swallow him, tried to peer down the endless aisles of the years which led to the future, to see what that future held for him.

To be married to a wife whom he did not love. Well, love did not always figure in marriages in China, and it were best perhaps as Tzu Hsi had arranged. Though the difficulty lay in the fact that he loved Tzu Hsi, had loved her passionately when she had been Lan Kuei, The Orchid; and, as long as life lasted, there would be the hope that one day things might be different, and that some time, somewhere, he might possess the sweetheart of long ago—as he knew that, deep in his heart and hers, he possessed her now.

So Yung Lu paced the floor.

There were two elderly ladies at the home of Yung Lu, as there were two at the home of Duchess Hui, so that four elderly ones, after the custom, might impart of their knowledge of life and marriage to the two who thus were setting sail on the stormy sea of a new life.

The two old ladies, as a noise came from the courtyard, passed from the dwelling place of Yung Lu, as did Yung Lu himself, to receive the bride. Following the chair were the two elderly ladies who had been with Lady Mei at the home of Duchess Hui. These were joined at the chair by the two who had waited at the home of Yung Lu.

The Marriage

The poles were withdrawn as before, the chair-bearers sent away, so that none might gaze upon the bride.

The chair door was unlocked. Lady Mei's face was daubed swiftly with rice powder, not for beautification, since the powder was applied helter-skelter, but for good luck, and the red veil of her maidenhood dropped over her face. Then she stepped from the chair, her head bowed so that she could see only that part of the courtyard floor directly below, otherwheres being hidden by the red veil—and, two steps from the chair, was compelled to step over a Mongolian saddle (an emblem whose meaning is lost in the ages of antiquity, save that it is supposed to indicate good fortune) which lay across the pathway she must follow to reach the house of Yung Lu. Beyond the saddle, after a few steps, was a charcoal fire in a tiny grate, over which she also must step. The charcoal fire was another aged bit of ritual, with something of the same significance as the saddle. This is only the Manchu ritual. The Chinese have something different, though the meanings are approximately the same.

Then Lady Mei entered the home of Yung Lu for the first time, accompanied by the four elderly ladies.

Inside the hallway, midway down, was a table on which were two candles, red candles, upon whose bulbous stems were carved the shapes of a phoenix and a dragon. Symbolism, all of it, as were the symbols on the banners of those who accompanied the bearers. Symbols of happiness, when so few marriages, because they were loveless things, arranged by parents or monarchs, were happy. Farcical, yet binding for all time, provided that the bride were a virgin, lacking which essential the groom might put her aside, returning her to her parents.

An aged man friend of Yung Lu's family, who had witnessed many marriages, officiated here as master of ceremonies. In a sing-song voice he told the bride and groom what was required of them to fulfill the ritual.

Yung Lu took place on the right of the table at the end, Lady Mei on the left, facing the door by which the bride had entered.

"Kneel!" commanded the aged master of ceremonies.

Yung Lu and Lady Mei dropped to their knees.

"Bow three times!"

The True Story of the Empress Dowager

The twain kowtowed, rendering thanks to the God of Heaven and of Earth.

"Rise!" commanded the master of ceremonies.

They rose again.

Twice more, at the sing-song command, the two dropped to their knees, bent and kowtowed deeply—nine kowtows to the God of Heaven and of Earth.

Then Lady Mei and Yung Lu, with the four old ladies following closely so that no part of the ritual be neglected, entered the room of the marriage bed, upon which Lady Mei sat with Yung Lu, side by side. They sat down together. There is a quaint old belief to the effect that whichever of the twain sits upon part of the clothing of the other, will rule the home. Yung Lu sat upon the hem of the robe of Lady Mei, and the four old ladies smiled. It was right and proper that the man should rule the home.

Then two bowls of wine, each enwrapped by a red ribbon, were tendered the bride and groom. Each drank sparingly from his own glass, which was then exchanged, so that each drank from the glass of the other. Another omen of good fortune, a part of the age-old ritual which might never be neglected.

Then rice cakes were brought, of which the two partook also sparingly since the wedding feast was to follow. The rice cakes were for fruitfulness and to eat of them was to assure of many children to the union.

"Multiply and be fruitful!" was the silent command of the rice cakes.

Macaroni for long life formed part of the wedding feast.

It was a great feast lasting many hours, interminable hours for Yung Lu, who did not love his bride, though he had taken her because Tzu Hsi had chosen her for him.

Then, when all was finished, and they still sat on the side of the marriage bed, Yung Lu, using the fulcrum of a Chinese weight scale, drew back the red veil which covered the rice-powdered face of Lady Mei, and gazed upon the face, the sparkling eyes, the tremulous lips, of Lady Mei.

There was happiness in her face, though she knew herself already for an unloved wife. Yung Lu was a great man and a good one. His was that human compassion which makes for

The Marriage

understanding of mankind—because he himself had suffered so much, and had seen so much of suffering. He knew what it meant to be denied love, knew what it had cost him in heartache and sorrow; and this little Manchu lady, who loved him, had been delivered into his keeping.

"I shall cherish thee always, Lady Mei," he told her then.

He made no mention of love. Lady Mei had not expected it of him.

That he was going to cherish her, to give her a modicum of happiness, his words had already promised. She would be near him always, her face would be always before him when he returned to his home, tired with the responsibilities of his office. This much was denied Tzu Hsi, whom Yung Lu loved and worshiped. This much possessed Lady Mei beyond the possessions of the Empress Dowager who, despite lack of love, possessed the wealth and power of the greatest Empire in the world—at least in point of numbers.

Had hers been the choice, Lady Mei would rather have possessed Yung Lu, without love, than to have had his love and been denied his companionship.

Thus far, at least, were her possessions greater than the possessions of Tzu Hsi.

She would not have changed places with Tzu Hsi for all the wealth in Christendom.

Tzu Hsi might have changed, yet she had crossed the Rubicon of ambition, and for her there could be no change, ever.

XVII. TUNG CHIH

Tung Chih was a handsome youngster of five or six. Tzu Hsi loved him as she loved nothing else. She thought of him continually, as the fruit of her ambitions. She had forsaken love, and in place of love, life had given her Tung Chih, a handsome youngster—who might almost have been called beautiful had he been a girl—whom she worshiped, watching over him as her heart's dearest treasure, dearer even than her own ambitions.

At the age of four Tung Chih started his studies, studies which every Chinese boy and Manchu boy of those days must undergo. There were tutors of course, no schools, because Tung Chih was Emperor. The tutors must teach Tung Chih how to read, and how to make the sprawling Chinese characters, before the watchful eyes of Tzu Hsi herself. Tzu Hsi was tyrannical where Tung Chih was concerned. She watched his diet, she watched his studies and his tutors, and even the most important of ministers walked small when Tung Chih was near. A little tyrant was Tung Chih, and because he was Emperor his tutors were not allowed to sit in his presence, so that they stood the long hours away, striving obsequiously to teach him what he should know, when they feared him almost as much as they feared his regal mother.

Custom provided, moreover, that tutors should never praise their students.

"That is well, Your Majesty," a tutor would say, referring to something Tung Chih had done, "but you are capable of doing so much better! Chien Lung did far better at your age."

A rather dull existence. A growing boy, even an Emperor, enjoys being praised—and little praise ever went to Tung Chih, save when his mother saw fit to lavish her love upon him. Busy was Tung Chih, busy as any boy of five or six could possibly be. He had some idea of what it meant to be Emperor of four hundred millions of people, too, for Prince Kung had ordained that a woman as beautiful as Tzu Hsi, and young moreover, should not hold audience with the ministers, which made an official job for Tung Chih. In order to avoid comment, or to avoid being considered immodest, Tzu Hsi caused a bamboo screen to be built behind her throne; and when the ministers came to hold audience with her she placed Tung Chih on the throne, baby as he was, and from behind the bamboo curtain directed the destinies of China through the mouth of Tung Chih, who looked very dignified, despite the fact that his feet did not reach the floor, and repeated his mother's words with all the accuracy of the thoroughly trained parrot. It must have been an ordeal for Tung Chih, but he was properly trained. The tutors, under the direction of Tzu An and Tzu Hsi, saw to that.

But when the audience was finished, there were several things that more entirely engrossed the attention of Tung Chih; he loved ponies, of which he soon possessed a goodly number, since his royal mother could refuse him nothing that money would buy; he liked archery—as what boy does not?—and he liked the toys which were allowed children in China; but above all he loved a certain Grand Councillor, whose name was Yung Lu.

Yung Lu worshiped Tung Chih as he would have worshiped his own son and Tzu Hsi's. Perhaps he saw in the slender, handsome child the child of that union-that- might-have-been; perhaps he saw Tzu Hsi in the eyes of Tzu Hsi's child. We may never know what he saw for Yung Lu was quiet and taciturn; but the fact remains that he loved Tung Chih. He was with him much. If Tung Chih, during his hours of recreation, wished to ride ponies, Yung Lu encouraged him to ride, taught him what he himself knew about riding, and about ponies. He helped the boy choose the ponies he was to ride that day, taught him how to care for them, taught him to understand them, taught him to love them—though in Tung Chih love of horses was inherent. His father, Hsien Feng, had been a great rider, who took delight in dashing about the countryside atop his shaggy Mongolian ponies, with all the saddle-trappings, the red tassels, the fiery eyes and stout hearts. From Hsien Feng, Tung Chih inherited this love of animals, and of the outdoors, and Yung Lu helped him to cultivate it, so that ponies became part of the life of Tung Chih.

As an archer, Tung Chih was skilled. Yung Lu, knowing archery, being an excellent archer himself, taught him all he knew.

What did Yung Lu gain from companionship with Tung Chih?

What did Tung Chih gain from Yung Lu? What did he read in the sad eyes of his friend?

The True Story of the Empress Dowager

What did Tzu Hsi, who seldom permitted Tung Chih out of her sight, see in the companionship of Yung Lu and Tung Chih? And what did the court, who had heard so many whispers anent the days before Tzu Hsi's arrival at Hsien Feng's court as his Secondary Wife, see in the friendship of Yung Lu and Tung Chih?

It is difficult to tell. Suffice it that Yung Lu loved the boy, and that the boy gave unstintedly of his own affection in return.

It is easy to see them, almost, those two whose love lives were so strangely entangled with that of Tzu Hsi; Tung Chih, imperious little martinet, Yung Lu delighting in being ordered about by a child of five or six, especially since, because that child was Emperor, his word was law. Among Tung Chih's ponies, which were the best that money could buy, which had been broken and trained purposely for Tung Chih by handlers who knew they must properly discipline the animals to keep their own heads safely on their necks, the Little Emperor would move, gaily laughing, eager to talk to his little four-footed friends, calling out at intervals to Yung Lu, commenting in boyish shouts on the good points of this pony or that. A normal life—away from books and tutors—was that of Tung Chih, upon whose shoulders the cares of state rested lightly. Not that Tung Chih did not understand, in a measure; for he could not have been reared at court without absorbing something of the court-atmosphere, especially since, being the Emperor, everyone did him honor, until he came to regard honor as his due, which it was, and realized that he was Emperor, in spite of ponies, toys, and archery.

"Yung Lu, instruct the *mafoo* to saddle the white pony for me this morning! Have him made ready instantly!"

"Yes, Your Majesty, immediately!"

Both meant it; but they were friends, just the same, and their laughter over the situation rang out the next instant. Perfect companionship. Yet the pony was saddled forthwith, and "made ready instantly." The two might laugh together, enjoy the companionship of each other; but Tung Chih, son of Tzu Hsi, was Emperor, and his word was law, regardless of the fact that there was sometimes lamentable lack of judgment in his words. Time would change all that, yet now he must be obeyed.

There was, for example, the case of the tutor who wore chin-whiskers. Tung Chih hated chin-whiskers, or whiskers of any kind. For many weeks he said nothing to a certain tutor whose hirsute adornment particularly offended the taste of Tung Chih.

This tutor, moreover, was an efficient tutor. He knew classics, and the characters he made were made with a brush which was skilled, because the hand which wielded it was schooled far beyond that of the average tutor. He never smiled, and was not given to levity of any kind. He appreciated the responsibility of being tutor to a Little Emperor. But when he talked, as he was required to do at times in his duty as tutor, the whiskers on his chin reminded Tung Chih of the whiskers on a particularly aged ram which, of all the animals Tung Chih loved, seemed to have a particular aversion for Tung Chih, despite the fact that Tung Chih was the Emperor. This ram, many times, might have treated Tung Chih quite roughly, had it not been for the stoutness of the pen in which the ram was kept.

This tutor reminded Tung Chih of that ram.

Finally, one day, Tung Chih could stand it no longer. It happened that Tzu Hsi was present in the study when Tung Chih's outburst so disturbed the tutor of the chin- whiskers.

"I wish you'd cut off those whiskers, at once!"

The proper answer of course for the tutor to make would have been: "Immediately, Your Majesty!"

But he didn't make that reply. It was exceedingly bad luck to cut off chin-whiskers. The tutor was, therefore, in the position of keeping his whiskers, offending the Emperor and maybe losing his head for disobedience, or losing his whiskers and the good fortune which had so far attended him. So he said nothing. Tzu Hsi heard the command of Tung Chih.

"But, my son," she expostulated, "if he cuts off his whiskers he will have bad luck henceforth! He dare not cut them off!"

"Then I no longer wish him as a tutor!"

The tutor of the whiskers was therefore banished forthwith, and returned no more to the court. A new one came, a new one who was smooth of chin and cheek, and Tung Chih kept him standing interminably, ordered him about with great enthusiasm, and absorbed learning from him as a sponge absorbs water from a fountain.

From which it may be seen that Tung Chih was quite a healthy, normal specimen of childhood, who played at being Emperor as any child of imagination plays, without actually being Emperor, and indulged his childish likes and dislikes as normal children indulge those likes and dislikes everywhere.

Always, in the life of Tung Chih, as long as he lived, there was the presence, and the love, of Yung Lu, the Grand Councillor; the love that amounted to worship of Tzu Hsi, his mother; his own love for animals, toys and archery, and the fun of playing at being Emperor of four hundred millions of people.

Sparkling eyes, laughing eyes—Tzu Hsi's eyes. Fragile hands, delicate hands—the hands of Tzu Hsi.

Healthy body, inherited from Tzu Hsi and his sportsman father, Hsien Feng.

Life and laughter, life that was full of everything that any child could wish for—

Tung Chih, during whose reign Tzu Hsi began the first of her three regencies.

Lady Mei, since her marriage to Yung Lu, was no longer lady-in-waiting to Tzu Hsi, though Tzu Hsi still loved her, and often received her at court, where she often kept her for days on end, as though reluctant to let her go. Why did she feel thus towards Lady Mei? And why did her love for Lady Mei go out to Lady Mei more and more after Lady Mei had been joined in marriage to Yung Lu, by the express command of Tzu Hsi herself?

A strange tangle. A tangle that affected, in one way or another, all China, for the court of the Manchus was the pulse of the Middle Kingdom.

XVIII. THE STAGE OE EMPERORS

In the center of Peking is the vast yellow-tiled-roofed stage over which moved the Emperors, Empresses, Empress Dowagers, Prince Regents, of the Manchu court from the beginning of the seventeenth century to the fall of the Empire.

The Forbidden City is the holy of holies of the Manchus. It has known the loves and hates of the Manchu court from Shun Chih to Pu Yi. It has echoed and reechoed to the footfalls of ladies-in-waiting, in their high- heeled shoes, who strode majestically along the walks of aged cobblestones; it has heard the high-pitched laughter of thousands of eunuchs; it has known court murders, court suicides; has been hushed, brooding, over the deathbeds of the great ones of the Manchu Dynasty. Every stone in its many courtyards could tell a story if it could speak. Here a prospective mother stood, pondering, after the death of her husband, wondering whether to follow him by committing suicide, or to live on and permit her son—if son it should be—to ascend the throne of the Middle Kingdom; there at the brink of the aged well, stood the ghosts, on many a cloudy evening, of two ancient maidens, dressed in the court costumes of the Mings, striving to urge others to commit suicide by plunging into the well in order that the ancient ladies might be loosed of their bondage; yonder is the closed door of an ancient palace, locked for over a century, where a royal concubine slew herself because her lord and master had spoken to her impatiently. The great walls which surround this city, for so many decades a city of mystery, are hoary with age, and frown forever upon the passersby of all nations.

Nan Chi Tsu is the street which passes eastward of the Forbidden City, and it is always crowded with Chinese who shout to one another in a dozen different dialects, lowering their voices only when they must pass yawning *Tung Wha Men*, the East Gate of the Forbidden City.

A place, the Forbidden City, where the audience halls, the palaces of the court, the houses of concubines, the living quarters of the eunuchs, all with the yellow-tiled roofs of royalty, are set so close together that there are many narrow little alleys, their floors worn deep with the passing feet of many centuries, upon which the sun seldom shines, even at midday. Gloomy places, places which seem to whisper of bygone glories, of gorgeous costumes of great ones dead and gone these many years. Vast courtyards, huge buildings, the great wall and the lotus-clogged moat—that is the Forbidden City of today, silent and deserted, save for the shouts of soldiers who guard the City's treasures for the warlords of today.

In the days of the Empire, the Forbidden City was a place that was crowded. An endless concourse of eunuchs, serving maids, ladies-in-waiting, court-ladies, ebbed and flowed through the streets and the little alleyways, the courtyards and the terraces. The Imperial Gardens were a place of laughter and beauty; actors, eunuchs usually, played their puppet shows upon the stages erected for the entertainment of Manchu royalty; aromas from the best food in all China came forth from the royal kitchens; dressmakers, shoemakers, artisans of all kinds and classes, labored to clothe the court and to keep beautiful the grounds and buildings of the Forbidden City.

It was a beehive of industry, this city which knew the greatest of the Manchus.

The Forbidden City, while the most famous seat of the Manchu court, was not the most beautiful. The palace called "Yuan-Ming-Yuan," which had been destroyed by the English and French soldiers as an act of reprisal, an aftermath of the "Opium War," just before the flight of Hsien Feng to Jehol, where he died, as already written, was the most beautiful of all the palaces; and Tzu Hsi never ceased to mourn the fact of its destruction, nor to bemoan the fact that it was practically impossible to rebuild.

The Stage of Emperors

ENTRANCE TO TAI HO TIEN AUDIENCE HALL, FORBIDDEN CITY, PEKING, CHINA

Then there was the famous Summer Palace, built during the reign of Chien Lung. It lies between Peking and the Western Hills, on an artificial hill, and while it is called a "palace" the name is somewhat confusing to the westerner, because of the fact that it covers so much ground, and is a composite of so many palaces, audience halls, and dwelling places of the court. It faces a huge artificial lake, upon whose surface the Dowager Empress, Tzu Hsi, took such great delight in exercising her unwieldy launches and houseboats. A beautiful place, in a marvelous setting, yet it is a palace of sadness now, because the feet it knew will come no more; the audience halls and the dwelling places are the sleeping places of coolies in soldier uniforms, and the ancient glory is day by day vanishing because of China's neglect.

The famous Marble Boat rests on the floor of the lake, at the end of the Great Colonnade which Tzu Hsi loved so well, and its story, in more or less garbled form, has been given countless times to the reading public from the pens of prolific—and sometimes careless—writers.

The Winter Palace, with the White Dagoba rising on a hill in its center like a great sentinel, is visible in the heart of Peking. It, too, is ringed about by a moat, lotus-clogged; and once upon a time it was one of the pleasure places of the Manchu Court.

Then there was Jehol, already described in another place.

These form the great stage across which moved the royal puppets of China's dynasties. These places knew the footfalls of Emperors, Empresses, Princes and Princesses, from Shun Chih to Pu Yi.

What stories they could tell if they only could speak! What tales of sorrow and of heartache, what tales of joy and laughter, of sentiment and tragedy!

They knew Lan Kuei, The Orchid, Tzu Hsi, the Imperial Mistress and Empress Dowager—and the ill-fated boy emperors, Tung Chih, Kwang Hsu and Hsuan Tung.

Each came on to speak his part, moved across the stage, posturing for an hour or a day, each called great in his time; and vanished from the stage to be known no more, save in history's musty pages, while the bodies of which they were once so vain now molder in tombs that are rapidly being forgotten, and have been neglected for decades.

An empty stage, echoing to ghostly footfalls—

Only, in the days of Tung Chih the time when the stage was to be vacant and deserted was many years in the future, and the Forbidden City and the Palaces were domiciles of life, laughter, love, intrigue, tragedy; and every day wrote new chapters in China's already voluminous history.

It is of these days we had best remember, for there is little pleasure in the contemplation of a tomb, however vast and awe-inspiring it may be.

So let us people the empty stage again, if only for a few hours or days, glance back down the corridors of the years, re-etch the registry of the footprints on the cobblestones, re-create the people of the long ago who lived, loved and had their being within the almost sacred walls; for it is only thus that we may comprehend the greatness, or the meanness, of the players who once spoke their parts upon this stage; it is only thus that we may be brought to understand that, behind the garb of greatness, underneath the rich costumes of royalty, behind the customs of courts and of countries, beat the hearts of human beings like ourselves, who lived and loved as we do, and were only Nature's children, with those children's faults and faculties, after all.

Take one glimpse at the stage, for the stage holds within itself emanations from the hearts of those who crossed it in their time, whose footfalls still echo on the rotting boards for those to hear who understand. It is only by noting the stage, the scenery, the properties, that we may thoroughly understand the players.

For the players are the play, and the stage is the world they lived in—and one may not understand the one without an equal knowledge of the other two.

XIX. THE JOURNEY OF AN TEH HAI

The law of the Manchus stated that no eunuch might leave the City of Peking. The penalty for disobedience was decapitation, of course after trial and conviction. A eunuch who thus disobeyed was compelled to answer to the nearest local tribunal, and since the fact of his absence from Peking was prima facie evidence of disobedience of the law, the local tribunals invariably moved with speed and dispatch, and a headless eunuch paid the penalty.

An Teh Hai knew this. So did every eunuch in the court.

Yet An Teh Hai, after the death of Hsien Feng, became impatient with court life, and yearned for a glimpse of the fields which were invisible beyond the horizon. He went to Tzu Hsi.

"I pray Your Majesty for leave of absence for one month, because of illness."

"An Teh Hai," replied Tzu Hsi, "tell me the truth! You are not ill, that I can plainly see!"

And An Teh Hai told the truth, because he trusted Tzu Hsi, knowing her own faith in him, a faith that made him the most powerful person at court. Petted and pampered was An Teh Hai, and his words of advice to Tzu Hsi were always favorably received. Officials, high and low, outside the court, knew An Teh Hai's standing at court. That's why they feared him, knowing that if they gave offense to the Chief Eunuch there were countless ways in which he could do them injury. That's why, because she believed in him, liked him very much because of his faithfulness to her own interests, An Teh Hai told her the truth—as much of it as he thought she should know— and why she listened to his words.

"I wish, Your Majesty," he told her, "to leave Peking for a short time. I desire to make a visit to Suchow."

"But the Manchu law, An Teh Hai! You know it well. No eunuch is allowed to leave the city of Peking!"

An Teh Hai, wise eunuch, held his peace! He merely waited for Tzu Hsi to continue, well knowing her faith in himself, well knowing that she wished to please him where possible.

"I think, An Teh Hai," she said at last, "that this is the best way to manage the matter: take two months leave of absence on account of illness. Then if any local officials, in the places you go to visit, insist upon following the law in your case, I shall order your immediate return to Peking, so that you may he tried at court. That is as far as I dare go in the matter. I am as amenable to the law as you are."

An Teh Hai, realizing that this was practically permission to leave Peking, realizing that his own popularity with Tzu Hsi had caused the granting of his request, proceeded at once to Suchow.

He called first on the governor, who received him somewhat dubiously. The governor knew the law, as well as did An Teh Hai. The Chief Eunuch had already condemned himself, dared the executioner, by leaving Peking. But the official knew the might of An Teh Hai at court, and feared the Chief Eunuch as he feared the Empress Dowager herself. An Teh Hai, a student of human nature—as he must have become since, through knowledge of the weakness and vanity of men, he had managed to amass a huge fortune for himself—saw instantly how much he was feared by the governor.

"I am here," he said, "at the express command of Her Majesty, to investigate conditions in the silk industry, and in your realm of influence in general. I desire your full cooperation in all things."

The governor, knowing the ruthlessness of An Teh Hai, and realizing how such a man could abuse power, then made a fatal mistake. He gave An Teh Hai the same honors he would have given Tzu Hsi, and bent before him in the servile kowtow which is the right of royalty; and An Teh Hai became almost instantly frantic with the lust to exercise the power which had been thus mutely placed in his hands.

He had not mentioned to the governor, or to Tzu Hsi, that Li Lien Ying, wily Li! had informed him of the far- famed beauty of the girls of Suchow. He had thought it best to keep this knowledge, and the real purpose of his visit to Suchow, from Her Majesty and from the governor.

Just why An Teh Hai, in the circumstances, was interested in maidenly beauty, may not be discussed in this book. But the fact remains, just as folks at court knew that many of the eunuchs of the court had sweethearts among the serving maids, sweethearts who really loved them, were almost slaves to them, and married them after the fall of the court.

When it is considered that the eunuchs at the court were really eunuchs, that there was no opportunity to falsify the record and enter the service unless a man were a eunuch, this desire of eunuchs for companionship with women seems incomprehensible. The fact, however, as I have said, remains. It is one of the dark horrors of court life. It suggests unmentionable orgies.

"My *yamen*, An Teh Hai," said the frightened governor, "is your home as long as you remain in Suchow. Go and come as you will. My house, my servants, are yours to command!"

But An Teh Hai had other ideas. He did not believe he could put them into operation within the sacred walls of the governor's *yamen*. He therefore refused the kind, frightened offer of his Excellency.

"Then, if you do not wish to honor my humble *yamen* by accepting it as your own, I shall arrange for you the best house in Suchow!"

This An Teh Hai accepted, learning that the house intended for himself was the house of Suchow's richest man, ejected from his home for An Teh Hai, and that it was a long, long way from the governor's *yamen*.

To this house went An Teh Hai, with his retinue of servants, of whom there were enough to satisfy the vanity of a reigning prince. The house became An Teh Hai's, and none other lived there, save as An Teh Hai desired.

The house became the house of orgies such as no pen may describe, by which no book may be sullied in the printing. An Teh Hai discovered that the little ladies of Suchow were beautiful, as Li Lien Ying had informed him, and many there were who went to the abode of An Teh Hai, either of their own will, because they were flattered in that a great man desired them, or because An Teh Hai sent his servants to fetch them, and their parents dared not refuse. A little king was An Teh Hai, a king to whom the populace of Suchow kowtowed as they would have kowtowed to Her Majesty, the Empress Dowager of China, and An Teh Hai most grossly abused the power which had been given into his hands.

Little ladies of Suchow went to the house of An Teh Hai, and came away weeping, faces pale with horror of the unnamed and unnamable, with red and blue marks on their arms, their cheeks; or they remained prisoners until, at word of An Teh Hai, their parents came for them, bearing ransom money to the sums of many thousands of *taels*. And none dared refuse An Teh Hai, none thought of refusing, though the populace of Suchow muttered under its breath. A scoundrel, meriting all the punishments of the nameless Hells, he nevertheless was a power at the court of the Manchus, and there was none with courage to deny him anything.

An Teh Hai went forth into the streets, into the marketplaces, purchased such goods as took his fancy—and those which captured his fancy were the best the tradesmen possessed; but An Teh Hai paid not a cent for the things, never intended paying, and the tradesmen dared not stir up trouble. So they thought, at least, during the first weeks of his reign of terror and of horror in Suchow.

"Send for the governor!"

That, invariably, was the way in which An Teh Hai began his day.

An Teh Hai should have called upon the governor, after seeking audience, and waited according to custom to be announced; but An Teh Hai did not. He sent for His Excellency, and the frightened governor, fear of the beheading knife at the command of Tzu Hsi stealing away all his wits, always obeyed the summons of An Teh Hai, went to him at the house the governor had set aside for him, kowtowed as to Her Majesty, and waited for the great man's permission to speak.

"I have some questions to ask of you."

The governor would wait, and would answer the questions as best he could. That the questions were framed without rhyme or reason, that they were utterly ridiculous as questions, frightened the governor even more. For he knew then that An Teh Hai had sent for him, not to question him, but to show him, the governor, that he, An Teh Hai, was all-powerful in Suchow, and that the governor had best walk with circumspection.

In the breast of the governor, fed by his abject fear of the power at court of An Teh Hai, grew a hideous hatred of the Chief Eunuch.

Yet there was nothing he could do. He sat awake nightly, striving to think of some plan whereby the Chief Eunuch might be undone, and he always ran against the same obstruction: An Teh Hai was the Chief Eunuch at the Manchu Court, was a favorite of Tzu Hsi, and his was, literally, the power of life and death. He had disobeyed the law, and though he was not above the law, as his famous successor was destined to be above the law, there was still a mysterious something behind his visit, perhaps his own egotistical bravado, which caused officials outside the court to fear him—and to hate him with a hatred that fed on itself.

An Teh Hai would then dismiss the governor, and his reign of terror in Suchow had been resumed for the day.

Lord of creation was An Teh Hai. Money, chattels, dwelling places, girls and women, were his for the mere taking; and when he did not choose to take he sent for them, commanding their parents to bring them to him where he lived.

But the governor of Suchow, fearful as he was of consequences, could not fail to heed the mutterings of his people. They depended on their governor. He could not afford entirely to ignore them. Something must be done. But he knew that sharp reprisal might follow on any attempt of his to bring An Teh Hai to punishment. What was he to do? He could not send a memorial to Tzu Hsi, for he believed that An Teh Hai was in Suchow with her permission, which was fact, as what she had said to An Teh Hai might be easily so construed.

So, thinking the thing over—while at Suchow kowtowed to An Teh Hai, did him honor ceaselessly, gave him right of way as though he had been the Emperor, only muttered in their hearts when he stole their girls, abused them, held them for ransom, even slew them if they were not amenable to his unreasoning reason—the governor of Suchow decided upon a course to pursue. He sent trusted messengers to Peking, with orders to find out exactly what lay behind, the unprecedented visit of An Teh Hai—direct disobedience to Manchu law. They brought back their story, and it was a strange story. It told of friction at court, of hatred between the Empresses, who, together, held in their grasp the destiny of the Middle Kingdom. It told that, though Tzu Hsi and Tzu An were equal in power as regents to Tung Chih, Tzu An had issued not one decree since the death of Hsien Feng, though, with Tzu Hsi, she always sat behind the bamboo screen while Tzu Hsi, through the lips of Tung Chih, on the throne before which ministers came to audience, directed the affairs of China. Tzu Hsi's hand was the hand that ruled, though her power expressed itself through the lips of a mere child, who listened for his mother's whispers from behind the bamboo screen.

That An Teh Hai, at court, was listened to with rapt attention, the story also authenticated. He was a power at court. The governor of Suchow must act circumspectly. An Teh Hai, he reasoned, was a favorite of Tzu Hsi. But there was deadly enmity, born of jealousy on the part of Tzu An, between Tzu An and Tzu Hsi.

There was also a story to the effect that once, during morning audience, an important audience, Tzu An had blundered grievously in her part of the routine—and An Teh Hai had openly laughed at her! Naturally, because Tzu An had been powerless, since An Teh Hai's laugh had been born of his knowledge of the hatred between the Empresses, and the fact that he was Tzu Hsi's favorite, Tzu An could scarcely entertain any great affection for An Teh Hai.

Tzu An, then, nominally with authority equal to that of Tzu Hsi, was the proper regent through whom to take action against An Teh Hai.

But how?

The whole story of how matters stood at court was brought back to the governor, and it proved that the whole court, to the least eunuch, knew the circumstances —that Tzu Hsi had failed to punish An Teh Hai for rudeness to Tzu An, the story of the royal jealousy, everything—and that, therefore, everyone knew that An Teh Hai, in leaving Peking, had forfeited his head.

But he had forfeited his head by being rude to Tzu An, and still lived—and his power was even greater than before!

The governor of Suchow had a friend at court, Prince Kung.

LI LIEN YING, CHIEF EUNUCH TO HER MAJESTY TZU HSI

Prince Kung, as we have said, was own brother to Hsien Feng, and he was utterly and completely faithful to Tzu Hsi, save in one thing; he deprecated the overbearing authority which had been given into the hands of An Teh Hai since the death of Hsien Feng. He knew of the jealousy of Tzu An for Tzu Hsi, as who did not? but decided that it was no affair of his, and tried to be faithful to them both—a trial that required diplomacy of a high order—succeeding to the extent that both Empresses listened to him when he spoke.

He received a memorial from the governor of Suchow. He read the memorial. Behind the departure from Peking of An Teh Hai he could see the fine hand of Tzu Hsi, who could refuse the grandiose eunuch nothing; therefore he could not take up the matter with Tzu Hsi. He carried the memorial to Tzu An, who had been waiting just such an opportunity as this.

"The departure of An Teh Hai from Peking is against Manchu law."

"It is, Your Majesty," replied Prince Kung.

"The punishment is decapitation!"

"It is, Your Majesty!"

"Is it not according to the wishes of Hsien Feng that I be regent with Tzu Hsi, and have equal power with her?" Prince Kung replied in the affirmative.

"And isn't it true that I have issued not one decree since the death of His Majesty?"

Prince Kung, the diplomat always, said nothing. He merely waited. He knew the law in the matter, knew that An Teh Hai merited decapitation, and wished to see him punished. But Prince Kung was a diplomat. He merely waited.

"Prepare a decree for transmission to the governor of Suchow, commanding that An Teh Hai be tried and punished, advising the governor that the punishment is decapitation!"

Prince Kung, a diplomat as I have said, not desiring some time in the future to find himself between the upper and nether millstones of the hate one Empress entertained for the other, offered a saving suggestion which, as he knew it would beforehand, only strengthened Tzu An in her resolve to act in this matter independently of Tzu Hsi.

"Hadn't Your Majesty best confer with Tzu Hsi before making this decree?"

"No, Prince Kung! I have equal rights with her! I am capable of making this decree! An Teh Hai should be punished! If Tzu Hsi knows, he will escape punishment!"

As Prince Kung left the presence of Tzu An, after the customary kowtows, his diplomatic mind was pondering on the proper method to handle this matter, in order that he might still play with both the hare and the hounds —keep the good will of both Tzu An and Tzu Hsi, bitter enemies though they were.

He caused the decree to be written, and dispatched to Suchow, with a message to the governor to act quickly, as another decree might be expected any moment.

Then Prince Kung waited exactly thirty hours—and went to Tzu Hsi with the first memorial he had received from the governor of Suchow, placed the governor's report before her exactly as he had placed it before Tzu An, and asked for instructions in the matter.

"I have already spoken with Her Majesty, Empress of the East, on this matter, Your Majesty," he said, as though it were an afterthought.

And then Tzu Hsi received the story from Prince Kung, and was so angry at the precipitate action of Tzu An that she overlooked the manipulations, in point of time, of Prince Kung. After all, Prince Kung was in the right. Orders from either Empress must be obeyed by him.

"Prepare a decree immediately, for transmission to the governor of Suchow, instructing him to the effect that An Teh Hai be immediately returned to Peking, in order that, since he is a court eunuch, he may be tried at court!"

Prince Kung, after the customary kowtows, withdrew from the presence of Tzu Hsi, and prepared the decree which she had bidden him to prepare. He prepared it slowly and carefully, a heavy task that required much thought, much rewriting, much labor, so much labor and thought, indeed, that ten hours more elapsed ere Tzu Hsi's memorial was dispatched to the governor of Suchow.

Meanwhile, in Suchow, the governor had received the decree from Tzu An. He knew it came from Tzu An, knew that there might be aftermaths of various kinds. It was no small thing to molest a high-powered official of the court.

An Teh Hai must be tried, too, according to the law.

The governor of Suchow sent for An Teh Hai, and received word from the Chief Eunuch some time later that if he, the governor, wished to see him, An Teh Hai, he must come to An Teh Hai's residence, where he would be admitted if it happened to please An Teh Hai.

Perhaps the governor smiled grimly. In any case, he went to the house of An Teh Hai, with soldiers at his back, and made him prisoner.

No eunuch dares leave Peking," said the governor.

An Teh Hai laughed.

"I am An Teh Hai," replied that worthy, as though that were sufficient answer.

"The penalty is decapitation," went on the governor.

"I am An Teh Hai!" snapped the Chief Eunuch.

And then the governor of Suchow, smacking his lips with relish, unrolled before the suddenly staring eyes of An Teh Hai, the decree he had received from Tzu An.

"It is a mistake!" snarled An Teh Hai.

"You have abused women of this town, An Teh Hai, said the governor inexorably, his eyes telling the Chief Eunuch of his enjoyment in the situation. "You have held girls for ransom. You have cheated tradesmen. You have purchased thousands of *taels* worth of goods, and have made no payment for them—"

"It is a mistake," repeated An Teh Hai, though terror was beginning to creep into his voice.

"And further," continued the droning voice of the governor, "you know full well that the very best foods, such as the largest capons—and the largest capons come from Suchow—must be sent to the court; yet you have compelled me, when shipments were to be sent to court, to allow you to make your own choice from among the articles in the shipment first; thus, you placed yourself above the throne. You ate capons destined for the tables of Their Majesties—"

"A mistake," groaned An Teh Hai.

And then his eyes brightened.

"The decree, you say, is from Her Majesty, Empress of the East?"

(You must know, of course, that none in China was allowed to mention an Empress, Empress Dowager or Emperor by name. An Teh Hai could not use the name "Tzu An"—which usage also would have been punishable by decapitation.)

"It is," replied the governor.

"Then it is sent without the knowledge of the mother of His Majesty! You must wait until I can communicate with Her Majesty!"

"And disobey this Imperial Edict? I cannot do it, An Teh Hai! You are to be tried immediately!"

And tried he was. The trial wore on into its second day. The preponderance of evidence was all against An Teh Hai, since the fact of his absence from Peking was ample proof of his disobedience of the law.

The second day was drawing on to a close. An Teh Hai would be beheaded very soon.

Then came the second decree. The governor knew what the second decree contained. It was odd that it followed so tardily upon the cooling heels of the first decree.

The governor, wondering if he had read aright the message, unwritten though it was, which Prince Kung the diplomat had sent him—had sent him in spite of the fact that he had sent him no message, traceable message that is, at all—placed the second decree under a weight on a desk in his yamen and went on with the trial of An Teh Hai.

An Teh Hai, as might well have been expected, was found guilty of disobeying the law.

He was sentenced to decapitation, and the sentence was carried into execution immediately.

After the head of An Teh Hai had parted forever from his obese body, the governor of Suchow opened the second decree.

"Return An Teh Hai to Peking immediately, for trial!" was the gist of the second decree.

Obviously, in the headless condition of An Teh Hai, he could not now be tried in Peking. The governor returned his body, nevertheless, and sent ahead of it a memorial to the court.

The Journey of An Teh Hai

"The first decree ordering the trial of An Teh Hai received and carried into effect. An Teh Hai has been convicted and summarily beheaded! The second decree was received exactly forty hours too late!"

But even though he had succeeded in ridding himself, and China, of An Teh Hai; when he thought it all over after sending his reply to the second decree to Peking, the governor of Suchow began to worry.

That he dreamed that night of bending his own neck under the knife of the executioner was very probable.

That Tzu Hsi received his memorial is history. That it made her furiously angry is also history—though told here for the first time as written history. She blamed Tzu An for the decree; but she could do nothing to avenge herself upon Tzu An. Tzu An was an Empress, shorn of power though she was. Tzu Hsi blamed her, and hated her thereafter with a terrible and bitter hatred. Tzu Hsi, since blame could little effect Tzu An, blamed the governor of Suchow for the death of An Teh Hai. She blamed Prince Kung, too, for the death of the Chief Eunuch; but Prince Kung was a diplomat, and succeeded in convincing her that he was not at fault.

The person who was really to blame, whose tempter's words to An Teh Hai had caused the erstwhile Chief Eunuch to desire to make the trip to Suchow, was a onetime "little eunuch" who had kept his eyes for years upon the position held by An Teh Hai—and that eunuch's name was Li Lien Ying, "Cobbler's Wax" Li, who many said was not a eunuch—a statement that is automatically branded as a lie, by the way, by any who know anything of how such matters are certified at the court of the Manchus.

"Cobbler's Wax" Li, Pi Siao Li, or Li Lien Ying—the most famous eunuch in China's history, because of the position he held with Tzu Hsi, China's most famous Regent.

Tzu Hsi blamed Tzu An for the death of An Teh Hai.

She blamed the governor of Suchow for An Teh Hai's death.

She blamed Prince Kung.

But the neuter who was really to blame, whose words had started all the trouble, she blamed not at all! Li Lien Ying had played his cards quite too well to be caught in any trap which might so easily be eluded by one who was clever, as were Prince Kung and Li Lien Ying.

A eunuch named Wong was senior to Li Lien Ying at the palace. He should have succeeded Ah Teh Hai as Chief Eunuch.

But he didn't. He hadn't the courage of Li Lien Ying, the superb self-confidence, and lacked the pockmarked eunuch's cleverness.

When An Teh Hai came not back from Suchow, the place of Chief Eunuch was vacant, and into this place stepped Li Lien Ying, naturally and without fuss or feathers, because, next to An Teh Hai, he had tried with greater concentration than all the others together to keep in the good graces of Her Majesty Tzu Hsi.

Li Lien Ying, Chief Eunuch to Tzu Hsi, the Empress Dowager!

These two whose lives were so strangely alike, from both of which lessons may be learned, were destined never to be forgotten in the Middle Kingdom!

The governor of Suchow? Of him there is little need to say more, save that Tzu Hsi bided her time, waiting patiently, and at last, after perhaps a year, found occasion to find certain faults with his administration of the affairs in Suchow, from which post she transferred him to the most difficult, the most thankless post in all China, a post which none might have managed.

In such a place it is not surprising that he failed to acquit himself with honor.

In a short time after his new and disgraceful appointment, he was hauled before the court to answer charges of negligence, fraud, and scores of others, to which no answer he could make served to satisfy the Empress Dowager. In the end, he was banished forever from court—his banishment to affect his descendants to the end of time—which meant he might never again hold office, that his children might never take the examinations for official positions, in short that the erstwhile governor and his descendants were doomed henceforth to live on a par with humble coolies.

It was not good to interfere with court eunuchs—a fact of which Li Lien Ying, in the years that followed, took full advantage—especially with those eunuchs who stood quite close to the throne.

XX. THE NEW CHIEF EUNUCH

Li Lien Ying, Pi Siao Li, "Cobbler's Wax" Li!

The most famous Chief Eunuch, without doubt, whoever served at the court of the Manchus.

Oily, smooth, supremely ugly, was Li Lien Ying. Face covered with smallpox scars, drooling lips, perpetually ready to snarl—though before his royal mistress he was the personification of servility. He knew how to please, was the toady *par excellence.* The strangest part of his relationship with Tzu Hsi—he paid little heed to Tzu An save when it was expedient and could not be avoided—was that she trusted him to the very end. Discerning where everyone else was concerned, she never could see that Li Lien Ying was the brute everyone else knew him to be.

Even before word came back that An Teh Hai had been beheaded, Li Lien Ying had stepped into the place of the Chief Eunuch, without so much as by your leave. He did not wait to be made Chief Eunuch. Incomparable aplomb was his. An Teh Hai had scarcely disappeared from the Forbidden City before Li Lien Ying had taken his place. When Tzu Hsi gave orders which should have been carried out by the Chief Eunuch, Li Lien Ying was the first to step forward, as though he already were Chief Eunuch. Tzu Hsi did not forbid him, and he was so careful, during the time between An Teh Hai's departure and receipt of word that he had been decapitated, to cement his standing with the Dowager Empress, that when the memorial anent the fate of An Teh Hai came to Her Majesty, it seemed only fitting and proper that Li Lien Ying take the place the ex-Chief Eunuch had vacated.

The eunuch named Wong was senior eunuch, but years later, in relating the incident, he stated that Li Lien Ying gave him no opportunity, that by sheer self-propulsion, he usurped the place that should have been Wong's. Then An Teh Hai's death, and the appointment of Li Lien Ying to succeed him, authorized to wear the blue button of the highest official rank to which a eunuch, at that time, might attain.

As soon as secure in his appointment, Li Lien Ying sent for all the most important eunuchs to come to him in his room.

"I have just been made Chief Eunuch," he told them. "I had nothing to do with the appointment. Her Majesty placed me in the position, and I cannot help myself. However, it is done, and there is nothing to say about it further, save this: I am not going to conduct myself as did An Teh Hai. When there is any money coming to me, such as cash presents for favors to officials, presents to assure the givers audience with Her Majesty, I shall not be selfish as An Teh Hai was selfish. I shall see that each of you receives his due proportion."

Long years later, Wong, recalling this conference of the neuters, made a certain cryptic statement which forms an excellent characterization of Li Lien Ying.

"He was a man with sugar on his tongue, and a dagger in his hand."

When the neuters left, having assured Li Lien Ying of their faith and support, he must have grinned wryly after them. He had managed the matter very neatly. After all, he was Chief Eunuch, and there was nothing any of them could do against him, save in an underhand way—and Li Lien Ying knew all about underhand methods.

When they had left his room, Li Lien Ying sat back comfortably in his chair, prepared himself a smoke of opium—his greatest vice, save for greediness—and looked the future over in the rosy clouds which rose from his gurgling pipe. No opium was allowed inside the Forbidden City, and for any to possess opium was to be punished by decapitation. But Li Lien Ying had already so frightened the "little eunuchs" that he rested secure in the knowledge that he would never be caught in the act of smoking, a knowledge that served him faithfully, as he never was caught. To make sure of it, he always smoked when Her Majesty was sleeping, or in another part of the Forbidden City, where his own presence was not required, and the little eunuchs stood guard at various coigns of vantage, ready to signal a warning if Her Majesty approached the room of Li Lien Ying. Since no matter how much he smoked, he never lost consciousness, it was an easy matter for him to remove the evidence of his smoking, so that, though Her Majesty may have suspected her new Chief Eunuch, she never caught him in the act of smoking, nor did she ever find opium in his possession.

Li, as Chief Eunuch, had many "little eunuchs" who served him in the capacity of menials, and his treatment of them further shows his character.

"Bring my pipe!"

A little eunuch who knew the pipe's location would hurry to do the bidding of Li.

"Move, son of a turtle!"

The "little eunuch" would increase his stride until it became a run, and his hands would be trembling so much that he could scarce manage the pipe of the impatient Li.

The "little eunuch" would kneel before the Chief Eunuch, preparatory to lighting the black pill for Li—

And if he still trembled, it was not unusual for Li to send him sprawling with a foot planted squarely in his face.

A fiend was Li Lien Ying, with the sadist's delight in watching the suffering of others.

This was amply shown at those times when Tzu Hsi held audience, when it was the duty of Li Lien Ying to stand behind her throne in case she might have need of him, always obsequious, where Tzu Hsi was concerned. She never caught him off guard—until long years later, when she had grown to depend upon him so much that she could not replace him—and to her he was always the soul of courtesy, the acme of desire-to-please.

He was a master of what, for lack of a better term, we will call self-propulsion. First, last and all the time, the person for whom he did the most, was Li Lien Ying.

There were many audiences which, though dealing with internal affairs of the court nevertheless were official, gave Li Lien Ying opportunity to encourage his propensity for inflicting pain.

A eunuch would be brought before Her Majesty for some slight offense. He had, perhaps, frightened a serving maid with a live snake, so that she had cried out, perhaps while Her Majesty was sleeping, causing her to waken. The offending eunuch would be brought before Her Majesty, who would ponder on fitting punishment for the case. At these times, Li Lien Ying managed to stand behind the throne of Tzu Hsi.

135

"Beat him with the bamboo!" she would say. "Twenty lashes!"

Li Lien Ying would lean forward, so that his lips were close enough to the ears of Tzu Hsi for her to hear, and whisper.

"His offense is a grievous one, Your Majesty. He cannot have the proper respect for Your Majesty, else he would gladly have died ere he would have disturbed your slumbers. He deserves, not twenty, but one hundred lashes!"

"See to the matter!"

The order would then be amended so that the punishment for the offending eunuch would be one hundred lashes instead of twenty. The poor fellow would be stripped to expose his naked limbs, and the bamboo— split bamboo with a pliable end, capable of breaking the flesh—would be applied by other eunuchs told off to administer the punishment. Slowly the eunuchs would beat the offender, always on the same spot, until the flesh was broken, when the pain must have been unbearable; while behind the throne of Tzu Hsi, where she might not note his actions, Li Lien Ying, a snarl on his face, his eyes boring into the frightened eyes of the eunuchs who were administering punishment, would signal for the beaters to beat even harder.

Perhaps twenty lashes would be administered before the skin would be broken, in rear of the thigh; then twenty more lashes before the blood flowed as freely as Li Lien Ying felt it should flow. By which time the eunuch, half mad with pain, would be screaming, weeping, and fighting insanely against those who held him.

"Your Majesty," Li Lien Ying would then say in a pitying tone, "I much fear that this poor fellow will die under the lash. He has received forty lashes. He still owes sixty lashes on his sentence. Will Your Majesty, whose heart is so compassionate, not allow him to go now, so that his wounds may heal, upon which he may be given the remaining sixty lashes?"

To Tzu Hsi, who was a mere girl after all, with little or no experience of man's affairs, this seemed right and proper; and the eunuch would be allowed to go until his wounds were healed. But never would that eunuch be forgotten. Li Lien Ying would see to that. He would keep record of sentences to punishment for minor offenses, and he knew to a nicety how to eke the most suffering—

for the other fellow—out of punishment. Just long enough time would be allowed to elapse for the wounds previously received from the bamboo beating to heal partially, when the unfortunate eunuch would be haled again before Her Majesty to receive the additional sixty lashes; and the eunuchs who did the lashing, instructed carefully beforehand by Li Lien Ying, would take care that the remaining sixty lashes fell exactly upon the half-healed wounds of the previous beating.

Eunuchs sometimes went entirely mad under beatings of the bamboo, and in their madness cried out against Tzu Hsi herself; and thus to cry out merited decapitation, which punishment was immediately suggested to Her Majesty by Li Lien Ying.

Li Lien Ying, in his own way, knew exactly how to command the respect of the eunuchs; for the beaten eunuch, moaning with pain, would at once inform his friends among the eunuchs what had befallen him, laying the blame at the door of the new Chief Eunuch. Fear of Li Lien Ying became rampant almost at once among all the eunuchs, for from the highest to the lowest, there was not one to whom Li might not work injury if he so desired, because Tzu Hsi trusted him.

"A man whose tongue was coated with sugar, and who carried a dagger in his hand!"

A diplomat of diplomats was Li Lien Ying, the ugly.

If there were any among Her Majesty's court ladies upon whom Tzu Hsi showered favors, that one was treated with the greatest respect by Li Lien Ying, in order that her apparent influence might not in some way work to Li's detriment at court. If Tzu Hsi had a favorite court lady to whom she listened graciously, it was not beyond the bounds of possibility that—if he in any way offended that court lady—she might inform Her Majesty of the fact, and lessen Her Majesty's faith in the new Chief Eunuch.

Favorite officials were likewise treated with gracious courtesy by Li Lien Ying—while behind their backs, in little ways, Li Lien Ying bent every effort to lessen the influence of those favorites with Her Majesty.

Drooling lips, snaky eyes, a figure of terror was Li Lien Ying. Ruthless, self-seeking, a born toady—perhaps one of the most skillful toadies who ever graced a court, since he was able for so many years to fool Tzu Hsi, who was the wisest of the wise. The other eunuchs feared and hated Li Lien Ying as they feared and hated neither death nor eternal damnation.

This fear grew by leaps and bounds. It extended finally outside the court, to the officials in distant provinces, all over China, until Li's name was anathema on the lips of everyone who had courage to voice their fear; but there were few of these, because Li Lien Ying soon developed an arm that was long, and he delighted in vengeance for real and fancied wrongs.

Li Lien Ying, the most sinister figure in the court of the Manchus.

And henceforth, he was to march side by side with Tzu Hsi as, each in a different way, these two moved into the future to meet their destinies.

XXI. THE DEATH OF TUNG CHIH

Tung Chih, son of Tzu Hsi, married at the age of seventeen, and, from the moment of his marriage, Tzu Hsi disliked the wife whom he had taken. This is difficult to understand, when we realize that Tzu Hsi had chosen Tung Chih's wife for him; but dislike the woman she did, a dislike that rapidly grew into bitter hatred that she tried with all her will to hide—because she loved Tung Chih, and the woman was his wife.

Perhaps this is the very reason Tzu Hsi hated the wife of Tung Chih. She loved Tung Chih to the point of worship, and it is probable that her hate grew out of jealousy toward a woman who could and did possess Tung Chih beyond the power of his own mother to possess him.

But still Tzu Hsi lavished her love upon Tung Chih.

She chose his concubines, of whom Tung Chih had four, one of whom was very beautiful.

The regency of Tzu Hsi ended with the marriage of Tung Chih, who thus became sole ruler of China, deferring, however, to his mother in all things, because in China it is almost the law that a son honor his mother and take orders from her. Ruler of China in name, and legally, Tung Chih nevertheless, was not ruler; since his mother's voice could be loudly heard in affairs of court, at least by those who were close to the court and understood these things. A proud mother, Tzu Hsi, who doted on her royal son.

Tung Chih became Emperor in fact at the age of seventeen, with one wife and four concubines.

He ruled for two years.

Considering the life of Tzu Hsi, as told by many historians who were prone to draw conclusions, and who knew little or nothing about Her Majesty—it was always her practice to hide from everyone the intimate details of her life, save that she sometimes, in impetuous moments, confided in her favorite court ladies—it is not difficult to understand the hideous charge that has been placed against her.

She has been accused of slaying her own son, in order to regain the regency.

Nothing could be farther from the truth.

Tzu Hsi loved Tung Chih as few mothers love their sons. He was a wild lad, inheriting the tendencies of his father. He enjoyed going forth in the highways and byways, accompanied by many eunuchs, all incognito, for horseback rides away from the rigors of life at court. He liked good wine, and enjoyed in unusual measure the companionship of women. He was a handsome lad, handsome enough to be almost feminine in appearance. Tzu Hsi could deny him nothing. If he wanted other concubines, other concubines were provided for him. If, as a child, he desired new ponies, of rare breed, those ponies were procured for him if all the facilities of the court were thrown into the effort to secure them. If a tutor displeased him, another tutor was secured for him.

Nothing in life that he could wish for, nothing in life that he even dared to aspire to, was denied him.

To Tzu Hsi, this son of hers was just a little less than a god, and she worshiped him accordingly.

The charge that she slew him, by slow poison, or any other way, in order to reassume the regency, is one of the basest lies ever perpetrated by a careless, prevaricating, or sensational historian!

Tung Chih, in his nineteenth year, died of smallpox— and most of the heart and soul of Tzu Hsi went with him to the grave.

She loved him, she worshiped him, and that she killed him is unthinkable. That he did die of smallpox is the exact truth, no less.

His death changed Tzu Hsi overnight. From a woman who took great satisfaction in living, who enjoyed life as few women enjoy it, who took pleasure from nurturing her great ambitions, she became a saddened, embittered woman—who retained only her ambitions, her love for Yung Lu, and began to place more and more faith, more and more of court responsibilities, upon the shoulders of Li Lien Ying, whom she trusted next to Yung Lu, her Grand Councillor.

For her action after the death of Tung Chih, in the matter of Tung Chih's wife, who soon was to bear a child, no excuse is offered.

Tzu Hsi was ambitious. Is ambition an excuse? I do not attempt to answer.

There was no way of telling, of course, whether the expected child were male or female. If female, Tzu Hsi might still be regent;

The Death of Tung Chih

if male, he would be the heir, and Tung Chih's wife would become Empress Dowager. It was a chance Tzu Hsi did not care to take.

She sent for the wife of Tung Chih.

"You are a very brave woman," she told her. "Your husband loved you."

The wife bowed.

"He would wish you to be with him."

The wife said nothing.

"Do you not miss him?"

"I miss him, yes, Your Majesty, for I loved him more than life!"

"Did you love him enough to desire to be with him always, even though you must die to be with him?"

When the wife hesitated to answer a question whose trend she did not understand, Tzu Hsi continued.

"When a wife loves her husband, loves him more than life, and the husband dies, it is not a disgrace to follow him. To follow him, the wife must have courage. I know you are very brave."

Tzu Hsi left it there, in order that the intimation she had given might have an opportunity to produce results —and the wife of Tung Chih, who was despondent over the death of the young man whom she loved so dearly, was ripe for the suggestion Tzu Hsi had given her. Saddened, bereft, ill from her expectancy, the suggestion of Tzu Hsi seemed to show her the way out of her troubles.

She committed suicide before her child was born.

That Tzu Hsi was responsible there can be no doubt.

Tzu Hsi then named, to succeed Tung Chih, Kwang Hsu, son of her own sister, who had married Prince Chun, a brother of Hsien Feng.

She sent for him at midnight, to make him Emperor of China.

He was four years of age.

When he ascended the throne, in spite of protests on the part of many officials, Tzu Hsi became regent a second time, Kwang Hsu's mother dying very shortly after the coronation of Kwang Hsu.

With the coronation of Kwang Hsu, the fragile hand of Tzu Hsi became a mailed fist.

She had need of Yung Lu, who loved her in spite of the mistakes she made.

She could have chosen no better Chief Eunuch than Li Lien Ying to stand at her back in her bitterness.

XXII. THE CORONATION

Tzu Hsi never forgave Tzu An for the betrayal of An Teh Hai. She had disliked her from their first meeting, and Tzu An had hated Tzu Hsi. But it required the appointment of Kwang Hsu to succeed Tung Chih to make their mutual hatred a terrible thing.

Kwang Hsu was the son of Tzu Hsi's sister, who had married Prince Chun, brother of Hsien Feng. He was a sickly child, pale and anemic, listless, with no interest in anything or anybody. At first Tzu Hsi loved him as she had loved Tung Chih, in that she watched over him carefully, supervised his feeding, selected his tutors—though there was never another human being who could completely take the place in her heart that was held by Tung Chih.

After the midnight coronation, one of those ill-fated midnight coronations of which we will have more to say in a later chapter, Kwang Hsu, of course, remained at court, where he was watched over carefully by eunuchs and serving maids, and as thoroughly spoiled as such children usually are. Nothing he wished was denied him. He was Emperor, though but four years of age.

The eunuchs loved him, save Li Lien Ying, who was incapable of loving anyone save Li Lien Ying.

There were times when Li Lien Ying teased the little Emperor, sometimes to the point of making him cry. At this point, began the hatred of Kwang Hsu for Li Lien Ying, a hatred that was to grow with the years, and to have a strange effect on the latter-day history of the Manchu Dynasty.

Here also began the most trying period of life for Tzu An and Tzu Hsi in their relations with each other. Tzu Hsi knew something of children, and always loved them. Her love for children was one of the things that brought unjust criticism upon her, caused veiled disparaging things to be said about her outside the court—to the effect that neither An Teh Hai nor Li Lien Ying was a eunuch, and that she had borne a child by the former—as evil a lie as was ever told against a proud woman. She watched over Kwang Hsu, as I have said. The little Emperor was inclined to be something of a glutton. Like most boys, he liked best the things that did not agree with him. Tzu Hsi, who knew many things about food that would have surprised the calorie experts of today—she weighed food and knew food values, whether instinctively or otherwise, as well as most of the aforementioned experts, fifty years before this business of calories became such a fad with people desiring to reduce waist lines— denied these things to Kwang Hsu.

"This food is not good for him, Sister," she would tell Tzu An. "It will make him sick."

Since the food in question was a mixture of various kinds of dough, ofttimes only half cooked, there was justice in her contention, despite the fact the Kwang Hsu wanted the food Tzu Hsi was denying him.

"But you are starving him, Sister!" Tzu An would reply.

"I am not!"

When Tzu Hsi spoke in this manner, that settled the matter, on the surface of things—and Tzu An would lead Kwang Hsu away from the presence of Tzu Hsi, and give him the very foods he wanted, which Tzu Hsi had just denied him. That they straightway made him sick, did not detract from Tzu An's belief that an Emperor should have the things he desired, nor did the fact of Tzu An's opposition add to Tzu Hsi's love for the Empress of the East.

"He must not play with the little eunuchs!" Tzu Hsi would insist. "They are an evil-minded lot, despite the fact that they are eunuchs—or because they are eunuchs —and they will teach him things he should not know!"

Tzu An, seemingly in agreement with Tzu Hsi, would lead Kwang Hsu away, and, after a time, after thinking the matter over thoroughly, deliver him to the eunuchs in order that he might play as he desired. There is probably little doubt that Kwang Hsu, as a child, did learn things from the eunuchs which ruined his later life, almost despoiled him of his manhood, and made him an object of pity of all who knew his story—of whom, by the way, there were only a few at court.

While playing with the eunuchs, Kwang Hsu fell into the hands of Li Lien Ying, the nearsighted, bestial Chief Eunuch, who plagued him so unmercifully that Kwang Hsu wept; and the story was taken to Tzu An. Furious at Li Lien Ying, whom she always hated because Li was rude to her, Tzu An forgot that Tzu Hsi had decreed that Kwang Hsu be not allowed to play with the eunuchs,

The Coronation

and carried to her the story that Li Lien Ying had deliberately mistreated Kwang Hsu.

"Li Lien Ying should be severely punished, Sister!" insisted Tzu An.

Tzu Hsi commanded that Li Lien Ying be brought before her.

"Did you mistreat His Majesty, the Little Emperor?" "I did not, Your Majesty," replied Li Lien Ying. "I was trying to amuse him, because I love him. I always try to amuse him. I try to do things for him whenever I have the time to spare from my duties. I am sure I do not know what I could have done to displease His Majesty! I understood that this was part of my duties, which are to please Your Majesty, and knowing that Your Majesty loves the Little Emperor, I thought if I should amuse him, it would please Your Majesty."

Thus, skillfully as always, Li Lien Ying gave the lie to Tzu An, and further cemented his standing with Tzu Hsi. Naturally, Tzu An disliked Li Lien Ying intensely, and this engagement served to increase that dislike. It planted in Li Lien Ying, moreover, a dislike for the Little Emperor, whom he blamed for the fact that the story of his mistreatment had reached Tzu Hsi; and that hatred grew as the years passed and Kwang Hsu approached manhood.

Then, thinking things over, Tzu Hsi decided that the time had come to have a final understanding with Tzu An. No one knows exactly what took place when the two Empresses quarreled bitterly over Kwang Hsu. But there is little doubt that Tzu Hsi, proud, merciless in her bitterness, lashed Tzu An with the tongue of the termagant, that she told Tzu An things that might never be forgotten; and that Tzu An became so angry in consequence, realizing that there was some justice in what Tzu Hsi had said, that she, Tzu An, took to her bed—and never again left it.

Tzu Hsi went to her in her sickness.

"I am terribly sorry to see you so ill, Sister," she began.

"I shall not be here to bother you much longer," replied Tzu An.

"You are not going to die, Sister," replied Tzu Hsi. "You will be up and about again, very soon."

"I do not believe it. I am dying. However, there is nothing to fear, I suppose. You are thoroughly capable, and do not need me to assist you in ruling our Ch'ing Dynasty."

Tzu Hsi commiserated with her, said she did not believe she was dying and said that she hoped Tzu An would soon be well of her illness—well knowing that fury had prostrated Tzu An, fury at Tzu Hsi herself, that Tzu An was dying, and that she, Tzu Hsi, was glad of it.

That the choice of Kwang Hsu to succeed Tung Chih was not a popular one is history. As a matter of sober fact, since Kwang Hsu was of the same generation as Tung Chih, he was not the proper choice to succeed Tung Chih. However, the word of Tzu Hsi was law, and Kwang Hsu became Emperor in spite of protests, written and otherwise, against his coronation.

There is one story to the effect that a high official, securing a private audience with Her Majesty, which she granted rather thoughtlessly, brought his protest in person. This man's name was Wo Ko Tu. He entered the presence very dramatically, and failed to kowtow, a failure that amounted almost to treason against the throne.

"What is it you wish?" questioned the Empress Dowager, frowning.

"I wish," began Wo Ko Tu, wildly, "to follow my written protest against the coronation of Kwang Hsu with a protest in person. He is not in the direct line of descent, as you well know! You've chosen him because he is your sister's son, so that you may continue to rule China as Regent! Prince Pu Lun, direct descendant of the father of His Majesty Hsien Feng, should have been named. But no! Desiring power for yourself, and realizing that Prince Pu Lun as Emperor would deprive you of power, you set over him as Emperor this mere boy, who really has no claim at all upon the throne of China! It is monstrous! All China is against it!"

"You realize the penalty for saying such words to me?" asked Tzu Hsi, her face pale with fury.

"I do," replied Wo Ko Tu. "It is treason! You might torture me, beat me to death or have me beheaded for what I have said to you; but I have beaten you! You are selfish! In the end you will ruin China! You pay no heed to the Board of Censors, will take no advice even from your wisest Ministers, and are a menace to the wellbeing of the Middle Kingdom! But I have beaten you! You would torture me for treason, because what I say is the truth, as you know, and it injures your colossal vanity. But torture me you shall not! I have already eaten raw opium, and my death is a matter of minutes. But I could not leave this life without making you understand that all China abhors this selection you have made of the successor to Tung Chih!"

But Wo Ko Tu was a useless martyr, as martyrs usually are. He died, as he had said he would, from eating raw opium. He died at the grave of Tung Chih—

And Kwang Hsu became Emperor of China. The death of Wo Ko Tu, more particularly his words, added to the bitterness of Tzu Hsi. It hardened her, and moreover, it proved to her beyond the shadow of doubt that though Ministers and Censors might protest, ever so vehemently, against her actions, if she insisted on having her way, have it she did.

Tzu Hsi was beginning to close her mailed fist.

Kwang Hsu was a mere boy of four.

Tzu An had died of her anger against Tzu Hsi— though, save for angering the Empress of the East, Tzu Hsi had nothing to do with the death of Tzu An, as some pseudo-historians claim—and the Empress Dowager had entered on the most important part of her career.

It was a far cry, this Tzu Hsi, from Lan Kuei, The Orchid. One wonders whether, had she had her life to live over again, she would have again chosen ambition in place of love, had the choice been hers. One wonders if she found the fame, power, and wealth, which she had coveted as a girl, all she had expected. Did it satisfy her for the loss of Yung Lu?

Did it satisfy her for her loss of the companionship of women of her own age—who now were so far below her in station that she dared not show her friendship, dared confide in but a few of them? Did this solitary grandeur, with all its emoluments, balance the happiness, now lacking, which had been hers when there had been no solitary grandeur, but only a doting father and mother who were not too watchful—and a sweetheart in a drowsy Manchu garden?

She never said, directly, but there were times when she did confide in her friends, of whom this writer was one, the fact that her life had been filled with hardships, lacking in happiness; and that the sum total of it all had embittered her, destroyed her faith in men and women equally, and made her a martinet, though an efficient one, whom China would remember always.

So Kwang Hsu and Tzu Hsi take place in the center of the stage.

In the wings are two who might also be called great, each in his own way—Yung Lu, who loved Tzu Hsi, and Li Lien Ying, the famous Chief Eunuch.

All others fade into the background, and of the four named above the two whose names will be remembered the longest were Tzu Hsi and Li Lien Ying.

XXIII. THE ILL-FATED WEDDING

Tzu Hsi chose a wife for Kwang Hsu, when Kwang Hsu was about seventeen years of age. She chose the daughter of her own brother. The husband and wife, therefore, were first cousins. Here entered again the pride of Tzu Hsi. She wished to have another Empress from the Yehonala Clan, to which she herself belonged.

The Young Empress, before she became the Young Empress, was much at court. Kwang Hsu knew and thoroughly disliked her before he even knew that she was to be his Empress, and the Young Empress-to-be held Kwang Hsu in contempt because he was so plainly a weakling. A weakling in the sense that he lacked stability, and what we commonly term "backbone," despite the fact that he had a good mind—a mind capable of doing great things for China—but lacked the force of character necessary to do those great things.

The Empress Dowager informed Kwang Hsu that her own niece was to be his wife.

"I don't want her!" he told Her Majesty, bluntly. "I don't like her! However, Your Majesty's will is my law, now as always."

There was nothing else to say. The Empress Dowager had made a decision, no law of God or the prophets could make her change it. This Kwang Hsu knew full well. She had chosen her niece for him, and her niece would therefore become his wife.

But what an ill-fated wedding it was, promising the heartbreak which it later developed!

The evening of the wedding, which is to say, the evening before the actual ceremony, the canopies which had been built to cover the courtyard just inside the entrance to the Forbidden City—that place where the ceremony was actually to take place—burned down, taking with them a goodly portion of the buildings which occupied that portion of the Forbidden City. All the preparation which went forward at the hands of the eunuchs—who, if they were not, pretended to be jubilant in anticipation of the great event in the life of their Emperor—went for naught.

To the superstitious, this was an evil omen; and so it later proved, though perhaps the omen had far less to do with the matter than ascribed to it by the superstitious.

The True Story of the Empress Dowager

The wedding took place next day, and there were several unpromising things in connection with the ceremony: it was a dreary day, raining, and the wedding candles would not burn; Kwang Hsu would not look at his wife; the Young Empress would not look at Kwang Hsu—they hated each other from the very first. However, the fact that Kwang Hsu slighted her so cruelly was a terrific blow at the pride of the Young Empress, who was heartbroken over the matter, despite the fact that she cared nothing for Kwang Hsu, and never was his wife save in name. Tzu Hsi was furious at the neglect of Kwang Hsu for her niece; and, with the ill-fated wedding of her nephew and niece, Tzu Hsi began to hate Kwang Hsu— a hatred that became a terrible, relentless hatred, souring her life, Kwang Hsu's life, and making the Young Empress the most unhappy woman at the court.

It was just about this time that Tzu Hsi acquired the name by which she is best known—that of "Old Buddha."

Li Lien Ying gave her the name, and she liked it best of all the names to which she had every right.

To digress: it was at the time when there was little rain in Peking, and crops all over North China were suffering in consequence. Tzu Hsi and her court, in accordance with custom when rain did not come, began a routine of prayers to Buddha—all her life Tzu Hsi was a devout Buddhist—which lasted until rain finally came. On this particular occasion, rain came on the third day and Li Lien Ying was so excited and happy—wise eunuch!—that he could not forbear the opportunity to compliment Tzu Hsi.

"Rain has come," he said. "Your Majesty is great! See how Buddha answers her prayers! It is almost as though she were Buddha herself!"

This compliment pleased Tzu Hsi. She always did appreciate compliments, especially when they seemed as sincere as those Li Lien Ying concocted for her ears. Li Lien Ying, who knew how to please, who never missed an opportunity to practice his woefully effective toadyism, saw that the idea pleased her. To him, thereafter, she was "Old Buddha" and he thus referred to her when he addressed her. Old Buddha she became shortly thereafter to all the court, to Peking, and to all China.

The Ill-Fated Wedding

Old Buddha she will be called until the end of time, or as long as there is a history of the Middle Kingdom. And this is fitting and proper, because she herself liked the title best.

But Old Buddha disliked Kwang Hsu, a dislike that rapidly grew into overpowering hate. She had chosen a bride for him, and, instead of pleasing him, that bride had offended him, in that she was not a bride he liked! It was an offense against the Empress Dowager herself, since she had chosen the Young Empress. But she put the best possible face on the matter, though it was shortly apparent to all that the Young Empress would never be the bride-in-fact of Kwang Hsu.

It was a rule at court that the Emperor, upon his marriage, should also take concubines. Usually the number was four. The concubines of Kwang Hsu also were chosen by Her Majesty, though she chose two instead of four, a fact for which no explanation has ever been given—and it is unimportant anyway, save that of the two chosen by Old Buddha, daughters of the Viceroy of Canton, one was the famous Pearl, known to history and to romance as the Pearl Concubine.

Kwang Hsu was devoted to the Pearl Concubine, which was an added insult to the Young Empress, though even the Pearl Concubine never was a real concubine to Kwang Hsu, for a reason that deals with masculinity, and which we may not enter into here. Kwang Hsu disliked the sister of the Pearl Concubine almost as much as he disliked his Empress, because the sister of his favorite was fat and not too greatly endowed with intelligence.

He, Kwang Hsu, paid entirely too much attention to the Pearl Concubine, to the secret anger and chagrin of the Young Empress, which was another shortcoming laid at his door by Old Buddha.

Adding this to the many other items Old Buddha began to charge against Kwang Hsu, after his indifferent treatment of the Young Empress, there is little wonder that her hatred of him developed into a sinister obsession that contributed, in no small degree, to the final downfall of the Manchus.

XXIV. THE RETIREMENT OF OLD BUDDHA

With the accession of Kwang Hsu, Old Buddha turned over the reins of rule—nominally at least—and retired to the Summer Palace, near the Western Hills. Her retirement was a triumphal procession; for everyone, including Kwang Hsu, knew that as long as old Buddha lived, there would never be another actual ruler in China. Her procession which wended its way from the Forbidden City to the Summer Palace was like the march of a conqueror.

Kwang Hsu, a young man whose head was filled with thoughts of reform, who really wished to do great things for China, was left alone to occupy the throne—with an Empress whom he hated, who hated him, and yet who was jealous of the Pearl Concubine because Kwang Hsu adored, in his abstract fashion, this beautiful daughter of the Viceroy of Canton.

A long file of sedan chairs. Court ladies, scores and hundreds of eunuchs, Li Lien Ying—all went with Old Buddha to the Summer Palace. Seemingly going into retirement, Old Buddha practically took with her the entire court.

Kwang Hsu was Emperor, seemingly with the power of life and death over his subjects, with the right to make laws or break them to interview ministers and foreign diplomats; yet he never decided a single important question without seeking the advice of Old Buddha. He went to the Summer Palace—and in those days it was a long, trying journey by sedan chair—sometimes three times a week; so that Old Buddha, seemingly taking no part in the affairs of court, directed the destinies of China just the same. She had once directed the destiny of China through the lips of Tung Chih, from behind the bamboo screen in rear of her son's throne. She now directed affairs from the Summer Palace, through the lips of Kwang Hsu.

That Kwang Hsu was a weakling there can be no doubt. One of the pathetic great ones of the Manchu Dynasty, he might have altered the whole latter-day history of China, had he possessed the courage of his convictions, and courage to proceed without the advice, assistance and consent of Old Buddha.

The Retirement of Old Buddha

One can still see Old Buddha, whose hand had been heavy upon China for many years now, on her triumphal retirement to the Summer Palace; one can see the swinging wide of the gates of the palace, in order that Old Buddha might enter and make the place a home—and, actually, the new seat of government.

The Summer Palace became a hive of industry. Old Buddha now had an opportunity to gratify her lust for beautification. Flowers soon grew in profusion throughout the Summer Palace. Eunuchs in bright robes and gowns were busy everywhere. Old Buddha's houseboats came and went on the bosom of Kun Ning Lake, threading their way through mats of lotus. Eunuchs wore runways on the sides of the houseboats, just inside the rails, or where the rail would have been had there been any rails, exerting themselves to take the boats whithersoever Old Buddha desired. She was getting along in years, and seemed intent upon getting some enjoyment out of the latter years of her life. Her court ladies went with her everywhere, and her favorite eunuchs, all of whom tried their very best to please her, waiting on her hand and foot as they had always done.

Every day, almost, there were other triumphal processions, but these were inside the Summer Palace, where Old Buddha strolled in the gentle sunshine of North China, followed by scores of eunuchs, each carrying some toilet article which Old Buddha might desire before her walk was completed.

The yellow tiles on the roofs were burnished, and gave off the light of the sun like polished gold. Bees droned in the trees and among the flowers. Shadows under the famous Colonnade sheltered the fragile bodies of beautiful court ladies, who had little to do save wait on Old Buddha.

In the great boathouse where Old Buddha's boats and launches were kept, pigeons cooed endlessly under the eaves.

Eunuchs labored in the gardens. Female attendants made dresses, socks and handkerchiefs for Old Buddha.

In retirement, she was apparently enjoying life to the utmost—yet she held audience as punctiliously as she had ever held audience as Dowager Empress; and when Kwang Hsu came to see her she directed him in matters of state, and he obeyed her because he knew full well that she was the most powerful person in China.

In those days she was even called the "only man in China," which gives an intimation of the actual state of affairs during her retirement, while Kwang Hsu nominally ran the affairs of the court.

What a place the Summer Palace was in those days! Old Buddha loved the Summer Palace. She took pleasure in beautiful things. There was nothing she desired that she might not have. She merely spoke, and miracles were performed.

But the rules of court life pertained here as in the Forbidden City. There was no let-up on the matter of courtesy, subservience to Old Buddha, who knew her rights and made sure they were accorded her, or in labor to make the Summer Palace a beautiful place that was at the same time a home such as the greatest person in all the world might have envied.

Buildings which were the homes of court ladies nestled under the sprawling limbs of huge trees, and through the limbs the sun shone, dappling the roofs in patterns of shifting sunlight and shadow. A drowsy place.

A place of ease and contentment—apparently.

Underneath the calmness of the Summer Palace's exterior, a volcano smoked and smoldered.

Yung Lu had not gone to the Summer Palace.

He had been made Viceroy of Tientsin.

The Retirement of Old Buddha

SOME OF THE OLDER PARTS OF THE SUMMER PALACE BUILD BY CHIEN LUNG

The True Story of the Empress Dowager

SOME OF THE OLDER PARTS OF THE SUMMER PALACE BUILT BY CHIEN LUNG

XXV. THE HAIRLESS MAN

At this time in the Summer Palace there began a strange reign of terror. Though it happened many years after the naming of Kwang Hsu to succeed Tung Chih, it nevertheless was the aftermath of that selection of Old Buddha's, and was a sort of revenge for the death of Wo Ko Tu, who had committed suicide at the grave of Tung Chih, after heaping all sorts of opprobrium upon the head of Old Buddha.

It began in this way:

There were no men in the Summer Palace, save the eunuchs, after a certain hour each afternoon, when the gates were closed, locked and barred against intrusion.

Yet, after the gates had closed one evening, and darkness had begun to settle over China, a lady-in-waiting burst into the presence of Old Buddha without the usual formalities, and made a somewhat dramatic announcement.

"Your Majesty, I was just walking along the pathway which leads to Your Majesty's boathouse, when I saw a man, who was hairless, and looked like a Tibetan monk, striding swiftly up the branching pathway which leads to the top of Ten-Thousand-Years Hill. I called to him, thinking at first that he was one of the court eunuchs, wondering what he did in that place alone, and he slipped out of sight in the shrubbery!"

"What, child?" replied Old Buddha. "Surely you must have been imagining things! No man is inside the Summer Palace at this hour. If there were, his presence would long since have been reported by the eunuchs."

"But, I saw him, Your Majesty!"

The lady-in-waiting was so much in earnest, so badly frightened at what she had seen, that Old Buddha finally believed.

She sent for Li Lien Ying, to whom the lady-in-waiting told her strange story. Old Buddha herself went forth with the eunuchs to assist in the search for the mysterious stranger of the hairless cranium.

But though they searched the Summer Palace from end to end, through every nook and cranny, and the eunuchs continued the search long after Old Buddha, infuriated and disappointed, had desisted, the mysterious man was not found. But that the lady-in-waiting had not been imagining things was amply proved by the red placard which Old Buddha found in her own palace after returning from the search. On the placard in well-made characters were the words:

"Your lady-in-waiting told the truth! It is useless to seek me, for I am greater and more skillful than you and all your eunuchs. I hold your life in the hollow of my hand!"

The hairless man, then, was a real flesh and blood man, and a man, moreover, so skillful that he had been close enough to hear the conversation between Old Buddha and her lady-in-waiting; and yet neither had seen him nor known of his presence. Old Buddha was very badly frightened. She had had things her own way so long that she scarcely knew how to conduct herself in the presence of the almost-uncanny. Not since the attempt on her life by Su Shun and Prince Yi, or rather the tool of these two, on the memorable return to Peking from Jehol, had she been so frightened. Diabolically clever was this hairless man, too, in that he perpetually eluded capture, and yet remained close enough to Old Buddha, much of the time, to be able to taunt her with a repetition of her own words—words in which she had commanded that he be hunted down at any cost.

The eunuchs hunted again through every nook and cranny of the Summer Palace, after Old Buddha had deciphered the characters on the red placard.

But they did not find the hairless man.

Old Buddha went to her sleeping chamber, uneasy and perturbed. She gave strict orders that she was not to be left alone a single second during her sleep, and took two court ladies with her into the chamber. On her bed was another red placard:

"I shall slay you in my own good time! Your life is in the hollow of my hand! I may slay you in your sleep, while you are walking or while you are eating. It pleases me to keep you in suspense!"

There was no sleep that night for Old Buddha.

In the early morning another court lady came to her before she was completely dressed, and this court lady was as badly frightened as had been the first to make the report of the appearance of the hairless man.

"I got up," said the court lady, "and happened to look out of my window. A man's face was just outside the window, and the man was looking in at me! His face, however, was upside down! He was hanging down from above by his toes, swinging back and forth like an ape! I cried out for help and the face disappeared, upward, from my window! I came here immediately to tell Your Majesty!"

Old Buddha made haste to follow the court lady, forgetting for the moment the exaggerated courtesy of the court. With a crowd of excited eunuchs trailing the procession, Old Buddha stopped just outside the building in which the court lady slept, and the frightened little lady explained once more, in detail, what she had seen. Old Buddha, her face pale, whirled upon the eunuchs.

"Turn the palace upside down, but find this man! When he is found, bring him to me!"

Eunuchs hastened away to do the bidding of Old Buddha, while Old Buddha herself entered the room where the court lady slept, there to find a third red placard, addressed to Old Buddha herself.

"I knew you would come here! I make sport of you all! I shall slay you in my own good time!"

Furious, frightened more than she would have cared to admit, Old Buddha returned to her own palace, where she found a fourth red placard.

"Your life is in the hollow of my hand! No eunuch is clever enough to catch me!"

The search for the hairless man continued throughout the day. Eunuchs darted from place to place, beat through trees and bushes, seeking the maker of placards. But they did not find him, though the search never ceased. When they would go over the ground they had just traversed, the eunuchs would find it literally plastered with those red placards, each one threatening the life of Old Buddha; but they did not once catch sight of the hairless man.

That night a veritable cordon of eunuchs stood watch outside the sleeping chamber of Old Buddha, while frightened ladies remained awake beside her bed. Eunuchs were scattered everywhere throughout the palace, watching, striving to catch glimpses of this mysterious hairless one who had so swiftly put the Summer Palace in an uproar.

A month passed, and still the hairless man remained at large, and his red placards were becoming day by day more insulting, more threatening, more obscene.

Two months passed. The Summer Palace was like a bedlam. Eunuchs had little sleep, being constantly on watch, and were peevish and difficult to manage. Court ladies became wan and pale from the almost ceaseless vigil beside the bed of Old Buddha.

Then came the night of his capture.

The lights were out in the sleeping palace of Old Buddha. Eunuchs, two deep, were lined up silently on either side of the hallway which led to her sleeping chamber. The outer door was closed.

Then, slowly, silently, stealthily, the door began to open. Instantly the eunuchs were on the alert. They watched, without a sound. The man thrust in a black-clad leg. Wider and wider went the door, opening slowly. Finally, against the moonlight, the eunuchs could see the outline of the hairless man. He was dressed in black from head to foot, a tight-fitting suit, something like the tights which are worn in circuses by performers.

The man was looking into the darkness, and could not see that the hallway was crowded with eunuchs. He moved in a bit farther. Then a slight sound, or perhaps he felt presences there, caused the man to withdraw, and start silently, as he had entered, to quit the palace. Instantly the eunuchs broke into full cry and gave chase.

The hairless man ran like a deer, easily distancing his pursuers; but their shouts into the darkness brought results, for other eunuchs, who had been patrolling the Summer Palace grounds, came on from all directions.

The hairless man was captured in the shadows behind a huge artificial rock, and made prisoner. Old Buddha had left orders that she be instantly awakened when the man was captured.

He was, therefore, led immediately into her presence. "Who are you?" she demanded.

The man smiled easily.

The Hairless Man

"What difference does it make? My name cannot interest you! Oh, I know that I am to be executed, and that you will question me; but I warn you that you shall learn nothing from me."

"Who sent you here?"

"I am sent to avenge the martyrdom of Wo Ko Tu, as a protest against the accession of Kwang Hsu!"

"That is not the real reason! Wo Ko Tu has been dead many years now! Who sent you?"

"A certain party. You may decapitate me if you wish, but I will give you no names! I have nothing against Your Majesty. I am merely carrying out the orders of my masters."

"Who are your masters?"

"I decline to name them!"

"Search him!"

Search the hairless man they did, and not any too gently; but they found not a single thing by which to identify him, no scrap of paper, nothing. The man submitted to the search without protest. He had lost, and he knew it, and it did not seem to trouble him overmuch.

"Has His Majesty, Kwang Hsu, anything to do with your presence here?"

"I decline to mention names, Your Majesty. I am merely carrying out orders, as I have said."

Old Buddha looked at the black-clad, hairless man, for many moments. Her right hand opened and closed spasmodically. Her cheeks were pale and drawn. It had been a terrible vigil, and this man had caused the vast uneasiness which had possessed the Summer Palace for months. What fitting punishment could she find for him?

Li Lien Ying, present then as always when weighty affairs were to be managed, leaned over and whispered to Old Buddha.

"Torture him!" he said. "Under the torture he may give us the names of his masters!"

"You may take care of the matter," said Old Buddha. "Beat him slowly and steadily, until he confesses, and gives the names of those who sent him."

The hairless man, nonchalant to the end, was led away. Li Lien Ying, the fiend, who delighted in the suffering of others, went with the guard to supervise the beating of the culprit. The bamboo withes, with the ends cut down to make leathery lashes, were brought. The hairless man was stripped and spread-eagled on the ground, under the expert supervision of Li Lien Ying; and two eunuchs, with two others standing behind them to relieve them when they tired, began to beat the naked back and legs of the hairless man.

Slowly, steadily, mercilessly, they lashed the back, arms, and legs of the hairless man. He groaned, finally, after a long siege of the almost unbearable torture.

Li Lien Ying gave the signal to pause.

"The names of your masters?" he demanded.

The man moaned and shook his head:

"I refuse to give them," he said.

Li Lien Ying signaled again. The beating was resumed. The two first beaters tired. The two reliefs took their places and the beating continued. After a long time, Li Lien Ying, who was enjoying it all very thoroughly, who signaled imperiously when the beaters lagged, bidding them beat harder, brought them to pause again. "The names, son of a turtle?"

The man shook his head.

Many hours later, Li Lien Ying reported the result of the beating to Old Buddha.

"He steadfastly refused to divulge the names of his masters, Your Majesty," said his report.

"Beat him until he does name them!"

"It is useless now, Your Majesty," replied the fiendish eunuch. "The man is dead! He would not give the names, so we beat him to death!"

XXVI. THE STRATEGY OF KWANG HSU

The results of the China-Japan War aroused Kwang Hsu to the sure knowledge that China needed reform. She was far behind other countries in matter of workable government, still following routine which had been inaugurated by the first Manchu Emperor, who in turn had taken something from the Mings, so that her form of government, having been handed down for generations, had changed little in the last several hundred years. The sad, humiliating results of the China-Japan War opened the eyes of Kwang Hsu, who really desired to gain for China a place in the limelight, among the great nations of the world.

He had a tutor whom he trusted entirely—Weng Tung Ho.

This man was highly educated, and had for years been a favorite of Kwang Hsu—and was disliked exceedingly by Old Buddha, mostly because Kwang Hsu trusted him. Old Buddha's dislike of Kwang Hsu required little to feed it. It was insatiable, feeding on itself.

"What are we to do, Weng Tung Ho?" asked Kwang Hsu. "China is no good! She is not taking her rightful place among the great nations of the world. We need reform, yet I am doubtful of the proper way to go about effecting reforms. And then, there is Old Buddha. She is a conservative, and is against any reform. I can scarcely do anything that she does not interfere. I feel now that something should be done, and intend to take steps as soon as a plan has been decided upon."

"I know a great scholar, Your Majesty," replied Weng Tung Ho, "a man who is a voracious reader of books, who is a great student of the mode of foreign governments, and who would be exactly the right man with whom to confer on this matter. Unfortunately, however, he is of inferior rank, rank too low to permit of his having a private audience with Your Majesty."

"But if we are to make reforms, we must begin in the proper way to make them. This matter of arranging audiences for men of certain rank must be discontinued if we must go below the designated ranks to find men who are suitable. What is the name of the man to whom you refer?"

"His name is Kang Yu-wei, and he is a great scholar. His rank, Your Majesty, as I have said, is not high enough to entitle him to private audience with Your Majesty." "The audience shall be granted, in any case."

The decree was issued forthwith. In such cases it was usual for decrees to be passed upon by the Board of Censors, who immediately pounced upon the fact that Kang Yu-wei was of inferior rank, and made memorials protesting against the private audience. Many of the Censors followed their memorials in person, to add their verbal protests to their written memorials. Kwang Hsu listened to what they had to say. Then he deliberately tore up the memorials, threw them to the four winds, ordered the Censors from his presence, and sent for Kang Yu-wei.

Kang Yu-wei was a great man in many ways. He was a voracious reader, student of Chinese classics, student of foreign modes of government. He might have been able to assist Kwang Hsu materially, had it not been for Old Buddha. But she was a conservative, loving the old ways, and Kang Yu-wei was too drastic, desiring reforms to be effective too quickly, reforms which, in a country that had followed the old rules for so many centuries, were too swift to be possible of accomplishment, even without the prospective opposition of Old Buddha.

Kwang Hsu went right to the heart of the matter upon receiving Kang Yu-wei. He told him something of what was in his mind, what he desired to do for China, how, in a general way, he wished to reform the existing form of government of China. Kang Yu-wei immediately made a proposal that may seem peculiar, even silly, at first sight, but which struck at the very roots of the government:

"First, Your Majesty," began Kang Yu-wei, "we must do away with the queue! Among all the nations of the world we are the strangest! We are like a race of animals in consequence, in that we have tails on our heads! We should begin by decreeing that all queues be removed immediately!"

"That is very difficult. It will cause uproar throughout China. The queue has for centuries been a sign of allegiance to the throne. It has become a part, almost, of China's religion."

The Strategy of Kwang Hsu

"Nevertheless, we must begin by doing away with queues! It will be a symbol that we are no longer a race of strange animals, laughingstock of all other nations of the world."

"But how about Old Buddha? As soon as she hears of the proposed reforms, she will come out of the Summer Palace to interfere—and Old Buddha, despite the fact that I am Emperor, has much more influence in China than I have. The people will listen to her."

"But if she were kept inside the Summer Palace until the decree had been issued and carried out?"

"How could we do that? There is nothing to prevent her quitting the Summer Palace any time she desires, and when she leaves the Summer Palace the people bow down before her, do her homage as of old, forgetting that there is an Emperor on the throne of the Manchus."

"My advice, then, is that Your Majesty send for Yuan Shih Kai who is in charge of the army."

Yuan Shih Kai was sent for. Meanwhile, Old Buddha, who had spies in the Forbidden City, eunuchs who listened everywhere and brought stories to her wise old ears, had carried to her the story of the private audience with Kang Yu-wei.

Old Buddha sent posthaste for Kwang Hsu who, obedient to Her Majesty as always, went immediately to the Summer Palace.

"Who is this Kang Yu-wei?" demanded Old Buddha, without preamble.

"He is a very wise scholar," replied Kwang Hsu, "in whom I have the utmost confidence. He knows much about foreign governments and is very valuable to me in many ways."

"He is a Cantonese! I do not trust Cantonese!" "But he has been recommended very highly by my trusted tutor, Weng Tung Ho, and has already proved to me his capabilities!"

"I should watch him very closely! Remember that you have already broken the old rules by granting an inferior official private audience. Moreover, the man is Cantonese!"

The True Story of the Empress Dowager

THE BRONZE PAVILION, SUMMER PALACE, PEKING, CHINA

KUN MING LAKE, SUMMER PALACE, WITH HER MAJESTY'S PRIVATE RESIDENCE IN THE BACKGROUND

However, Old Buddha did not forbid Kwang Hsu to deal with Rang Yu-wei at this time, though she expressed her opposition to the unprecedented proceedings quite forcibly. She did not, however, wish to take direct action against possible reform, lest she be too severely criticized for trying to manage the affairs of the government when she was no longer Regent or Empress Dowager.

Wise Old Buddha, in her way!

She practiced the old saying: "Give a calf enough rope and he will hang himself."

Kwang Hsu returned to the Forbidden City, and, in spite of renewed protests on the part of Censors and high officials, promoted Kang Yu-wei to rank sufficiently exalted to allow of Kang Yu-wei's permanent retention at court.

Shortly after this two important things happened: Yuan Shih Kai came in obedience to the Imperial Command; and a spying eunuch took a Bible, translated into Chinese, to Old Buddha, informing her that Kang Yu-wei was a Christian, and that Kang Yu-wei was by way of making a convert of Kwang Hsu, which wasn't far from correct. Kwang Hsu, though of a long line of devout Buddhists, was inclined to listen to the teachings of Christianity. Old Buddha had always hated foreigners. She had especially hated missionaries who, she claimed, and righteously enough, had come to her country to reform it, despite the fact that there was probably plenty of opportunity for exercising their reformatory proclivities in their own country. Moreover, and facts were with her, the missionaries, exponents of this same Christianity, had caused untold suffering, much misunderstanding, in China,

Naturally, then, she did not take kindly to the fact that there was a possibility of Kwang Hsu becoming a Christian.

But Old Buddha was never one to act with undue haste. She bided her time.

Yuan Shih Kai was received in private audience by Kwang Hsu and was informed by him, seconded by Kang Yu-wei, of his plans to reform China.

Yuan Shih Kai listened without a word.

Kwang Hsu gave Yuan Shih Kai all the details of his scheme, placing all his trust in the recommendation of Kang Yu-wei.

The Strategy of Kwang Hsu

"I wish no harm to come to Old Buddha," Kwang Hsu told Yuan Shih Kai, "but I do wish to prevent her leaving the Summer Palace before I can make effective the news and somewhat drastic decrees I have in mind. If she leaves before the decrees become effective, she will interfere and spoil all our plans. If she is held inside the Summer Palace until the decrees have been issued and put into effect, she may then come out as she wishes, since it will then be too late for her to nullify my plans. This is what I wish you to do: Take your soldiers and surround the Summer Palace! Make no attempt to injure Old Buddha in any way; but make sure that she does not leave the Summer Palace until I give orders to withdraw the soldiers. Bear this in mind, however, No harm must come to Old Buddha!"

Yuan Shih Kai agreed with every detail of the plan advanced by Kwang Hsu and Kang Yu-wei, even added some detailed suggestions of his own, and seemed fully in accord with the whole plan, even to surrounding the Summer Palace with soldiers. He, too, he said, appreciated China's need for reform. He was eager and willing to assist in inaugurating those reforms.

Yuan Shih Kai left the presence of the Emperor.

But he did not go to the Summer Palace, nor did he surround the Summer Palace with soldiers.

With all speed he set out for Tientsin, where Yung Lu, once Grand Councillor to Her Majesty, was now Viceroy.

Several days were consumed in the trip to Tientsin. It is certainly strange that Kwang Hsu remained in ignorance of the trend of affairs, strange that he did not remark on the continued absence of Yuan Shih Kai.

Stupidity. It is the only name for the carelessness of Kwang Hsu in this instance. When nothing happened, when no soldiers had been thrown around the Summer Palace, a fact of which he must certainly have been cognizant, he must surely have realized that something had gone amiss with his plans; yet apparently he thought nothing of it at all.

Meanwhile Yuan Shih Kai reached Tientsin and demanded immediate audience with Yung Lu, whom he knew, as did all of those close to the court, to be Old Buddha's most faithful retainer.

Yung Lu was awakened in the middle of the night, and informed that Yuan Shih Kai wished to see him on a matter of the greatest importance, a matter that could in no wise wait until morning. Yung Lu protested, wondering what a mere army official could have to tell him, half minded to deny Yuan Shih Kai's request for an interview.

However, after a space, he admitted Yuan Shih Kai.

"What is it?"

Yuan Shih Kai told Yung Lu exactly what had transpired on his, Yuan Shih Kai's visit to the court of Kwang Hsu, giving all details; but when he came to the part he himself was to play in the matter of preventing Old Buddha from interfering with the plans of Kwang Hsu, he changed the matter materially, to suit his own convenience.

"I am to surround the Summer Palace, by surprise, *and am then to go in and assassinate the Old Buddha!*"

Thus Yuan Shih Kai, destined to be numbered among China's great men, blackened his lips with one of the most ghastly lies that ever betrayed an Emperor. Kwang Hsu had no intention of injuring Old Buddha, and so stated in his instructions to Yuan Shih Kai. Yet Yuan Shih Kai, the first Judas of the Republic which came years later, told this terrible story to Yung Lu who, once upon a time, had been sweetheart to Lan Kuei, The Orchid, and had been faithful slave, retainer and protector to Tzu Hsi, Grand Councillor to Old Buddha.

Immediately Yuan Shih. Kai and Yung Lu made ready for the exhausting journey to Peking. It was a long journey in those days, there being no trains, and the only methods of transportation were by Peking cart and by water.

Yuan Shih Kai and Yung Lu traveled day and night to reach Peking and proceeded immediately to the Summer Palace, sending in word that they must see Old Buddha immediately. Since this came from Yung Lu, whom she still trusted above all living men, and from Yuan Shih Kai, who, spies had informed Old Buddha, had been closeted with Kwang Hsu, closeted so tightly that eavesdroppers had been unable to catch one word of what had transpired, Old Buddha received them at once.

Yung Lu stated tersely what Yuan Shih Kai had told him.

The Strategy of Kwang Hsu

Yuan Shih Kai, when called upon by Old Buddha to verify his own words, flung himself at the feet of Old Buddha, kowtowed deeply, and completed the betrayal of his monarch by repeating the lies he had told Yung Lu.

Old Buddha wasted no time; just how much she might have believed of the story there is no way of telling. Whether she believed none of it, yet saw in these disclosures her chance to return to power, may never be known. There are many stories current. One takes one's choice. Old Buddha said several times, before her death, however, that she thoroughly believed the story of Yuan Shih Kai. In any case, she proceeded on the assumption that Yuan Shih Kai had spoken truth.

Still that strange stupidity of Kwang Hsu. Many days had passed since he had given orders to Yuan Shih Kai. The Summer Palace should have long since been surrounded by Yuan's soldiers. Had this been done, a peremptory summons must long since have been received from Old Buddha, demanding that Kwang Hsu report to the Summer Palace with an explanation of Old Buddha's incarceration.

That no such summons came must certainly have warned Kwang Hsu, who knew the fiery temper of Old Buddha, that something had gone very much awry.

Yet he seems to have gone serenely on his way, with never a thought of the strangeness of things—and his carelessness, amounting to crass stupidity, might almost be blamed for the ultimate downfall of the Manchu Dynasty, if one may possibly seek out any one thing and say: "this is the cause." This, of course, is just the opinion of this writer, who knew Kwang Hsu for a serious young man who really had nothing against the Empress Dowager, save that he resented her interference in matters of state when he himself was supposed to be ruler of China. Had Kwang Hsu gathered about him the right type of advisors, had he insisted on his reforms being put into effect, China might not now be in the throes of chaos as she is. This is speculation, however.

Old Buddha, receiving the reports of Yuan Shih Kai and Yung Lu, made ready to go at once to the Forbidden City.

She told no one what she intended doing there; but her face was a mask of fury, her hands opened and closed like talons, and

171

her wise old eyes almost gave off sparks. She had done much for Kwang Hsu. She had treated him, during his youth, as well as she had treated her own son —and this was the way he had repaid her for her treatment.

Yuan Shih Kai, the arch-Judas, together with Yung Lu, who had carried the warning to Old Buddha in good faith, because he believed the words of Yuan Shih Kai, accompanied the procession of Old Buddha on the journey from the Summer Palace to Peking, and the Forbidden City.

At three o'clock in the morning, a eunuch saw a signal in the sky in the direction of the Summer Palace. He had seen that signal often during his years as court eunuch. He knew the meaning of the flare, while yet the procession of Old Buddha was a long way off.

The eunuch hurried to the bed chamber of Kwang Hsu, broke in without ceremony, awakened the Emperor, and made his report.

"Her Majesty, the Old Buddha, is approaching the gates of the Forbidden City! She will arrive in a very few minutes!"

Not until this very moment did Kwang Hsu know that something had gone awry.

"I knew instantly that I was lost!" Kwang Hsu told this writer five years later. "I did not know what to do. So I dressed myself, sent word to Kang Yu-wei that he must leave the Forbidden City, and Peking, at once, and make no attempt to return as he valued his life—and prepared to go out to my accounting with the Old Buddha!"

When the procession halted inside the gates, Kwang Hsu hurried to meet his royal aunt, flung himself on his face at her feet, trembling in every limb, almost too frightened to speak, for he knew the power in China of this harsh old lady.

He saw among her procession a face that he knew. He saw several that he knew; but there was one face that stood out from the others, a face Kwang Hsu would remember always, remember in hatred, despair, and loathing—Yuan Shih Kai, the man whom he had trusted, who had betrayed him, and who was destined to mount by the steps of this dastardly betrayal to the First Presidency of China before he died.

The Strategy of Kwang Hsu

Old Buddha said nothing to Kwang Hsu, save that she bade him rise.

He followed after her, realizing that she was too furious to speak.

She proceeded to the hall of audience, whither hurried eunuchs ahead of the procession to make the hall ready, to light lanterns and candles against the needs of one of the strangest conferences ever held inside the Forbidden City.

Old Buddha lashed Kwang Hsu, then, with the fury of her scorn. She charged him with all that had been spoken in the lie from the lips of Yuan Shih Kai, she named him ingrate to the aunt who had treated him as a son and, since Yuan Shih Kai was there, and Young Lu, both of whom Old Buddha trusted now, Kwang Hsu felt there was no use denying what Yuan Shih Kai had said. Old Buddha intended to take the word of Yuan Shih Kai against the word of her nephew.

All of the many things that may have led to her decision, may never be known, save in oddments of hearsay gathered here and there. Suffice it that she did take the word of Yuan Shih Kai; and Kwang Hsu, having nothing to say, because he saw denial useless in the face of this preponderance of evidence, damned himself utterly by denying nothing.

XXVII. THE COUP D'ETAT

A Great hall of flickering candles and colored lanterns, oddly like a chamber of death. It was a chamber of death?—death to the hopes of Kwang Hsu for reform, death to his hopes of modernizing China.

Kwang Hsu, the culprit, standing before his Imperial Aunt, who looked at and through him. The fearless old lady, at first, entered the audience hall alone with Kwang Hsu.

This was the first question she put him:

"Do you know the law of the Imperial Household which deals with punishment for one who raises his hands against his mother?"

This was the first intimation Kwang Hsu had of the real seriousness of the offense charged against him. It had been an evil thing to throw soldiers around the Summer Palace, yet it merited no such punishment as Old Buddha's first question seemed to indicate. Ergo, something was very much wrong; Kwang Hsu's plans had miscarried much more badly than he had expected.

Old Buddha did not wait for a reply from the kneeling man. She lashed him with a bitter tongue.

"I have treated you as a son! You have taken the place with me of the son I lost, and this is the way you repay me! I save your life and you seek to take mine. You are ungrateful! You are unfit to rule from the throne of the Manchus! You have fallen into the trap set for you by the Cantonese, whose one desire is to drive out the Manchus and usurp the throne! What you have done may be instrumental in causing the downfall of the great Ch'ing Dynasty. You have listened to the Cantonese and their suggestions for so-called reforms, designed to lead you into the very trap into which you have fallen! Do you know the punishment for raising your hand against the person who stands as mother to you in the Imperial Household?"

And Kwang Hsu made reply.

"Punish me according to the law! I deserve it! I am a weakling, as Your Majesty says, and am unfit to rule!"

"You have four hundred millions of people to look to you for advice and guidance, and you have betrayed them!"

"Punish me according to the law. I deserve it!"

The Coup D'Etat

Old Buddha then called in Yuan Shih Kai and Yung Lu; and Kwang Hsu, the degraded Emperor, whose heart a few days before had been so full of great plans for the betterment of China, was face to face with the Judas who had betrayed him.

Kwang Hsu told me about it later, several years later.

"I stared steadfastly at Yuan Shih Kai, and my betrayer could not face me. He kept his eyes on the floor. He realized the depth of his infamy, yet now, if he would save his life, he could not rectify the wrong he had done me. So he stood there, pale as ashes, looking everywhere but at the sovereign he had betrayed, and every expression on his face showed that he realized the horror of his betrayal. Yet there was nothing I could say. I *had* ordered him to throw soldiers about the Summer Palace to prevent Old Buddha's leaving until I could put my decrees into effect; and this act merited punishment in itself. But I had never even suggested that Yuan Shih Kai, or anyone else, raise a hand against Her Majesty."

One can almost see the arch-Judas there, fearful of meeting the accusation in the eyes of the man whom he had so foully betrayed. Yuan Shih Kai, the traitor, as evil as Benedict Arnold, since his betrayal ushered in chaos for China, and cost more lives than ever were lost through the activities of Arnold.

Li Lien Ying was there, too. Into his face Kwang Hsu looked also, striving to read the thoughts of this neuter who had been for so long the power behind the throne of Old Buddha. There was horror, and amazement in the faces of the other witnesses to the degradation of Kwang Hsu; fury and scorn in the face of Old Buddha; but in the face of Li Lien Ying there was an expression of smug satisfaction. He had always hated Kwang Hsu. Moreover, because she was the favorite of the Emperor, he had always hated the Pearl Concubine, of which hatred more later.

"Punish me as I deserve, as the law bids you punish me. I am not fit to rule."

"Make a decree, then, here and now, thou ingrate, abdicating the throne of the Manchus! Write that decree yourself, returning me to power, relinquishing the throne yourself."

Paper and brushes were brought, Kwang Hsu seated himself at a table arranged for the purpose, and silence fell over the hall of audience.

What a tense situation! With every character etched by the brush of Kwang Hsu, a brush that trembled because Kwang Hsu trembled as with the ague, Kwang Hsu was condemning himself to a future which held no hope. The candles flickered, guttered and hissed like reptiles.

There were weird figures on the walls, figures like wraiths of dying hopes, wrought by the dancing flames of the candles, by the shadows of the swaying lanterns.

Old Buddha, her face a thundercloud, stood impatiently nearby while Kwang Hsu signed away his birthright. In his decree he told of his own infamy, extolled the virtues of his Imperial Aunt, confessed himself a weakling; though, in the decree, he did not put the confession into words, the fact that he made the decree was confession enough.

A silent figure which trembled as though with ague. Motionless eunuchs, waiting the next commands of Old Buddha, stiff and stark as shadowed statues, amid the lights from the candles, lights which showed the drawn whiteness of the face of Kwang Hsu, lights which watched beside the bier of a man who, as a ruler, would soon be dead.

Yuan Shih Kai, whose betrayal had caused all this misery, stood there in silence. This was his first visit to court, since his rank did not entitle him to audience with Emperors, yet he was forced to come here to hurl his own lie, as though it were the truth, into the pale white face of the man whom he had betrayed. In the background was Yung Lu, whom Kwang Hsu suddenly hated because of his very faithfulness to Old Buddha, even though Kwang Hsu realized that Yung Lu was here in all good faith, believing utterly in the words of Yuan Shih Kai.

The decree was finished. Kwang Hsu was no longer the Emperor.

Old Buddha had begun her third Regency, four hundred million subjects once more returned to her hands—though they had never left them, save nominally.

The Coup D'Etat

Li Lien Ying, unnoticed by Kwang Hsu, who was tremblingly signing away his imperial heritage, slipped over to stand behind Old Buddha.

"It is the Pearl Concubine who has caused all this!" he whispered in her ear. "She has a bad influence on the Emperor."

Old Buddha said nothing though her eyes narrowed. She, too, hated the Pearl Concubine, since the Pearl Concubine held the love of Kwang Hsu which had never been Old Buddha's. Old Buddha said nothing as Li Lien Ying, a greater Judas even than Yuan Shih Kai, since he was more of a smirking hypocrite, and did not even trouble to be ashamed of his lies, made his damning accusation of the Pearl Concubine.

That Kang Yu-wei was really the cause of the trouble Old Buddha knew; but here was an opportunity to be revenged upon the Pearl Concubine because of her influence upon Kwang Hsu, an influence greater than that of Old Buddha. After all, Li Lien Ying's words might be true since there was no way of proving them not, true— and Old Buddha wished to believe. The Pearl Concubine, just possibly, Old Buddha might have thought, might have influenced Kwang Hsu to admit Kang Yu-wei at court in the first place.

Li Lien Ying had planted a bitter seed in the heart and mind of Old Buddha, who believed absolutely in this smirking, evil-visaged eunuch. But she said nothing, for Kwang Hsu was writing.

A tense tableau, as Kwang Hsu signed away his birthright.

Then, when he had finished, he flung himself once more at the feet of Old Buddha.

"Punish me according to the law! I deserve it! I am a weakling, unfit to rule!"

Old Buddha said never another thing to Kwang Hsu at this fateful conference. She was once more ruler of all China. What would be her first commands.

She spoke briefly to Li Lien Ying.

"Imprison the Emperor on Ying Tai! Give him only the barest necessities in the way of food! See that he is never unguarded! Assign a eunuch you can trust to be at his side perpetually!"

"And the Pearl Concubine?" questioned the smirking Li.

"She will not accompany him! Keep her here, but confine her too! I will give detailed instructions in her case later."

Old Buddha paused for a moment in thought. Then she continued.

"Prepare a decree banishing Weng Tung Ho forever from the court! Neither Weng Tung Ho, his children nor his children's children, to the end of time, may ever again serve at the court of China."

Imperiously then Old Buddha turned, looked not once at the deposed Emperor, and quitted the audience hall, that mausoleum of dead hopes, leaving Kwang Hsu behind her on his knees—destined henceforth to be a pitiful prisoner in his own palace.

All because a man, whom later China grew to regard as great, had played the Judas for his own ends.

With four eunuchs to guard him, Kwang Hsu was taken to Ying Tai, a little island in the lake which occupies part of the grounds of the Winter Palace, where he was incarcerated, and where he caused to be written no small part of the diary which has caused so much controversy among historians.

And the Pearl Concubine, the only ray of light in the life of pathetic Kwang Hsu?

She became a prisoner, too, in the building which had been set aside for her as concubine, and orders were given that no change of raiment be given her, that she be compelled to wear the clothing in which she entered her prison house, until the clothing should fall from her, and common decency compel that she be furnished with other clothing.

But for all of that, it was an evil day for Yuan Shih Kai, the betrayer.

For as he betrayed his Emperor, so was he himself betrayed in later years when, in his complete unseeing egotism, he strove to take the throne from which his lies had hurled the one Emperor who, had he been less a weakling, might have prevented the chaos which today is China.

Weng Tung Ho, who also had tried to aid China in the best way he knew, was banished forever, and today is only an unimportant name in history.

XXVIII. THE PRISONER OF YING TAI

Kwang Hsu was banished to Ying Tai, a little island in Nan Hai, which is part of the Winter Palace. It is not an island exactly, being but a four-roomed house built out in the water among the lotus. It is a roomy place, but it is a prison, just the same. And the bitterness of the pill for Kwang Hsu lay in the fact that when he looked in one direction he could see the Winter Palace, which now was denied him, while when he looked the other way, he could see the yellow tiles of the many roofs in the Forbidden City, whence he had been banished.

Part of his punishment lay in the fact that he could see, like Lucifer, how far he had fallen.

Naturally, in the long months he spent in this place his love for Yuan Shih Kai did not increase, nor for Yung Lu, nor yet for Li Lien Ying, the famous eunuch. He thought several times, as he later told, of the last words, which he had heard fall from the lips of "Cobbler's Wax" Li immediately after the abdication.

"I spoke many good things about your Majesty," Li Lien Ying had said. "Had it not been for my good offices the Old Buddha had not been so lenient. I explained to her that the Pearl Concubine was to blame!"

Cursed be Li! A hypocrite, Li Lien Ying, par excellence. With one sentence he tried to keep in the good graces of Kwang Hsu, who might one day return to power, while with the other he thrust a knife into the heart of the sovereign, and twisted on the haft thereof—this with the seemingly casual mention of the Pearl Concubine, whom the Emperor, if he did not love her, regarded as his one true friend at court.

So the Emperor Kwang Hsu was banished to the island of Ying Tai, where he entered his four-roomed hermitage —a prisoner from his own kind, with only a few yards of water between himself and liberty. Yet those few yards might have been thousands of miles, since they were impassable. They might better have been thousands of miles, since from his prison house Kwang Hsu could look forth daily upon the Empire he had lost—

Through the betrayal of Yuan Shih Kai!

Here Kwang Hsu began his famous diary, about which so much has been written. Some of that diary he later showed to this writer. This writer knew and respected Kwang Hsu, knew him for a good man, highly educated, yet lacking in the driving force so necessary if a ruler is to protect himself against the perpetual intrigues of court life.

In that diary he told of day-by-day events in his life, of visits made to him by the four eunuchs assigned by Old Buddha to safeguard him, to see that he had no opportunity of leaving Ying Tai, and to report back to Old Buddha every act of the deposed ruler.

But there was one that was faithful to Kwang Hsu, aside from the Pearl Concubine. That one was Huang, a eunuch. This man, presumably a spy for Old Buddha, reporting to her all that Kwang Hsu did, conferred first with Kwang Hsu to make sure that he reported nothing that would in any way injure His Majesty. Him only Kwang Hsu trusted with the details of his diary. Into his care was it placed when Kwang Hsu was not writing upon it. It went into hiding when the four eunuchs, who really were spies for Old Buddha, were near.

Huang would report to Old Buddha:

"The Emperor is studying painting, writing, and the classics. He employs his time in useful things. I shall stay by his side to see that he does no mischief."

Thus, by seeming to be on the side of Old Buddha, Huang did the best he knew for his master, and lessened a little the hardships of his daily life on Ying Tai.

Unhappy Emperor! When there was no writing to do he could sit for hours on the broad verandah of his prison house, gazing out at the world which he had lost, toward the Winter Palace, and the Forbidden City. But he might not visit either. The furniture in his prison house was the very plainest that could be found, the simplest that could be given him, and that made shift to serve his purposes. A table, a chair or two, rough benches—these were the furnishings of the prison house of Kwang Hsu.

The Prisoner Of Ying Tai

EMPRESS DOWAGER TZU HSI IN A SNOW COVERED GARDEN

YING TAI IN THE WINTER PALACE, WHERE EMPEROR KWANG HSU WAS IMPRISONED, AND WHERE HE DIED

The Prisoner Of Ying Tai

And he worked on his diary. In that diary many names were mentioned—the names of Yuan Shih Kai, of Yung Lu, and of Li Lien Ying. And it was by the latter that a terrible use was to be made of the famous diary.

A small dock led out toward the house of Kwang Hsu; but it did not touch the house. There was a gap of water in between, which could not be bridged. By keeping those four eunuch spies on guard over Kwang Hsu, Old Buddha made sure that no boat could be procured by which Kwang Hsu could escape.

So the unhappy Emperor sat on the verandah of Ying Tai, idly, with hands clasped in his lap, looking out at the treasures which had been his, or he slept at night on a rough bed while the lapping sound of the water that held him prisoner lulled him to fitful sleep, a sleep perhaps which was full of nightmares.

For almost two years Kwang Hsu was a prisoner on Ying Tai.

For the same length of time, the Pearl Concubine, who had nothing whatever to do with the troubles of Kwang Hsu, whose only fault was that she worshiped the degraded monarch, was a prisoner in her own room.

Kwang Hsu's food was the rough fare of the coolies, which was brought to him by seemingly servile eunuchs who sneered at his plight behind their hands, or even openly, because they knew him powerless to punish; the Pearl Concubine's food was also the poorest that could be found, which would keep body and soul together, and she received new raiment only when that which she wore literally fell from her in rags.

Her food was brought to her by the eunuchs and slipped into her room through specially prepared apertures, or through doors ajar for the purpose, as though she had been a dangerous animal.

And months moved on, toward the fateful dawn of the twentieth century.

XXIX. THE PEARL CONCUBINE

Of the two daughters of the Viceroy of Canton, Kwang Hsu appreciated most the Pearl Concubine. Her sister was too fat, too dull of wits, to appeal to the fine tastes of Kwang Hsu. So he ignored the fat sister, as he ignored the Young Empress, and made the Pearl Concubine his favorite—

Which sealed the fate of the unhappy little lady!

A strange jealousy, the jealousy of Old Buddha for the Pearl Concubine. It is difficult to explain, save in Old Buddha's hatred of Kwang Hsu, a hatred that began back in the days of Tzu An, when the boy Kwang Hsu had turned to the Empress of the East to find the understanding he had been unable to find in the Queen Mother.

Now, Kwang Hsu had betrayed his Imperial Aunt, and Li Lien Ying had convinced Old Buddha that the Pearl Concubine, because of her beauty and wisdom, because she encouraged Kwang Hsu to do things he wished to do, was a bad influence upon the Emperor, directly responsible, therefore, for this attempt on the part of the Emperor, to "assassinate" his aunt.

Unhappy Emperor! Unhappy Pearl!

Never again might they see each other—save only once, which we shall cover in its place. Kwang Hsu was the only living person who really cared for the Pearl, save perhaps her fat sister; the Pearl Concubine was the only true friend of Kwang Hsu; and now the two friends they had never been lovers for a reason already alluded to—were separated for always.

I can see her there, this unhappy little beauty of the court, alone in her room save for the necessary serving maids and eunuchs, waiting at a window for the friend that never came. Ignorant of the reason of her imprisonment, she must have suffered agonies.

That she left her food many times untouched, there is ample reason to believe. Food was tasteless, when the hands which tendered it—tendered it swiftly as something unclean, which it ofttimes was—were the hands of people who did not love her, and who fed her merely because they could not allow her to starve and thus escape punishment for something she had not done.

The Pearl Concubine

Through the holes in her garments her flesh could be seen, flesh that was white and sickly from the long incarceration. Her cheeks were pale, and never again would feel the rose blushes of the little lady who is truly happy.

An unhappy lady by a high window, looking out, her hands clutching the bars of her prison, toward another prison house whose occupant she could not see, but who she knew was there, probably looking toward the place where she waited in silence for the lord and master who never came. Sad eyes in a face that was never broken by a smile. A bird in a cage, a cage too small to allow the bird to preen its wings, a cage whose gloom forbade melody—another mausoleum of hopes.

Food untouched on plates, meal after meal. Wan cheeks pressed against a window. A face that drew hack when passing eunuchs looked, saw the face, and sneered— a face that drew hack hurriedly while the heart of the Pearl Concubine suffered the agonies of the outcast who does not understand his ostracism, or why friends, at least the one friend, does not come again.

A headdress of wilted plumage, because there never was a new one offered her, clothing that was vile with too long use—

How terrible must the nights have been! The wan face at the window staring at a moon which, purporting to understand the troubles of friends, lovers and sweethearts, seemed callous to the suffering of one of the God of Heaven's noblewomen. A prison house, hers, of sighs, of heartaches, of perpetual sadness.

A room whose walls, as the months passed, seemed to crowd in upon the frail little lady, whom sickness soon was wasting, to crowd in, all four walls together, as though to smother her, and release her forever from her sufferings.

No wonder they say that the spirit of the Pearl Concubine still roams at night about the place where she was imprisoned, and about the well in the gloomy courtyard where—hut wait. Her moans must often have been heard in her darkened chamber after nightfall when the moonlight came through to make a silvery patch on the floor, a silvery patch all crisscrossed with the shadow of steel bars. As though the hands of the Pearl Concubine could have done injury to any living thing!

I do not strive to arouse sympathy for the Pearl Concubine, save as she deserves sympathy. I do not tell of her sad fate in order to make a monster of Old Buddha— for I loved Old Buddha and was her favorite. I am merely trying to tell the story, without swerving from its proper sequence, and one must tell the story, all of it, the good with the bad. Else how may one regard Old Buddha as human, instead of a creature of habit and of custom, a statuesque figure out of history, dressed in imperial robes, wearing a coat of mail, and with hands clinched in gloves of iron?

So, I ask pity for the Pearl Concubine—who has long since passed beyond the need of pity—for there was greatness in her. When all the court hated Kwang Hsu, when all the court, even to the smallest eunuch, sneered at him, either openly or covertly, the Pearl Concubine dared to love him, and paid in prison, and later with her life, for her fidelity.

A little noblewoman, slender and graceful as Lady Mei, and as beautiful, was this ill-fated Pearl Concubine, who dared to love the Emperor whom Old Buddha hated.

XXX. THE HATRED OF OLD BUDDHA

Old Buddha always hated foreigners, and with good reason, probably, since so many of the foreigners took it upon themselves to criticize her government.

Her especial dislike were the missionaries, and from them her hatred spread to include all foreigners, wherever found.

The bit of flame that started the holocaust, however, had to do with a certain follower of that famous revolutionary, Dr. Sun Yat-sen, and it was ignited by the famous eunuch, Li Lien Ying.

There was a certain man named Kao Yung Ming whom Li Lien Ying suspected of designs against the government. This man, for some reason or other, aroused the ire of the famous eunuch, who had him followed. He had been accused of inflammable utterances against the government, and a certain article had even appeared in one of Peking's papers which dared to criticize the government. Li Lien Ying, who always seemed to have the best interests of Old Buddha at heart—naturally enough since his own power depended upon hers—caused Kao Yung Ming to be followed.

It was discovered by agents of Li Lien Ying that Kao Yung Ming lived in quite a good hotel, just outside of Chengyangmen. Li immediately instructed the Chinese police to make a thorough search of the man's room to discover, if possible, what his purpose was in Peking.

Among his effects they found all sorts of literature, among other things a printed pamphlet addressed to the throne, in which Old Buddha was instructed to leave the Forbidden City before a certain time, with all her court, relinquishing all power, else death would be the penalty. This pamphlet was merely in the possession of Kao Yung Ming, and had not been sent anywhere as yet. Li Lien Ying had set the police on the man's trail before he had been ready to act.

There was a strange letter, too, instructing Kao Yung Ming how to get the pamphlet into the Forbidden City, since it was impossible for him to take it in. Copies of the pamphlet according to this wild letter, were to be dropped into the Forbidden City from balloons. The letter purported to be the work of Sun Yat-sen and the pamphlet to be inspired by him, though he had then been an exile from China, with a price on his head, for many years.

Li Lien Ying, satisfied that he had unearthed a deep conspiracy against the throne, took the story to Old Buddha, who was naturally furious.

She had Kao Yung Ming brought in, questioned, learned much of the details of plans under way by Sun Yat-sen, and then had Kao Yung Ming beaten to death.

When the word of the slaying went forth among the foreign legations, there was an uneasy stirring and muttering among them; and, with the usual I-am-better-than- thou attitude of many of the foreign ministers, some of them made open remonstrance. Old Buddha heard of these mutters, since Li Lien Ying's spy system was unbeatable, but she said nothing.

Then came her spring garden party. This was ordinarily attended by representatives of all the foreign legations.

But the British legation ignored the invitation to attend!

Trust Old Buddha not to miss the implication in this rudeness, and trust her to comprehend exactly why it had transpired!

"What right had they," she said, years later, in explaining many of the things which happened as an after- math of this affair, "to be so rude to me? This is not their country, and they have no voice in its affairs! Haven't I a right to punish my own subjects? Suppose my ministers in foreign countries were to criticize the actions of the governments to which I send them? Would those governments like it? Suppose my ministers were to ignore a royal invitation of the English sovereigns, because they did not like something that had been done by English law? Would those sovereigns like it? Most assuredly not! Yet they allow their own ministers to be guilty of the most unpardonable rudeness to me. They don't like our way of living, but it is our way and we like it. If they don't, they should leave. We never asked them to come here. They are here on sufferance, yet they have the unbelievable effrontery to criticize my actions because they happen not to be in accordance with the manner in which the same offense, such as that of Kao Yung Ming, would be punished in their country!

The Hatred Of Old Buddha

THE FAVORITE FLOWER, THE ORCHID, OF HER MAJESTY TZU HSI,
HER FAVORITE PIPE, AND A JADE TEACUP

"Our country was a civilized country while the people in so-called civilized countries were still swinging by their tails from trees; yet those same countries have the audacity to send missionaries to us, to teach us religion and civilization! Suppose I were to flood foreign countries with Buddhist priests, to teach foreigners the religion which has been good enough for us, whose dictates have made us a happy country—until the foreigners came in!

"They inoculate our people with the virus of Christianity and the Christian Chinese immediately lose all respect for our laws and customs. Most of the trouble in inland China is caused by Christian Chinese. They refuse to honor their rulers, and the lesser officials set over them by those rulers, all because of the teaching of foreign barbarians who would probably have plenty of reforming to do at home if only they were less prying, less eager to carry nonsensical religious doctrines to other countries, intent on forcing them upon the people of those foreign countries whether or not those countries approve. And we let them come here because we are more polite than they!

"What have they to offer us that is better than what we have? Nothing at all! We are taught from time immemorial to reverence our parents. Foreigners do not do this. When they reach a certain age they may leave the parental roof and never again obey their parents, while with us the parents must be obeyed as long as they live, no matter how long that may be!"

Here are some of the different viewpoints which are essentially Chinese, yet which are easy to grasp by the foreigner, when one explains the reason behind them. Old Buddha was talking with this writer when these things were expressed.

"Take their marriage customs," continued Old Buddha. They marry for love! Here we arrange marriages, and the husband trusts his wife. In foreign countries when a man loves a woman and she loves him, and they make love to each other before marriage, how can the man trust the woman after marriage? Surely he must realize that if his wife will make love to him she will make love to someone else! It is inevitable and reasonable! Moreover, a wife may have a lover, and no one seems to think ill of the matter, least of all the husband. They even have signals for this sort of

The Hatred Of Old Buddha

clandestine arrangements. When the lover comes in during the absence of the husband, he leaves his hat and cane in the hall. When the husband returns, finds the hat and cane, he knows that the lover is with his wife—and goes away again until the hat and cane shall have been removed!

"However, do we object to their silly customs, as long as they do not try to force them upon us? Most assuredly not! We permit them to live as they please, asking only in return that they accord us a like privilege, which they consistently refuse to do.

"By treaty we have placed the foreigners in regular settlements, leased to them for terms of years, yet the missionaries buy up land outside the concessions, and strive to compel us to recognize property rights; and, when we fail to do so, they call upon their governments to step in and protect their rights. If we invited the missionaries here it would be a different matter; but we don't want them! Yet they come, disrupt our customs, scoff at our religion, strive to supplant it with a religion of their own, and are inexpressibly rude to us when we refuse to be remade according to their pet ideas!"

It is little wonder perhaps that Old Buddha hated foreigners. Foreign ministers were never received at court, until the time of Kwang Hsu, save when they presented their credentials, made their speeches of reporting for diplomatic duty, heard the Emperor's speech in turn— all of which required no more than five minutes from time of entry to time of departure; yet in many cases, foreign ministers were guilty of the most inexcusable rudeness to the throne, either direct or indirect, because the ideas of China were not their ideas, and they were too narrow-minded to comprehend that China's ideas suited China, and that for centuries China had been the foremost, potentially, of the countries of the world.

So old was China; and upstart nations, scarce out of their swaddling clothes, attempting to dictate to this woman who was perhaps the greatest of the great Ch'ing Dynasty! There is little wonder that Old Buddha was impatient with foreigners, whose insidious religious teachings even broke through to the throne, when Weng Tung Ho tried to teach Christianity to Kwang Hsu, and succeeded to the point that Kwang Hsu was deposed by Old Buddha just before the dawn of the twentieth century.

"Then there is another thing, also blamable to the foreign barbarian missionaries; they take our poor children in the interior, and experiment upon them with their medicines. They have even been known to take the eyes of little children from which to make medicine. Suppose I were to send our doctors to England and America, to France and Germany, to force our medical knowledge upon those countries. Would those countries like it? Most assuredly not, and rightly, too. Let them live as they please, make such medicines as they desire—which may be good enough for all I know—and teach their own religion—but to people who are receptive! It is just because we are not receptive that they strive to compel then- own ideas upon us! The foreigners are the curse of China today, and I would be the happiest woman in the world if there were only some way to rid China of them forever!"

All of this recalls many audiences at court at which I was present. There were times when, as First Lady-in- Waiting, I was detailed by Her Majesty to keep careful eye on gold and silverware in order that foreign curio hunters might not carry these things away. Inexpressibly rude were many of the foreigners—oh, not all of them, for there were many of my acquaintance who were true diplomats, willing to live and let live; it was only the exceptions which embittered Old Buddha against them all— incidentally there were quite too many of the exceptions.

It was quite common for the foreign ladies to comment loudly upon the richness of dress of court ladies, and ladies-in-waiting, speculate on the probable price paid, and even to finger the rich materials, ignoring the wearers as of no account, while talking about the clothing in voluble asides to friends who were just as interested, just as curious, and just as inexpressibly rude.

In one instance, a woman darted directly away from Old Buddha toward a very stately young woman who stood at the door of the throne room. She grasped the neckerchief of this one, and called to one of her friends:

"Oh, come and look at this one! Isn't she cute?"

I made haste to the spot, hoping to avoid trouble, and to interfere before the unbelievable rudeness, downright boorishness, should attract the attention of Old Buddha. I touched the offending foreign woman—I cannot call her a lady—and said:

The Hatred Of Old Buddha

"Please, madam! That is Her Majesty, the Young Empress!"

Naturally Old Buddha did not miss this, nor did she miss the giggles of the woman whom I had reprimanded; and when the delegation had left, she asked me to tell her exactly what happened. No, I don't entirely blame Old Buddha for her dislike of foreigners.

But this is a digression.

Old Buddha continues her monologue, in almost her identical words, as nearly as memory serves:

"Then the contact of foreign men with foreign women. With us, the women are kept apart from the men. Our women are virtuous because they are taught to be, until virtue is their most valuable possession. But the foreigners! Women accompany men, not their husbands, to public places. They shake hands with them, and dance with them, even putting their arms about their waists while they dance! I think dancing is rather nice, if girls dance with girls. But when men, not husbands of the girls, dance with girls, no one can convince me that it is proper. I know too much of life! Could anyone convince me that a man could put his arm around the waist of a woman, press her body against his own, and still think no evil concerning her? I do not believe it. If the girl is innocent, she does not remain innocent long. Nature takes care of that, and repeated contact with the opposite sex, as in dancing, cannot help but have harmful effects on the girl, whatever it may do to the man. No, the foreign ways are not our ways, and I am bitterly opposed to making them our ways!"

Insignificant, some of this monologue which I have reported, yet it is important in view of what happened later. It explains some of Old Buddha's deep-rooted prejudice to foreigners, which is understandable to the Orient at least. If I may be permitted another digression, I wish to say that much of Old Buddha's beliefs have proved peculiarly apt since China became a Republic, and Westernism has begun to surge across the length and breadth of the Middle Kingdom. Women are emancipated now, more or less, and they are going about the way of the western girl—except that they are going faster, releasing the steam that has been imprisoned for centuries; and there is much of unhappiness in China, since divorce became common, and the sexes have been allowed to mingle freely.

I am expressing no opinion, however, contenting myself with the statement, since it bears on Old Buddha's views.

Naturally, anything that tended to confound the foreigners found Old Buddha instantly interested, as the Boxer Uprising amply proves. Nor can she be too harshly blamed.

The foreigners of those days were insufferable, apparently desirous of remaking China according to their own standards, without so much as consulting the wishes of China as to whether she wished to be remade.

The matter of this same Sun Yat-sen, referred to above, also gave Old Buddha cause for dislike of foreigners.

"How can they," she once said, "deliberately harbor an escaped convict like Sun Yat-sen? He is in exile from this country, yet he is received with open arms in England, Europe and the United States! The countries which have received him, allowing him to strike at China at a distance, unobstructed, are themselves deliberately striking at China! Do they think we shall respect them for this?"

It may easily be seen that Old Buddha was in a receptive mood when the Boxer Beast was in process of being born, and that the Boxer Uprising was by no means an abortive thing, born of the moment, but was caused by something deep-rooted and significant—a nursling Gargantua for decades, awaiting only the affirmation of Old Buddha to break forth to slay and maim.

And Old Buddha, though she perhaps did not know it then, was almost ready to give the signal.

She had been pressed quite too closely by the asinine meddling of foreigners.

XXXI. THE CROWN PRINCE

Since Chai Ching there had been no Crown Prince. The Emperor, or Empress Dowager when the Emperor was a minor, could choose whosoever best suited his or her whim to succeed to the throne.

But Old Buddha, though this ruling in regard to a Crown Prince was a law governing succession, decided, just before the Boxer business, to have a Crown Prince. It was not the first time, nor yet the last, that she saw fit to override custom and tradition, in spite of the fact that she was a conservative, against all change and reforms— unless inaugurated by herself.

But she hated Kwang Hsu with a. bitter hatred. She treated him despitefully always, after the *coup d'etat*, and a Crown Prince would be just another thorn in the crown she had already fashioned for the deposed Emperor.

She bade Kwang Hsu attend upon her.

"You are always ill," she told him. "I am very much afraid because of your health, and you have no heir to succeed you."

Kwang Hsu guessed what was coming, and knew what Old Buddha expected him to say.

"I am useless as a ruler," he replied. "I am always ill, and probably will not live long."

But beyond this bare statement, Kwang Hsu did not help her. He knew the law, knew that a Crown Prince was not allowed by the rules of the court. But he said nothing of his knowledge. It was also the law that a son be obedient to his parents, and Old Buddha stood in the light of a parent to Kwang Hsu.

"I know it is not the law for us to have a Crown Prince," she said. "But I feel that, due to your illness and physical condition generally, we should make an exception in this case."

Kwang Hsu made no reply. He merely bowed his head in acknowledgment.

So Old Buddha, without further ado, named as Heir Apparent the man whom she had always intended naming —Ta-A-Ko, son of Prince Tuan, the degenerate who was later to gain world-wide notoriety as the leader of the Boxers.

Ta-A-Ko felt the weight of his responsibility keenly, and immediately upon arriving at court, proceeded to exercise the prerogatives of an Emperor, as he soon expected to be. However, he failed to question the Old Buddha in advance of his acts, and the acts which led to the rescinding of his appointment were discovered by her by accident——as will presently follow.

Ta-A-Ko was a son of his father, the degenerate Prince Tuan. Prince Tuan once having made his entrance, as related in a succeeding chapter, pushed his influence with Old Buddha to the utmost, having in mind the power that would be his as Prince Regent, or as the father of the heir —to the end that Old Buddha, up until the time of Prince Tuan's fall from grace, perpetually condoned the faults of Ta-A-Ko of which there were many.

To-A-Ko was a trouble maker of the first water from the very moment he appeared at court—as might have been expected of the son of his father. He was only about seventeen years of age, perhaps even a little younger, and his new responsibilities went to his foolish head like strong wine. He knew the power of the Emperor was absolute, extending to all his subjects, men and women—especially women—since the Emperor was the one man allowed to remain inside the Forbidden City or the palaces after nightfall, all others of masculine persuasion being eunuchs. With the arrival of the Crown Prince, however, there were two unemasculated males at court.

The heart affairs of Ta-A-Ko, all with serving maids— since court ladies were usually staid married women, and unapproachable because they were so near Old Buddha— were the talk of the court. Since the eunuchs were born gossipmongers, it was inevitable that stories of these heart affairs should go beyond the walls of the Forbidden City and the Palaces.

It began when, from some trivial cause, Old Buddha ordered one of the serving maids to be roundly spanked in the courtyard, and spanked exactly as westerners understand the term.

When the serving maid was prepared for the spanking, and the eunuchs who were detailed to the task were quite ready to begin their delectable duties—most of them delighting in inflicting pain on others because they had been indoctrinated with the sadist's virus by nature and by Li Lien Ying—it was discovered that the serving maid wore the underthings of Ta-A-Ko.

The matter was hushed up, for Old Buddha was of no mind to allow the public to know that she had chosen foolishly when she had named Ta-A-Ko as Crown Prince.

Even when some of the serving maids had to be sent away, quietly, to bear children to Ta-A-Ko, Old Buddha, furious as she was over the matter, could do no less than minimize the fault. She had gone too far to retreat, and retreat would have been a mute admission that she had chosen unwisely, a thing that Old Buddha could in no wise countenance. She cast about her, however, for a way out of her dilemma. It was common knowledge among all the court that Ta-A-Ko was quite at home in the servants' quarters, and Old Buddha cast about her for a way to gracefully undo the harm she had already done in naming Ta-A-Ko to be Heir Apparent.

But no excuse offered itself for almost two years, during which time the Crown Prince kept the court in an uproar.

XXXII. EVOLUTION OF THE BEAST

Now comes one of the strangest chapters in the life of Old Buddha—that chapter which treats of the Boxer Uprising, in which she played such an important part.

The Boxers, from time immemorial, were jugglers, mountebanks, purveyors of strange medicines and charms, and their number was legion. The word "Boxer" is a misnomer. The Chinese term is *mai yi te*, which means something like "doers of stunts." These jugglers, dressed in strange regalia, with painted faces, traveled here and there over China, doing their performances under grimy awnings, to the delight of the lower classes.

They carried all sorts of arms—curved swords, lances, daggers—and were remarkably proficient in their use. Two or more children were invariably members of each troupe of these strollers, and they came by the children in many ways. Some of them were kidnapped, some purchased for a few cents from poor families in famine districts, and a few were offspring of the Boxers themselves. These children began their training very early, and were taught to handle daggers, swords and spears with great proficiency, and to do all sorts of acrobatic turns. The adults were proficient with arms, with their hands, and other paraphernalia used in their profession, and personal combat, fast, furious, apparently bona fide—yet in which no one was ever hurt—was their forte.

They sold plasters for all sorts of skin ailments, but selling things was a small part of their business. They attracted crowds by their juggling, and crowds usually tossed them copper cash and pennies. They invariably kowtowed to whosoever threw them money.

During the day, the above routine was followed by the Boxer troupes. At night they were proficient thieves, capable of entering houses by upper windows, stealing from pockets or money belts, and of petty pilfering of all kinds.

They were much in demand a few years ago—a few may even be found today in China—and the upper classes often retain them to entertain guests. They, however, were never permitted nearer the

Evolution Of The Beast

homes of their employers than the courtyards, because of their thieving proclivities.

They were the strolling players of China, and there was little they would not do for money.

Their traditions were rooted in the dim and distant past of China. They were strictly a Chinese institution, as common as the sing-song girls.

Prince Tuan, who led the Boxers later in the dreadful uprising, was a degenerate. He cared nothing whatever for people of his own class, hating them most cordially, probably because he realized that, though he was prince by birth, he had been really born out of his class. He delighted in joining the Boxers, in making friends and confidants of China's riffraff. It was against Manchu law, at least outside Manchu custom, for even ordinary officials to witness the activities of Boxer strollers, to say nothing of taking part in their performance. It was outside Manchu custom for officials of any great rank even to visit Chinese restaurants.

But not Prince Tuan!

His delight was in the lowest kind of companions, and he was early attracted to the antics of the Boxers,

He was a man of independent fortune, yet nothing pleased him more than to attend the performance of the Boxers, attire himself in their regalia, take active part in their juggling, in which he became as proficient as they themselves—and to kowtow to the crowd when pennies were tossed to him! He was the arch-pariah of princes. Everyone, from the highest to the lowest, knew Prince Tuan, and his appearance at a Boxer performance, and especially if he took part in their antics, always assured the quick gathering of crowds—and many pennies and copper cash hurled contemptuously to the jugglers who, including Prince Tuan himself, kowtowed their thanks as though the coolie audience had been Emperors and Empresses.

Prince Tuan, of course, knew of Old Buddha's hatred of foreigners, and he thought the matter over so continuously that an idea came to him—an idea that was destined to bathe China in the blood of her sons and daughters, to make of Peking a flaming holocaust, and to make the name of Old Buddha anathema in the mouths of the countries of the world.

That his thoughts should single out the Boxers is natural, when we consider that they were, despite his princely rank, his own kind. They had that peculiar liking for him, mingled with strained contempt, which the lowly have for the upper class person who demeans himself by catering to those far below him in education, rank and intelligence.

For many months, therefore, Prince Tuan carefully went about the business of welding his Boxers, organizing troupe after troupe into a rapidly growing whole, into a truly formidable organization, with himself in the role of leader. The Boxers had never been molested severely by the law, and had come to regard themselves as above the law, so it was not difficult for Prince Tuan, in the carrying out of his scheme, to convince them that they were as invincible fighters as they pretended to be. He compelled them, by sheer force of his baleful personality, to the belief that no bullets could slay them, no foreign swords deal them wounds; and drilled them so thoroughly in this doctrine that their presumptuousness became remarkable, a formidable thing.

Prince Tuan undertook to weld the Boxers into a fighting organization more for his personal amusement than for any other reason, and later seized upon the idea of driving the foreigners out of China in order to try out the machine he had perfected. Of course he knew that Old Buddha deprecated most strenuously his mingling with the riffraff of China, and this, he thought, was an excellent opportunity to win his way back into the good graces of Her Majesty, by proving to her that his activities among the *mai yi te* had been for a purpose— the purpose of creating an instrument which should be turned to the use of Old Buddha, placed at her back as one of the greatest fighting organizations China had ever seen.

That he succeeded, history bears painful witness; and, in her various confidences with this writer, Old Buddha, though she did try to minimize her own part in the Boxer Uprising, placed the blame for all the horror at the door of Prince Tuan where, in a way, it belonged—though Prince Tuan's plans would certainly have failed had it not been for the support of Old Buddha.

I remember Prince Tuan very well. He was an evil visaged man; his face marked by smallpox scars, his eyes small and ferret-like. I

Evolution Of The Beast

have excellent reason to remember him, since my family were *er mao tzu* (Christians Number Two, or Christianized Chinese). My father, Lord Yu Keng, was very much afraid of Prince Tuan. He had learned of Tuan's activities among the Boxers, and when Tuan made some excuse to call upon my father—at which time I saw the pockmarked man—my father knew it was in the role of spy that Prince Tuan called, and that he had come to examine our foreign-built house, and to discover if possible if our family was "Christian."

It was because of Prince Tuan, to escape from certain death at his hands, that my father accepted an appointment as Minister to France, where I was educated.

But I digress.

Prince Tuan, once well under way with his plans, still had before him the task of convincing Old Buddha that they were practicable. He planned to play upon her hatred of foreigners to gain his ends, to convince her that his Boxers were invincible; and, despite her remarkable intelligence, Old Buddha had always been a believer in signs and portents, a profound believer in things occult, having the genuine atmosphere of "outsideness."

Prince Tuan's hopes of convincing Old Buddha lay in this weakness of Her Majesty's. He had the organization perfected to a point where he could convince her of its effectiveness—if only he could gain audience with her and prove his contentions. To do this it was necessary to prove to her, by the evidence of her own eyes, that his Boxers were invincible.

This meant an audience with Old Buddha, and a performance at court of the Boxers, an unheard of thing.

But he reckoned with Old Buddha's hatred of foreigners, and he reckoned to some effect.

Yung Lu, faithful vassal of Old Buddha, had by this time been returned to a post of honor at Peking, where he was once more in constant attendance upon Old Buddha. I am absolutely sure, from many conversations with Old Buddha, that the affection which these two entertained for each other had never once waned—though he was still an official, she China's Empress Dowager, too proud to give rein to her feelings, had it even been possible under Manchu law and custom, which, after all, are synonymous words.

Yung Lu had discovered something of the activities of Prince Tuan, and tried with all his faithful heart to prevent Old Buddha from granting the super-mountebank an audience. He knew, did this faithful retainer, that Old Buddha would make a terrible mistake to listen to the plans of Prince Tuan. He knew, too, that she was not the person to listen to objections once she had made a decision—even though those objections came from one whom she trusted as she trusted this man who had loved her when she had been merely Lan Kuei, The Orchid.

Prince Tuan's plans, as Yung Lu discovered, involved the destruction of every foreigner and Christianized Chinese in the Middle Kingdom.

Yung Lu knew that such a move would bring utter ruin upon the heads of the Manchu rulers, and tried to balk Prince Tuan at every turn—thus making himself a bitter enemy of that worthy.

Kwang Hsu, prisoner in his own palace now, could do nothing.

Old Buddha would not listen. Prince Tuan was granted the fateful audience.

XXXIII. THE SNARLING OF THE BEAST

None of those who attended this private audience with the Dowager Empress realized that it would be directly responsible for the worst horror ever visited upon China —save perhaps the Beast himself, Prince Tuan, leader and organizer of the Boxers. Prince Tuan was a showman. He hated foreigners and Christian Chinese, and knew that Her Majesty hated them even more furiously than did he. Yung Lu, friend and vassal of Old Buddha, knew that things were not right. He exercised his prerogative to remonstrate with the Dowager Empress.

"I beg your Majesty to order my instant decapitation rather than that I live to see such horror visited upon the Middle Kingdom!"

"Enough, Yung Lu," snapped Old Buddha. "Prince Tuan, proceed!"

"Our organization," began the showman, on his knees before Old Buddha, "is the most closely knit China has ever known. There is nothing we cannot do! We are the dragon of China, a dragon whose claws will fasten in the soft and pampered bodies of the foreign barbarians, tearing them asunder, so that not one of them will be left alive in the Middle Kingdom! We are invincible! Bullets will not slay us, no knives can maim us—and we know how to slay. Your Majesty has always hated foreigners. Now is the time to free China of these interlopers. The power, and the weapon of slaughter is in my hands!"

"But how, Prince Tuan, do I know you speak truly? There is no one, in these troublous days, whom I can trust. Prove me your words and I shall tell you my decision!"

The great door to the audience hall inside the Forbidden City in the heart of Peking, swung open, and into the room filed half a dozen of those brutal brethren who were destined to inaugurate a reign of terror that even now, almost thirty years later, has not been forgotten, which will leave its mark upon China until generations have been born, lived, died, and vanished into dust. Prince Tuan, his face stamped with the mark of the beast, a mask of smallpox scars, fingernails like the talons of an aged eagle, stood aside, speaking rapidly in the dialect of cooliedom to convey his orders to those who came in. Armed with knives, spears, daggers, were the half dozen, stripped to the waist, their nude torsos gleaming with perspiration because fright possessed them in the presence of the Old Buddha who, by a single word if she desired, could have them decapitated. The name of Old Buddha was a name with which to conjure in the China of thirty years ago. Not only the coolies feared the Old Lady—she was feared by everyone, man, woman, child, from the highest to the lowest, for her word was the law of China, and whatever she commanded was done, or the one whom she commanded lost his head or died by slow torture.

No wonder the Boxers were afraid!

Prince Tuan barked a command.

Two of the Boxers, in the full warlike regalia of their class, advanced to the clear space before Her Majesty. Between them walked a small man who carried no weapon at all. The two carried gleaming spears.

"I prove to Your Majesty that no weapon can take the life of a Boxer!" said Prince Tuan.

Her Majesty waited, watching every move with eyes that, even at sixty and six, still were hawk-like, missing nothing.

The two who were armed with spears set upon the unarmed man at once and a bewildering play of weapons caused the Empress Dowager to clinch her hands on her throne until her knuckles showed white with the strain. Thrust, parry, slash—from two sides at once the men with the spears drove at the man who was unarmed. The spearhead of one passed under his arm, just as the spear-point of another slipped across his right shoulder, missing his neck by a seeming miracle. The two with the spears warmed to their work, perspiring freely, apparently trying with might and main to slay the man who was unarmed. This one sprang aside as the gleaming point drove at his stomach, whirled about in mid-air to parry the point of the man behind him with his right forearm. He seemed to have eyes in the back of his head, this unarmed one, and strive as they might the two with the spears could not slay him—not even though they fought savagely, thrusting, parrying, slashing, stabbing, until the sweat streaked their bodies like rain, until their eyes stood out from their sockets with the pressure of their effort.

The Snarling Of The Beast

Yet the unarmed man, fighting back at them, kept his place before the Dowager Empress, covering no more space than might have been covered by the Empress Dowager herself, had she been standing on the spot, with her robes of office hanging down to touch the floor in an uneven circle about her. The Empress Dowager watched them in fascination.

Prince Tuan watched the Empress Dowager. She had already told him, the day before, that she would take no action against the foreigners, because, though she would not admit it, she feared what the armies of the foreigners would do to China—recalling what China had lost to Japan in the China-Japanese War. Now, however, it might be different, if Prince Tuan could convince her that he had an organization that was unbeatable. So he watched her handsome old face, and waited. He scarcely breathed. Could it be possible that he was actually convincing this superstitious old woman weapons could not slay the Boxers? Anyone with knowledge of weapons must have known the show a farce, its every move practiced for months on end until its actors were letter perfect. Every dodging movement of the unarmed man was ritualistic, as was every thrust and parry of the two with the spears. One variation of the ritual on the part of any one of the three, and the thing would go awry, the unarmed man might be slain—for the spears were sharp— and the plans of Prince Tuan, who had staked all on one bold throw, might topple into ruins about his head.

For ten minutes the three fought on, apparently one unarmed man against two doughty fighters armed with spears—three who fought for life because they knew failure meant death for themselves. If they failed, and one was slain, or even was wounded, Tuan's brags would be of no avail—and not only themselves, but Prince. Tuan himself might be executed for trying to hoodwink the wisest old lady who ever sat upon the throne of China.

Tuan barked a command. The two who were armed dropped their spears in a sort of salute. They were breathing heavily, absolutely soaked with moisture, until the odor of their unwashed bodies filled the air about the throne—and the man against whom they fought was absolutely unmarked, his breathing imperceptible! Prince Tuan looked at the Dowager Empress. Her nostrils were working like little pulses. Her eyes were narrowed. Her right hand was opening and closing on the arm of her throne. In all his long years at the court of Old Buddha, Yung Lu had not seen Tzu Hsi so moved. Spellbound, Prince Tuan and Yung Lu watched the Old Buddha, scarcely daring to breathe. The Boxers, at a signal from Prince Tuan, who saw that he had already convinced Her Majesty without showing the rest of his wares, withdrew silently, after making the customary kowtows, which Old Buddha noticed not at all.

For many minutes, the Old Lady was lost in thought. For many minutes, the lives of hundreds of thousands of her subjects, the lives of scores and hundreds of foreigners, hung in the balance. The face of Yung Lu was putty-like. He wrung his hands in anguish inside his long sleeves. Prince Tuan looked on imperturbably, waiting. Finally the Old Lady looked at Prince Tuan, who once more flung himself on his knees at the foot of the throne.

"What would you have me do, Prince Tuan?" she asked at last.

"Give me leave to send my Boxers forth to slay the foreigners! Give me leave to open fire tomorrow morning upon the foreign legations!"

Still, for a minute or two, Old Buddha hesitated. Then—

She rose to her feet, majestically erect, and stood forward from her yellow throne. Her right hand came forward, palm up. Then, slowly as though she crushed lives away in the tiny palm—which she actually did, because all power was hers at that moment—the right hand closed, closed tight, until the knuckles were white again.

She turned to Yung Lu, in whose face was all the agony of the damned, for Yung Lu, since the days when he had been a humble guard commander, and she the daughter of a retired general—before the fatal day when this woman had become the Secondary Wife to Hsien Feng, the ladder upon which she had mounted to the highest pinnacle of fame and power—had loved Old Buddha. And now, when she most needed his advice, which he had freely given despite the fact that she had not asked it, she was ignoring him, listening to the empty words of an ambitious prince whose will, loosed upon foreigners, would make the name of China anathema in the mouths of all the civilized countries of the world.

THE THREE STORY STAGE IN THE THEATER
AT EH SUMMER PALACE, PEKING, CHINA

The True Story of the Empress Dowager

COLOR SCHEME OF CEILING, PILLARS AND WALLS OF THE AUDIENCE HALL, JEHOL PALACE

The Snarling Of The Beast

The Empress Dowager looked into the eyes of Prince Tuan. He looked back at her boldly, exultation rising in his black heart because he saw already that he had won— and then the Old Lady's right hand came down, as she pronounced the fatal words which ushered in the Boxer Horror, and wrote the name of the Dowager Empress in the press of the world, in letters of fire almost, surely in letters of blood—for as a result of those words all China was crimsoned with the blood of her faithful sons, and with that of foreigners who, in their sudden dire extremity, knew not which way to turn.

"Fire on the foreign legations at daybreak!" commanded Tzu Hsi hoarsely.

Prince Tuan kowtowed enthusiastically, his eyes glowing. Yung Lu, unnoticed now, paced back and forth, back and forth. As Prince Tuan exited from the royal presence, he cast a triumphant look back over his shoulder at Yung Lu, Tzu Hsi's Grand Councillor. Tuan had accomplished the impossible. He had won out over the advice of Yung Lu, whom Tzu Hsi trusted as she trusted none other in all the world.

Prince Tuan quitted the Forbidden City, and we follow him, to see the horror that he planned. Outside the gates, his lieutenants awaited him—beasts they were, like Tuan himself, eager for the blood of the foreigner, eager for any blood whose shedding would profit themselves.

"To the gathering places with all speed!" commanded Prince Tuan. "Gather our men swiftly! Send out messengers, calling in recruits! Whip them into shape, utilizing all possible time before daybreak tomorrow. Gather weapons where weapons may be found! Gird your loins for battle! Pass the word that Prince Tuan commands that no Boxer retreat, unless that Boxer wishes to die on the weapons of his own brethren! Hurry, friends, hurry, lest Tzu Hsi change her mind—-for tomorrow at daybreak we fire upon the foreign legations! Tomorrow we start the slaughter, and when we have finished, when the Boxer dragon has traveled his relentless way the length and breadth of China, not one' foreigner will be left alive in the Middle Kingdom. Hurry! It is the watchword. Spare no labor. Whip them into shape. Tomorrow, I myself will lead you against the legations!"

The lieutenants of the beast departed swiftly, and word fled the length and breadth of Peking, the word which quoted Tzu Hsi, warning friends of foreigners to flee, warning Boxers to prepare; and at the grand meeting place, Prince Tuan himself talked with his lieutenants, encouraging them, firing them with the awful desire to watch the flowing of fresh blood—the blood of foreigners —from the points of their own weapons. Prince Tuan, with the permission of Tzu Hsi, had loosed the dragon of the Boxers, and before a week had passed China would be bathed from end to end in the crimson tide of wholesale slaughter. Women, young and comely girls, would commit suicide, clogging the wells of Peking, rather than accept lives of shame—or rather than live on after forced submission to the beasts whom Prince Tuan had provided with claws, and with the right to slay and maim.

And the first dread night, the night of terrible waiting, settled over Peking. There was no sound—save the inaudible snarling of the beast of destruction, who would be loosed of his chains when the sun came up from the direction of Tientsin.

In fear and trembling, because their own servants, who had fled, had warned them against the morrow, the foreign legations armed themselves during the hours of darkness, and prepared to hold out until the end against the Boxer dragon.

XXXIV. OMINOUS WHISPERS

That night of waiting! How freighted with terror, because none in Peking, save only the Boxers, knew what was to happen on the morrow. Servants of the foreigners, hearing the evil whispers that spread through the Capital City like wildfire after Prince Tuan's audience with Her Majesty, Tzu Hsi, the Empress Dowager, slipped quietly away from their masters, deserting those whom they had faithfully served for years—all because, when the axe fell upon the necks of those whom they had served they had no desire to feel the edge of that axe themselves.

Everywhere, among the shadows, beside raging bonfires, Boxers donned their forbidding regalia and rallied to previously designated meeting places. Eager they were, as eagles are eager, for the coming of the morning sun and the beginning of the slaughter! They lusted to kill. Prince Tuan and his minions had played upon their lusts, flaying them until their evil natures were uppermost, all their being filled with the lust to slay, to loot, destroy and ravish.

Throughout Peking went the whispers. The Boxers would rise when the sun came up. They would take their weapons in hand to destroy the foreigners and the foreigners would have no redress because their weapons would he useless against these invincible masqueraders.

The moon, against the sky freighted with sullen darkness, was blood red, darkened ever and anon by clouds of that Peking dust which flicked across its face ominously, silently, as though to mask from the eyes of Heaven the horror that was brewing, that would boil over, engulfing all China, when morning came.

Foreigners heard the whispers, for some of their servants were faithful in so far as they warned their erstwhile masters before deserting them. The legations were in turmoil. Weapons were brought forth, and tightly gripped in hands that trembled and would not be stilled. Children, babes in arms, instinctively sensing the approach of something dreadful, wept in the arms of frightened mothers—mothers who, brave as mothers always are, in spite of bodily fear, kept beside their husbands, waiting for news. Men in authority knew not what to do, which way to turn, and useless telegrams were sent out; though those who sent them realized that they would probably never get through, because the Boxer organization had already tied up all communication. Legation guards redoubled their sentries, and the clump-clump of heavy feet resounded the length and breadth of Legation Street.

"It will all blow over," said many officials. "These things never develop into anything serious."

But some knew better, and when the proper officials did not move to take action, themselves went quietly among the males able to bear arms, fitting them out as best they could with meager equipment, breathing words of cheer into their ears, striving to wipe the fear from their blanched faces. It was the fear of the unknown which obsessed them most, for, when bullets began to fly, most of them would straighten, smile a little, and answer the call to arms. Men who had been through things like this before knew this to be a fact, and did not worry—save that they knew themselves outnumbered by thousands to one, and that the Boxers, ably led, as they were ably led by such men as Prince Tuan and his lieutenants, would probably take the legations in time, slay and mutilate the male defenders. The women—

But they dared not think of the women. Each man, independently of his fellows, however, resolved to save two bullets when it should finally be seen that there was no escape—one for the woman, who might thus be saved from the lusts of the beasts, one for himself, saving himself from slow torture.

Lights were out over Peking, as though Prince Tuan and his minions would hide their beastly preparations from the eyes of men. Utter darkness possessed the alleys and the side streets. Here and there, had there been any in the alleys and streets to see, wedges of light showed in the chinks of tight-closed doors, behind which odorously unwashed men spoke in whispers, their hands opening and closing in anticipation as they fancied the feel within those hands of the throats of the foreigners. Men who were not Boxers by inclination became Boxers to save their own lives, well knowing that the Boxers, in their lusts against the foreigners, would include in the slaughter the Chinese who had been friendly to the foreigners—so that Peking was treated to the experience of seeing erstwhile servants of foreigners armed against the very people who had fed them, to slay them if they could.

The greatest fear, which filled the night air of Peking like an exhalation from some dank tomb, was that which gripped the hearts of Chinese who had become Christians. For them there would be no hope. The foreigners would be slain, perhaps tortured. The fate of the Christian Chinese would be the most terrible the Boxers could conceive—and the very roots of their organization were planted in age-old knowledge of the art of slaughter, of torture, and unnamed lusts.

Long before morning, as soon as the first mad whispers began to spread in fact, the foreign legations were filling with refugees—Christian Chinese, missionaries, and foreigners who lived outside the legations proper. Every bedroom in every legation was filled to capacity and more. Every dining room, every reception room, every hallway, was fitted with makeshift beds, made ready to receive the refugees. The refugees came and were cared for, and still others came, until the courtyards were tight-packed, and some should have been turned away, and weren't. Marksmen of the enemy, should they come close enough to see, could not possibly miss the targets made by those who filled the legations, men, women, and children. The children weeping and fretful, the women half dressed, their eyes dry with misery and awful expectation, some unashamedly nursing babes at breasts that had dried because of fear and because already food was at a premium. Wide-eyed men moved among the refugees, striving to keep up their courage—a futile attempt when the men themselves were blasted with worry and fear, and could not keep their feelings from showing in their drawn white faces.

Not even a dog moved on the deserted streets of Peking. Not even a dog barked. Silence, oppressive and all pervading, held Peking in its grip. Young women everywhere, foreign and Chinese—and especially the Chinese, because they had been through trouble of the kind before—did not sleep during that night of waiting, nor during many of the nights which followed. Now and again one of them would raise her hands in horror, covering her pale face, as though already she envisioned the staring eyes and the drooling lips of the beast or beasts who would come to take her, force her to submit a virgin body, give her to the soldiery, release her at last, so that she in turn might find release by suicide.

And always the silence, ominous and oppressive—Great God, how oppressive!—the atmosphere of brooding fear, and the waiting for sunrise.

Dark figures, as dawn approached, though yet a long way off, darted in ever increasing numbers through the black streets and alleys, and all wore the regalia of the Boxers—tools of Prince Tuan the Beast.

And through all, from end to end of Peking, from east to west, from north to south, went the ominous whispers, starting none knew where, yet moving swiftly and terribly, as though they utilized the wings of sullen darkness.

Then the dawn, the loosing of the Boxer dragon, and the first thin whine of a bullet!

XXXV. LOOSING OF THE DRAGON

But the legations were not entirely unprepared. I'd be going against recorded history to say that. The slaying of Von Kettler had warned them of possible contingencies that must be faced; and, after his passing and the conference of Prince Tuan with Her Majesty Tzu Hsi, the whispers whose ominous portents filled all Peking, all China.

The more practical ones among the defenders of the legations had been busy for two or three days preceding the firing upon the legations, while the night of waiting had not been wasted; for every hand that could use a needle had been forced to sew sandbags, and every hand which could wield a shovel forced to fill the bags made ready. Preparations for defense went forward with all speed. Men, and courageous women, worked until they fell exhausted, only to clamber to their feet after the briefest of breathing spaces to go on with the work.

Then, against the red glow of that first unforgettable dawn after the fatal words of Tzu Hsi, the Empress Dowager, the first fires of destruction, as the Boxers touched torches to the houses of foreigners, to houses built in foreign style by perfectly proper Chinese, to the houses of Chinese Christians—and the thin whine of bullets loosed to slay.

"Kill! Kill! Kill!"

The word, repeated until it became a sort of chant, filled the air above Peking, while those in Peking who had time to think of aught save their own plight, knew that it was the word oftenest repeated that day throughout China.

"Kill the foreigners! Kill! Kill!"

The mountebanks of Prince Tuan, trained to arms as they were—to give them all due credit—played up to the orders of the beast; and the streets and alleys of Peking, the shadows vanishing with the first flush of dawn, literally stirred and rustled into life with the whine of that first bullet which ushered in the horror.

Mao tzu meaning "people of unshaven crowns," or foreigners, and *Er mao tzu*, or foreigners "number two"— Christian Chinese—were taken where found, after the signal of the first bullet.

To add to the horror of the siege of the legations, Prince Tuan offered a bounty of five hundred *taels*— about three hundred and ten dollars at present writing— for every dead foreigner. Tzu Hsi was backing her orders with cold cash. She had given Prince Tuan full access to the Imperial Treasury—and Prince Tuan knew how to use it, how to fire his cutthroats to deeds of unprecedented valor. Five hundred *taels* for the dead body of a foreigner! No wonder slinking Boxers, frightening all who saw them, with their black painted faces, their turbans and warlike regalia, climbed to the roofs of houses adjacent to the crowded legations and strove to pick off foreigners with their Mausers and their *gingals*— long rifles of about fifty caliber fired by two men—until they were discovered behind jutting gables and paid for their temerity with their lives. More than one Boxer, despite Prince Tuan's claim that no bullet could slay them, took terrible chances in order to fire upon the foreigners, only to learn that bullets did not know they were invincible, and slew them in spite of it.

Fires glowed against the sunrise, red and angry, after that first bullet which signaled the fact that the Boxer dragon had been loosed of his chains. From the city outside the legations came the screams and moans of the dying, as the Mausers and *gingals* of the Boxers ripped huge bullets into the innocent bodies of *er mao tzu*, the Christian Chinese. In this house a dozen Chinese, Christians, huddled together for protection against the Boxer beast, while the Boxer beast in the shape of a hundred leaping mountebanks in regalia, brandishing knives, spears, and "choppers," circled the place outside, waiting —until the torch applied to the house of *er mao tzu* flamed into a sullen hissing glow, and those who were not suffocated by the smoke, who did not choose to remain inside to be roasted, came forth from the house of flimsy protection to die on the points of Boxer weapons. The males, that is, and the old women—for the young women were kept alive to feed the lusts of the beasts, and were then turned loose, white and drawn of face, to wend their ways to the deepest wells, into which hundreds of them plunged to efface their everlasting shame in the welcome waters, in which other young women of China already were floating, until before the end of that first day, many of the wells were clogged with suicides, and the moans of those who feared to die rose to high Heaven. Even the legations heard and could do nothing, though the legations offered asylum to all who could enter the already over-crowded courtyards.

Behind a rampart of sandbags, men in uniform, men in citizens' garb, watched and waited, seeking among the dust and debris before their improvised fortress for a moving hand or arm or body, which would indicate an enemy. Weapons barked, barked angrily and often, until their barrels grew hot in the sweaty hands which held them—- and ever and anon, as the cordon of the enemy closed in, always managing somehow to keep fair cover, Boxers in regalia stood upright, stiffening, to plunge on their faces after a moment, while their dead bodies shook and trembled with the bullets which poured into them from the firearms of those who wished to make them suffer the very acme of suffering before they breathed their last.

The Boxers brought brass cannon into play. Tiles flew in splinters from roofs of the legation buildings. The more flimsy buildings collapsed with the ceaseless pounding of shells, and came tumbling down upon the heads of their defenders who, through cracks left them in their sudden imprisonment among the debris, kept on firing, aiming at moving hands and heads, always taking toll of the enemy. But there were so many of them! Mausers and *gingals*, and always, gleaming in the sun which now was high enough to witness the slaughter, the threat of cold steel when the Boxers should finally carry the legation positions.

Shouts and screams of the dying, hoarse cries of the slayers, singing a mad paean of blood-lust. From their positions the defenders of the legations could see the flames of destruction, could hear the shouts and the screams of the dying, the bitter wailing of lost women— women lost in the mad vortex of an undisciplined mob.

Bullets thudded into aged walls. Men sprang to their feet, foreign men, their hands clutched to their throats. One man straightened, grasping with both hands at his throat, striving to close the ghastly wound made by a leaden slug fired at random from an unseen *gingal*.

Mauser slugs tore through tiles and flimsy walls. Women inside the compounds screamed and fell, coughing their lives away;

and the wounded who lived on were made as comfortable as possible, in an improvised hospital ward which was already overcrowded with refugees; so that refugees who were unharmed gazed always upon the wounded and dying, seeing in them the shadow of the thing which might come to them all.

Peking was a city of horror.

A great church to which had fled hundreds of *er mao tzu* — flocking to the standard of a missionary who would not desert his flock, which was too large to be taken whole into the legation quarter—was put to the torch. Out of the crackling flames, to the ears of the Boxers who hemmed the place in, came the shrieks of burning humanity— shrieks of terrible suffering, shrieks through which came other cries, cries of those who had accepted the teaching of the Living God and now were calling in vain upon Him for protection in the mad hour of their unbelievable extremity. But perhaps He did hear those prayers— and those who prayed died more swiftly, released from useless and prolonged suffering, the end to which would be the same in any case.

Closer and closer pressed the cordon of the Boxers, hemming in the beleaguered foreigners—who were already short of food, and whose ammunition was already being doled out—while those who had been through these things before, and who could not be brought to believe that relief would reach Peking before it was too late, commanded men who carried firearms to fire only when they saw targets that could not be missed. And there were so many against them! A thousand to one, some said, perhaps more. No one really knew, though there were a thousand guesses that first day and all knew that the numbers of the besiegers were increasing hour by hour, for bullets fell upon the legations like hail. Tiles burst into fragments under the ceaseless pounding of lead, and the fragments scattered to work havoc among the defenders who were just out of line of fire.

Buildings toppled and took fire, and, added to the necessity for fighting back against the Boxers, was the necessity of protecting themselves against the flames in their own compounds—in order that those flames should not drive them forth to fall under Boxer knives and before Boxer bullets. At first the Boxers believed what Prince Tuan wished them to believe—that no bullets could slay

Loosing Of The Dragon

them—and almost carried the legations in their mad zeal. It required a veritable hail of lead to convince them that their bodies were not proof against the bullets of the foreigners—after which they dropped to earth, all about the legations, and dug themselves in, indicating their determination to hold the place in siege, and to take the legations in the end. Tzu Hsi, the Empress Dowager, would have the lives of those who proved faithless—Prince Tuan had said so—and so the Boxers preferred to give their lives under foreign bullets, and fought on.

The day passed.

The night was horror-filled, for the fires in the city beyond the legations lighted up the skies in sullen glare. And out of the very flames, it seemed, came the ceaseless screams of the dying, the shouts of the beasts a-prowl, the bitter wailings of women who would get up courage to fling themselves into wells, or from the Wall of Peking, before morning.

The sullen roaring of flames, a roaring that mounted hour by hour in volume. Houses would fall, crashing into ruins, red and angry, hurling sparks in all directions, sparks that ignited the houses of the innocent, until the fire threatened to make a flaming waste of Peking. People fled from their burning homes, with the flames clutching at them as they fled—and many there were, women with babes in their arms, who could not outstrip the flames, and fell in their own doorways, where the flames crept up to their quivering, tortured bodies, and their clothes were burned from them, their bodies soon blackened, their screams of pain and anguish mercifully stilled.

An American led a forlorn hope in a sortie against the advance cordon of the Boxers, and, of the dozen or so in that forlorn hope, all fell before coming to hand grips— save the leader himself who, despite the repeated cries of his countrymen to come back, dashed on, a madman in his fury, to throw himself upon the numberless Boxers, who laughed tauntingly at the defenders who had not come forth, and hurled back the crimsoned body of the dauntless, foolhardy leader, upon the points of blood-smeared spears. The defenders, shouting sullenly, their faces white masks of horror, redoubled their fire, pouring hot lead into the Boxers—and many there were who fell. But always where one fell three others stepped into his place, and the endless fight went on.

Will relief arrive in time? The question was asked a thousand times, and none could answer, though there were those who tried, striving to keep up the courage of the defenders.

That mad night of carnage! The dead were unburied, because the living could not spare time from the tenacious defense to inter them—and they remained unburied for days. The Boxer toll was heavy too, and their dead also remained unburied, for days on end, until the stench of the corpses stung the nostrils of the defenders who could not escape the evil effluvium, because there was nowhere they could go. Penned in. Unable to do aught, during darkness, but watch for pinpoints of light, and fire at the light; to listen for slithery sounds, as of men creeping close, and to fire at the sounds. No wonder faces became white and strained! No wonder that, though the defense had lasted only thirty hours, it seemed to the defenders that they had been battling against a host of almost invisible enemies all the days of their lives. It seemed as though their lot in life was to hold back the Boxers, that they had been doing just that for days, weeks, months and years on end. Had they known actually how long they would be compelled to hold out, they might have given up, and the story would have a far different ending. But they didn't know, and hoping against hope sustained their wavering courage—until to have courage, to fight on, to move back only when compelled to move, fighting with the brave hearts of them for every inch of ground, was habitual, and those who had been fearful at first wondered why they had been fearful—

And raised their weapons to fire quickly at a moving hand or arm beyond their sandbag parapet, which had been slashed, pitted and torn by the ripping slugs of the Boxers.

Among the Boxers, Prince Tuan moved perpetually, never sleeping, exhorting his followers to fresh deeds of violence, inspiring them to make treacherous flank attacks, to find coigns of vantage whence they could hurl leaden hail into the women and children who were crowded behind the protection of woefully decimated rifles.

Loosing Of The Dragon

The fight went on. The eternal thud of rifle bullets, the crash of slugs from awkward *gingals*. The screams of the wounded, who begged for water when hands were too busy to bring water; the shouts of broken and mutilated *er mao tzu* in the outer city, where the Boxers continued to take terrible toll of the Christian Chinese; the pitiful screams of young and beautiful, hitherto virginal, Chinese women and girls. The Boxers were out of hand. Prince Tuan didn't care. What mattered a few dead Chinese, more or less, or the ravishing of otherwise useless women? If the women amused his men, they were more useful than they had been before. Let them take them. They would fight better, fighting for other amusement.

Stores were torn open, goods hurled into the streets, and tradesmen who tried to protect their wares were hurled after their goods, their bodies quivering from many knife slashes, because they had held out against the looters, fighting to hold their own—and the looters poured into the stores, ripping them apart, seeking for money, and for unmarried women.

The cordon of Boxers drew tighter about the legations.

Far away, in Tientsin, the relief column was forming, but it must fight every step of the way, battling against stubborn Boxers, ere it could reach Peking and relieve the embattled legations.

Would they be in time?

The legations hoped so. Prince Tuan determined that, if the relief column did arrive, it would reach Peking only in time to look upon the ruins, and upon the broken, mutilated bodies of the erstwhile defenders.

But the relief column was forming, uniformed men of many nations. Tzu Hsi, the Dowager Empress heard—and prepared to flee from the wrath of those countries whose nationals she had given into the brutal hands of Prince Tuan.

But none knew for sure. The Boxer Dragon was unloosed, rampant for blood—and there were many among the living, after that first day, who would be dead and buried before relief arrived.

XXXVI. THE FLIGHT OF OLD BUDDHA

Old Buddha had started an avalanche which she could not stay. It was Yung Lu who urged her to flee from Peking and the certain vengeance that would be visited upon her by the soldiers of the countries whose nationals had lost their lives because of her orders to Prince Tuan. Prince Tuan joined with Yung Lu in urging Old Buddha to flee from the Forbidden City and from Peking.

Old Buddha did not wish to go. She had a sort of superstition about the Forbidden City. She thoroughly believed that if she left it she would never be allowed to return, and that the Manchu Dynasty would pass in her absence. It was the same argument she had used when Hsien Feng had fled to Jehol after the Opium War. She did not fear death, she told her advisors, and did not wish to flee from the Forbidden City.

But her advisors prevailed.

Li Lien Ying was not endowed with great courage, and had no counsel to offer Old Buddha in the hour of her greatest need. He was a neuter bereft of all reason, afraid for his own life, and afraid for that of Old Buddha because he knew that if she were slain his own power would pass with her demise. But he did not know what to do.

And the other eunuchs, of whom there were some three thousand in the court, had begun to desert Old Buddha as rats desert a sinking ship. Worried, heartsick, remorseful, Old Buddha, the sovereign, was given a glimpse of the loyalty which, she had inspired among her underlings. The eunuchs whom she had treated kindly were leaving her, some even having fled without so much as by-your-leave.

It was a sad plight for China's greatest ruler. Over sixty years of age, she was scarcely in the best of condition to undertake a flight such as this one promised to be.

But her advisors prevailed against the better judgment of Old Buddha—which was best for her in the end, since the foreign soldiers did try to take her, and vengeance most assuredly would have fallen upon her head had she remained in the Forbidden City.

She knew, did this remarkable Old Lady, that foreign troops would doubtless ravage at will among the treasures she must

The Flight Of The Old Buddha

necessarily leave behind her. She had had too much experience at court with foreigners to believe that they would regard her valuable things as anything other than souvenirs to be carted away, diced for, and sold to dealers in the United States, England and other places, when the foreign troops should eventually return home.

So she adopted a unique way of safeguarding her treasures, such of them, that is, as she had time to care for.

Her treasure house, a room containing her wealth of gold and silver ingots—so many *tael* weights each—she had bricked up. Old bricks were used, to give the appearance of age, and the new wall was built well inside the old, and the riches of Old Buddha were left between the outer and inner walls, on the knees of the gods otherwise. Her jewels and gems, her gold and silver plate, she had made into easily manageable bundles and dropped into the wells which dot the Forbidden City. There were many things, of course, for which she could find no hiding place, and these things were either carried away or ruthlessly destroyed, first by the Boxers, second by the Foreign soldiers—the foreign soldiers and the Boxers between them, managing to make a fairly complete sweep of all valuables not hidden away by Old Buddha.

When Old Buddha was finally ready to take leave of the Forbidden City, taking with her, despite the fact that she fled, the power and authority which had always been hers, her flight was actually a clever move, since she not only escaped from the vengeance of the foreigners, but carried on court routine on her flight, as surely as ever she had while in the Forbidden City. There were but few eunuchs and ladies-in-waiting with her. Besides the Empress Dowager, there were Kwang Hsu and his Empress, Ta-A-Ko, the court ladies and Li Lien Ying. A pitiful remnant of a once mighty court.

When she returned to Peking, two years later, Old Buddha tried to make the foreigners believe that Ta-A-Ko had not accompanied her into her voluntary exile, but the fact is that he did go with her, and that he was one of the sources of her many troubles on that interminable two years away from the Forbidden City; for even in exile he considered women fair game, and was not above going afield among the country women to exercise what he seems to have believed to be his divine right as Crown Prince.

Sorrowfully, Old Buddha took a last look at her beloved Forbidden City, her Summer Palace and Winter Palace, before she was ready to trust herself to the tender mercies of China's interior, where she was to be in virtual exile for two years.

Her destination was Shi An, a journey by chair and Peking cart of almost one month, so slowly was the court compelled to travel.

Just before the departure, Li Lien Ying held converse with Old Buddha.

"We have forgotten the Pearl Concubine," he said.

"What shall we do with her?" replied Old Buddha.

"We can't leave her behind," replied the vengeful eunuch, this sadist who delighted in the pain of others, "for you must remember she was behind the defection of His Majesty two years ago, and is just the sort to talk. She will be found by the foreigners after we leave, and would be just the person whom they would depend upon to secure information as to our destination."

"No," replied Old Buddha, "she must not be left behind. Bring her out of her prison. We shall take her with us."

"What for, Your Majesty?" demanded Li Lien Ying. "She is of no use to us! She will be merely a burden to us on our journey to Shi An, and we already have more burdens than we can manage."

"Then what shall we do with her?"

"If Your Majesty will leave the matter in my hands it shall be properly disposed of!"

There can be no doubting the fact that Old Buddha understood exactly the meaning of Li Lien Ying's words.

But—

"I leave the matter in your hands," she told the Chief Eunuch.

Li Lien Ying gave sharp orders to the eunuchs who still remained faithful to Old Buddha.

But, before they could bring forth the Pearl Concubine, Kwang Hsu managed a last few words with her. He spoke with her through the window of her prison house. It must have been a sad parting for these two, who had not enjoyed each other's companionship since Old Buddha's *coup d'etat* of two years before.

Kwang Hsu found the beautiful Pearl Concubine no longer beautiful. Her clothes were in rags, her hair in ragged wisps about a face that had once so charmed the heart of the deposed Emperor,

The Flight Of The Old Buddha

and her prison house was like a pig sty, because little attention had been paid her during her long incarceration. A sad little woman, talking to her lord and master through a grating, knowing in her heart she would never see him again; that lord and master knowing, too, powerless to do anything about it, careless whether he lived or died, hopeless beyond words, he had but few words to say to the Pearl Concubine.

Then came the neuter-minions of Li Lien Ying who, as Kwang Hsu turned away from the one woman who had ever meant anything in his life, brought the Pearl Concubine forth from her prison house. The Pearl Concubine knew instantly what this meant. She could read their purpose in the hypocritical faces of the eunuchs. She begged for her life, begged the next minute that they kill her instantly, releasing her from her torture of suspense, but the eunuchs, headed by Li Lien Ying, turned deaf ears to her pleas.

She was dragged, disheveled, woebegone, frightened, pale as ashes, into the courtyard where Old Buddha waited impatiently the hour of departure.

"Save me, Your Majesty! Save me!" she begged of Old Buddha.

She flung herself on her face before the Empress Dowager, humbly begging that her life be spared. Li Lien Ying, his pockmarked face set in a smirk of enjoyment, forced her to kowtow more deeply by deliberately forcing her face hard against the cobblestones of the courtyard. There was a stain of blood on the face of the Pearl Concubine as, abjectly, she raised her face to Old Buddha, and repeated her pleas that her life be spared.

"I have never conspired against Your Majesty!" she pleaded. "I have always loved Your Majesty, have always been faithful! Please deliver me from the hands of the eunuchs!"

But Old Buddha, unrelenting, never ceased even for a moment to hate the Pearl Concubine, whom in some way she was wont to blame for most of her own troubles, disdained even to look down at the huddled form of Kwang Hsu's only friend and sympathizer. Kwang Hsu, though his heart must have been heavy within him, could do nothing, and knew it.

Old Buddha impatiently turned her back on the Pearl Concubine and strode to the ornate sedan chair which awaited her, the hearers cooling their heels as they waited patiently for the word which would start them on the long journey inland.

Li Lien Ying and his eunuchs carried the Pearl Concubine away. They took her to the famous well just inside the gate of Tung Wha Men, and hurled her in. They knelt above the well. The Second Eunuch affected to hear the moans of the ill-fated concubine as he cocked his ear to listen.

"The fall did not kill her," he said to Li Lien Ying.

Li Lien Ying said nothing. He merely looked questioningly at the Second Eunuch, who raised a huge rock above his head, aimed carefully down into the darkness which surrounded the shaft of the well, and hurled the stone.

Up from the darkness came the sound of a sickening thud, and the moans of the Pearl Concubine were heard no more. They covered the well over.

Even today, during the hours of darkness—so they say —the moans of the Pearl Concubine may be heard by those who care to listen.

Then Li Lien Ying, satisfied in that he had been allowed his own way of disposing of the "menace" of the Pearl Concubine, returned to the Old Buddha, who waited to take her departure from the Forbidden City-—into voluntary exile.

The journey to Shi An began, and Old Buddha herself, after her return, often dwelt upon the hardships and horrors of that, to her, unforgettable journey.

For almost a month they traveled inland. There is a story to the effect that, because of her fear of the foreigners, Old Buddha assumed the role of one of her own servants, and compelled that servant to take her, Old Buddha's, place in the sedan chair. Old Buddha later heard this story, and never ceased to deny it. Knowing something of the courage of Old Buddha, I feel that this is an unjustified slander, with about as much foundation in fact as most of the stories which have been told about Old Buddha.

Old Buddha rode in a sedan chair, the only member of the court to so ride. Kwang Hsu and the Young Empress rode in Peking carts. Kwang Hsu, all hope dead, seldom spoke on the interminable journey. He made no complaint about food or accommodations, seemed interested in nothing that transpired; and

The Flight Of The Old Buddha

the Young Empress was scarcely less resigned to the hopelessness of the situation.

Much of the way led through precipitous mountain passes, where a slip on the part of the chair bearers would have meant death to Old Buddha, since often her chair hung above the most appalling abysses. Yet the flight continued. The animals dragging the unwieldy Peking carts stumbled over the trails, were whipped back to their feet by brutal eunuchs and the journey continued.

Word went on ahead of the court, by that mysterious verbal telegraph which is a miracle to foreigners who know China, and places were always ready for her when nightfall came. Provincial governors and lesser officials had their yamens prepared against her coming, renovated and repaired, to offer her the best they had—poor enough thus far from Peking, whence there were no roads worthy of the name, no trade routes, and no communication.

The carping eunuchs never ceased to complain of the accommodations furnished Old Buddha by the various officials who acted as hosts to her on her long journey to Shi An, not because they were particularly solicitous for the welfare of Old Buddha, but because they missed the luxuries to which they themselves had been accustomed inside the Forbidden City, now so far behind.

The food was bad, but it was the best procurable. Old Buddha realized that her hosts reverenced her as much as she had ever been revered upon her throne, back in distant Peking, and she appreciated their solicitude. Not so the eunuchs, who quarreled with the officials, told them that what they offered was not good enough for Her Majesty, refused to listen to the officials' excuses to the effect that they offered the best procurable in these out-of-the-way places, and even had childish vengeance upon those officials by, just before departing, maliciously destroying furnishings and draperies which the officials had been at endless pains to obtain against the arrival of Old Buddha.

When Old Buddha discovered that such things were going on, she never failed to punish the offenders, and always took the opportunity to express her regret to the officials that these nuisances had occurred, and repeated her own appreciation of what the officials had done for her.

But on her journey to Shi An, she could never free her mind of her last view of Peking—a city in flames, whose orange glow lighted up all the soft night skies of North China. She never could, never would, forget the cries of the wounded and dying, Chinese and foreign alike, or the wailing of the ravished women, many of whom would have died by their own hands long before Old Buddha herself would return to Peking, if return she ever did.

A heartbreaking journey for an old woman, sick and weary, aged and despised. Her indomitable courage almost failed her at times. Kwang Hsu, whom she had compelled to precede her, so that she could watch him, until they had gone too far from Peking for him to make his escape successfully, was also very ill. Every member of the sadly depleted court was near to exhaustion long before the court reached Shi An.

At this place, the Viceroy had prepared his own *yamen* against her coming. What a pitiful place it must have seemed to the fugitive court, accustomed as it was to the splendor of the Forbidden City and the Palaces! Yet there was nothing else to do, nowhere else to go that might prove better. A small *yamen*, but it was tendered her whole-heartedly by the Viceroy of Shi An, and Old Buddha never ceased to be grateful, though her eunuchs complained continually, deluged her with trifling objections, and generally added to the misery which the court must endure until word should be received from Peking that it was safe to return.

The odyssey of Old Buddha, on the journey to Shi An, is an odyssey of heartbreak.

Her exile was to endure for two long, terrible years.

XXXVII. A CITY IN FLAMES

Red flames against the sky. Peking a roaring furnace, as the Boxers wrought with might and main to create such a chaos as the aged capital of the Middle Kingdom had never known. Cries cut through the roaring of the flames like keen knives, proof that there were many who fell in the flames, or who were taken in their light and slaughtered. There were running men, and women who could not run because their bound feet hindered them— pitiful women who must pay for an age-old heritage with their lives. Men running, as I have said, running blindly, with their arms before their eyes to shut out the terrific heat. Boxers dancing in the red glare in the streets, yelling like the beasts they emulated, brandishing their weapons, red with the blood of the slain. The streets were filled with milling men, men who knew not where to go, men who milled in the frenzy of fear, watching the dancing dervishes of Boxers, hoping against hope that the cup which had been tendered them would pass. Above all rode a moon whose face was blood-red, as though the stain which Prince Tuan had put upon the Middle Kingdom had smeared her countenance, once benign.

Then came the wind. The flames bent over, reaching out tentacles of flame, clutching tentacles that fastened to buildings hitherto untouched, so that it seemed that all Peking would be reduced to ashes. Always there came the rattle of musketry, the thudding crash of Mausers, the thud of the heavy slugs from the *gingals*—those strange weapons of the long barrel, which must be fired by two men, one man to fire the piece, the second to hold the barrel.

"I pray this cup to pass from me!"

That might have been the prayer of the *mao tzu* and the *er mao tzu*. Perhaps there were many who thus beseeched the God Who seemed to have forsaken those whom He had chosen. The truth will never be known, for the flames wiped out many of those who might thus have prayed; and most of those who remained alive, who came whole through the flames, fell in agony on the points of the Boxers' spears, were slashed by their knives, or met more merciful death before the leaden slugs of Mausers or *gingals*.

Hatamen Street, famous Hatamen Street, which is within shouting distance of the gates of the Forbidden City, was aglow with the fires which consumed the little shops to her east; and looters—some of them wearing finery taken from those same shops, some even wearing the clothing of women who never again would hold up their heads, because of shame, or because they had fled from shame in suicide—made of Hatamen Street a hideous thoroughfare.

Lantern Street and the other narrow streets and alleys became firetraps because in them the houses were set so close together. Many there were who could not escape from Lantern Street, even had there been no Boxers to watch the exits, because the fire hemmed them in, and cut them down, preventing all escape, so that bodies, black and charred, were found many days later, bodies of men, women and children who had scarcely left their own doorways before the terrific heat had struck them down.

"Kill! Kill! Kill!"

Always it was the word most heard. Boxers slunk like vultures through streets and alleys, seeking others to slay. Someone whispered that Christian Chinese, when they became Christians, had had the Holy Cross branded on their heads. The Boxers heard, and went forth to slay anew, and when asked whom they had slain, claimed to have slaughtered people who were branded with the Holy Cross on the crown of the head. Boxers seized the opportunity to pay off old scores and slew their best hated enemies, because there was no law to deny them.

And still the flames roared, painted weird pictures, blood-red pictures, against the sides of buildings not yet reached by the flames. Walls fell inward, or outward, pinning men and women under them, roasting them alive as they strove to win free and were not able.

Prince Tuan went still among his Boxers, his invincible Boxers, preaching his gospel of slaughter, reiterating his offer of five hundred *taels* for each foreigner slain; and his men heard, shouted approval, and went out to collect fresh bounties.

Inside the legations, starvation stared the defenders in the face before many days had passed. Word had come that the relief column was approaching Peking. The Empress Dowager and her

A City In Flames

court seized the opportunity to flee from the Forbidden City, heading into the interior, fleeing from the wrath of foreigners in uniform, foreigners with rifles and bayonets in their hands, foreigners who would go right to the heart of things, and deal out punishment to the lawgiver of China, that harsh old lady who had given Prince Tuan leave to begin the slaughter. The court fled, the word reached the beleaguered legations, but still relief did not come. Day succeeded day, with, fresh dead among the legation defenders, with many fresh dead among the Boxers who infested the legations, and still the relief column did not come. Night succeeded night, and though it seemed that there could not be a flammable house left standing in Peking, flames still roared, sending their red-tongued messengers up as wild salutes to the blood-red moon, making their crimson etchings on the walls of stone and brick buildings which the flames had blackened, worried, and had not been able to consume. Hatamen Street, for days and nights, was a thoroughfare of terror, forsaken by all save the Boxers, who ruled both night and day in Hatamen and all other streets and alleys, and danced their ritualistic dances, brandishing their weapons, mouthing threats that now were useless, because there was no one left to slay. Some had escaped slaughter, of course, but had made good their escape. Many had fled the city well knowing as they fled that North China lay in the clenched hands of the Boxers, that the Boxer Dragon was crushing out the lives of helpless and frightened fugitives; but eager to get into the open, away from the searing flames, where they might have at least a fighting chance for their miserable lives. Many died of hardship, starvation and exhaustion, but they died in the open, while the blood-red moon looked down upon them, and cool winds bathed their fright- fevered cheeks.

"Kill! Kill! Kill!"

The word went from mouth to mouth, becoming part of the Boxer ritual. The Boxers did not know, or refused to believe, that the relief column was an actual fact; that when it finally arrived their own dread word would be flung back in their teeth, and that the guns and bayonets of the foreigners would exact, to the uttermost farthing, payment for the horror Prince Tuan and his minions had visited upon Peking. They did not foresee that the

Forbidden City would soon not be "forbidden," that the cobblestones of its courtyards would be marked and indented with the wheel traces of enemy guns, that the Summer Palace, the pleasure place of Tzu Hsi, would feel the heavy tread of marching enemy feet, would echo and reecho to the rumbling roll of gun-carriages.

No, they did not see.

Perhaps the red glow of the fires which consumed the aged buildings, the rich treasures of Peking, blinded them.

But the relief column was under way, marching upon Peking; and though the Boxers might dance, though they might sing whatever hymns of hate they should compose, they would dance to another tune in the end, and would pay the fiddler in the very coin they had exacted of the *mao tzu* and the *er mao tzu*.

XXXVIII. MARCHING FEET

The legations received dully the report that relief had arrived. It couldn't be true—couldn't be true that all the terror was over, and that they wouldn't have to go on and on, fighting day and night, listening to the moans and shrieks of the wounded and dying, living on little or nothing in the way of food, tending the sick, repairing badly damaged parapets, watching the hours away for moving arms or legs of Boxers.

But it was true!

Though the horror was not over. Not easily had the foreign troops completed that long march upon Peking. They had fought every step of the way, had felt the bite of Boxer fangs, and, tired and exhausted as they were, they entered Peking through the great gates with the determination to pay up the Boxers for all they had suffered, and all they had compelled the beleaguered legations to suffer. White faced men and boys in the uniforms of many countries and conspicuous among them the men and boys uniformed in the fighting togs of Uncle Sam. What a brave sight for the eyes of those who had been under fire for so long in Peking, though they did not smile at the sight, because they had been through so much they had forgotten how to smile.

Into the city of Peking poured the foreigners; and Prince Tuan, realizing now that reports of the relief's expected arrival were true, massed his invincible Boxers to dispute entrance to the city.

The Boxers could not be slain, despite the fact that many of them had already fallen before the guns of legation defenders! Still that farce of invincibility, so convincingly propounded by Prince Tuan that the Boxers still believed it, and faced bravely the belching guns of the foreign troops. They rallied to his standard as never before they had rallied, and faced the new danger, shouting and brandishing weapons, baring their breasts brazenly to the leaden hail which the foreigners were not loath to drop upon them.

Every street and alley was filled with blood-mad Boxers, ready to face foreigners who, after seeing what the Boxer Dragon had done to Peking, were just as filled with blood-lust as the Boxers themselves. Who can blame them? Certainly not those who have never faced death as those men faced it! Certainly not those who have—for those who have known the meaning of heartless slaughter, and nature commands their very manhood to rise up in revolt to avenge the slaughter of innocents.

The Boxers presented a bold front to the foreign troops; and the foreign troops, the streets echoing to the steady tread of their feet, the morning sun glinting on the colors of half a dozen countries, moved straight to the front, like soulless Juggernauts, carrying everything before them. Bullets whined and whistled, and sang, when they ricocheted, flattened, to dull their song when the bullets thus dumdummed found sanctuary in quivering flesh, tearing it asunder savagely.

Relentlessly the foreign troops moved ahead, their white faces set with unflinching determination, facing bravely the bullets, the knives, and the spears of the Boxers. Boxers flung wide their arms, daring the bullets and bayonets of the relief, and fell sprawling—learning too late the fact that they were not invincible after all—while other Boxers, by scores and hundreds it seemed, moved forward to take the places of those who had fallen; and the foreign Juggernaut, decimated in places but with gaps immediately filled by those who closed up in the rear, moved steadily forward, stern and unfaltering as a mountainous tidal wave which carries everything in its path.

Prince Tuan moved among his men.

"Kill! Kill! Kill!"

The dread word, repeated again and again, the meaning almost blurred by countless repetitions, rang throughout the ranks of the Boxers. The foreign troops, hearkening only to the stern commands from their officers, loosed volley after volley, tearing the ranks of the Boxers asunder—yet the ranks of the Boxers seemed never to lessen, as they were filled at orders from Prince Tuan and his minions.

Crash!

Projectiles from brass cannons smashed against stone walls and were deflected into the ranks of the foreign soldiers, while direct hits smashed into the drawn white faces of American, Russian and French troops, who, nevertheless, without faltering, moved forward, firing at word of command, aiming their shots, making every shot count, intent on breaking the seemingly unbreakable

Marching Feet

Boxer wall of men. Dead, piled high in distorted heaps, filled the streets of Peking after the foreign troops had passed, and not all of the dead were Boxers. There were white faces among the dead, white faces set in masks of hatred and resolve, as though in falling the foreign dead had striven to urge forward their comrades who yet lived —and move forward those comrades did!

Like a flood, which separates into a thousand streams, where it may, the foreign troops poured into Peking. Large groups kept to the main thoroughfares; smaller groups filtered into the side streets, rifles, bayonets fixed, held eagerly to the fore; while even smaller groups separated from the main streams and the lesser streams to carry by storm the isolated strongpoints, buildings and dugouts, where stubborn Boxers still held their ground and poured leaden hail into the ranks of the attackers.

Human flesh could not stand the strain, unless that human flesh was inspired by a righteous spirit of revenge; and such spirit was the heritage of the foreign troops, a heritage which they had made their own on the terrible march upon the beleaguered capital of China. Nothing less than extermination or utter rout would satisfy the foreign troops.

The Boxers, here and there, in spite of all Prince Tuan could do, began to give way before the relentless march of the foreign Juggernaut, before the silent threat of the slatting colors of half a dozen outraged countries, before the angrier threat of bullets which hit the targets at which they were directed—bullets that hissed, snarled, and slew without mercy.

But the Boxers still were stubborn. They had visited unbelievable horror upon Peking. That had been when Peking was wholly and completely in their power. Now, as they began to break, the less courageous to flee in mad terror, they made of Peking a worse horror still. Then they had slain only those who had been named in the verbal edicts of Prince Tuan—the *mao tzu* and the *er mao tzu*— now they slew all whom they met, all who were not very definitely identified with the Boxers; and the bodies of those who fell before the Boxer rout were mutilated as by the hands of the most primitive and bloodthirsty of savages.

Torches were brought into play again, firing such houses as had not felt the flames which had already all but made of Peking a city of ruins and charred remains. While the Boxer wall, striving to hold yet being forced back in spite of their stubborn determination, brought the foreign troops to the most infinitesimal of pauses, looters ravished anew the stores and dwelling places of those who had escaped the previous mad orgy of destructions; and Peking carts, piled high with the wealth of a great capital, began to wend their slow and ponderous ways out of the city, their drivers and guards intent upon guarding their loot with their lives. Much of the treasure of Peking disappeared in this way, never again to be seen, vanishing from the sight and knowledge of all save that of Prince Tuan and his minions.

The end came on the ramp of the Wall of Peking. That was not the end, of course, but it exemplified the end—for on this ramp was fought the bloodiest hand-to-hand conflict of all the many hand-to-hand conflicts which had taken place, and were still taking place, in the ravished city of Peking.

Boxers fled to the crest, firing down upon the up-marching troops, who, no longer firing, their white faces masks of resolve, were climbing the age-old steps, gripping bayoneted rifles in white knuckled hands; and when the Boxers on the crest, realizing that nothing could stop these men in uniform, moved down in desperation to engage them on the ramp, the clang and clash of weapons could be heard for blocks. Nude torsoed Boxers fell upon the bayonets of the foreign troops, who hurled the bodies aside, over the blood-stained precipice of the ramp, and continued their march to the crest, slashing, parrying savage blows, thrusting crimsoned weapons home. Boxers toppled and fell, screaming, to break their bones upon the cobblestones below the ramp. Now and again, a foreign soldier fell, mouthing curses because death had cheated him of his just revenge. He, too, crashed to the harsh stones below, a crumpled heap that did not move, save only sluggishly, when bodies from the distant ramp above crashed down atop his motionless form. When the last Boxer on the ramp had fallen, filling the steps of the ramp with crumpled, bleeding killers, the foreign troops moved on, slowly, up the age-old stairs, toward the crest, where a few of the Boxers, afraid to engage on the ramp, afraid to fling themselves from the wall, stood their ground desperately, waiting with weapons in hand for the foreign troops to reach and cut them down.

And reach the Boxers the foreign troops did; and when the last Boxer had paid with his life for his faithfulness to Prince Tuan, the Beast, when the last Boxer, his arms flung wide, his weapons slipping from nerveless hands, plunged from the crest of the wall to the ground, far, far below, his fall was a signal that Peking, at long last, was in the hands of uniformed foreigners—protectors and avengers of those *mao tzu* and *er mao tzu* whom the Empress Dowager had given into the hands of Prince Tuan for slaughter. But the Empress Dowager herself, far away in the inland now, did not know that guns rumbled through the streets of the sacred Forbidden City, that gun-carriages dented with their wheels the pathways of the Summer Palace, pathways which had hitherto known only the touch of royal feet—until her return two years later, when she would never allow those pathways to be repaired, because she wished to be reminded until her death of the great mistake she had made in placing her trust in the keeping of the Beast, Prince Tuan, leader and organizer of the Boxers.

And after the deluge, like many another she had suffered down the centuries, Peking raised her head from among the ruins and began methodically to gather up her charred remains, bent upon rising like a phoenix, out of her own ashes, to even greater place among the capital cities of the world.

XXXIX. OLD BUDDHA'S RETURN

A sad homecoming was the return to the Forbidden City of the Old Buddha. She had aged ten years in the two trying years she had been absent, though during all her absence she had never once doubted that her good fortune would prevail in the end and that she would return to the glories she had lost because she had trusted Prince Tuan, the degenerate showman of the Boxers.

She came in in her sedan chair by way of Chengyangmen gate. From her chair she looked up at the high flanking walls, and was instantly reminded of the disgrace which she had undergone two years before.

For several foreigners stood upon the wall and looked down upon her pitiful procession amusedly. In the days before the Uprising they would never have dared. In those days, when Old Buddha went abroad, the streets were always deserted, since no one was allowed to watch the passing of Her Majesty.

With Old Buddha returned Kwang Hsu, the deposed Emperor, the Young Empress, Ta-A-Ko and Li Lien Ying.

The procession passed through the great gates, into Peking, and it was far from being a triumphal return. Old Buddha knew, long before she reached the Forbidden City, that the hands of the foreigners had probably ravished the place of all her treasures, had probably desecrated the holy of holies which for centuries had known no footfalls save those of royalty.

But the grim Old Lady hurried on, borne by faithful chair-bearer eunuchs, and passed through the central gate of the Forbidden City.

She was home at last from exile; but what a change!

Everything that could be moved, that possessed value at all, had either been stolen or carried away by the foreigners. Their triumphal entry ostensibly to relieve the foreign legations, had been made by the foreigners an excuse to rob and pillage.

One foreigner even went so far as to have his picture taken sitting in the throne which Old Buddha had occupied before her flight. He seemed, from the picture Li Lien Ying had been able to secure of him, the usual sort of person who would have been guilty of such an act. He sat low on her throne, a leg across either arm of

Old Buddha's Return

the yellow-cushioned chair, stared idiotically into the camera, while a cigarette was hanging from his long slim fingers. This made Old Buddha furious, naturally enough, and most assuredly did not increase her liking for foreigners. Nor may she be blamed. Foreigners had been meddlers since their first admission to China.

It must have almost broken Old Buddha's heart when she entered the holy of holies of the Manchus to discover the ravages the foreigners had made. Broken screens of priceless value; broken vases; oddments of valuable trinkets, which had been handed down from ruler to ruler for centuries, had either been broken and left where the hands of the vandals had dropped them, or had been carried away by the thieves.

The most important loss, in the eyes of Old Buddha, was her own priceless jade seal, which never was recovered.

Buildings had been all but wrecked, weeds grew in profusion among the cobblestones which paved the courtyards. A silent city then, silent as it is today, a place of memories, of loves, hates and heartaches.

But the indomitable old lady, once more inside the holy of holies, having been made welcome by countless thousands of China's citizenry which had stood afar off to watch her return to the Forbidden City, began straightway to repair the ravages which the Forbidden City and the Palaces had suffered at the hands of the foreign barbarians. She drew up from the wells the treasures which she had caused to be hidden before her flight and tore down the inner wall of her treasure house, exposing, untouched, the Imperial Treasury. How many foreigners, their hearts filled with the lust for wealth, had passed within a foot of that treasure house without knowing its existence? Hundreds, perhaps, for representatives of every foreign power which helped to overthrow the Boxers had a hand in the looting of the Palaces and of the Forbidden City.

Despite the fault which was China's, despite the fact that Old Buddha made a mistake when she ordered Prince Tuan to fire upon the legations, the fact remains that two wrongs never make a right—and that the actions of the foreigners, and those of the officers who took part in them or countenanced them, were inexcusable. Some of those officers today are famous, perhaps justly so, but they are still living and I do not name them—thus showing them vastly more consideration than they showed China during those evil days of the Boxer Uprising. There is no word too bitter to apply to thieves of this class.

Soldiers diced for precious baubles on the streets of Peking—and their officers knew. Precious baubles appeared in the show windows of shops in London, New York and San Francisco, brazenly offered for sale, and were mute proof that these foreigners who would have reformed China were actually less civilized than she. Even the war lords of today, some of whom are ambitious ex-coolies or ex-bandits, show more consideration for the treasures of the overthrown dynasty than did the foreigners of those days who entered Peking and laid it waste because there was no one sufficiently strong to stay their thieving hands.

But I digress.

Old Buddha returned. She learned all that had happened in her absence. She grew bitter as she listened to tales of vandalism, to stories of the rape of China's womanhood by Boxer and foreigner alike, to tales of wanton destruction, desecration and sacrilege. But she kept her head up, this old lady, and began to make repairs. She hated foreigners more bitterly than ever—she went to her grave hating them—but she had no intention of giving them the satisfaction of seeing that she was downhearted because of their inexcusable lack of the spirit of sportsmanship.

The eunuchs who had deserted her before the flight began sheepishly to return. She accepted them back because she needed them in her plans for reconstruction. Li Lien Ying unearthed his own vast treasure, which he had buried under the floor of his private quarters just before the flight, and took charge of the menials as he had done for years before. In a short period of time, so feverishly did Old Buddha prosecute her efforts to reglorify the Forbidden City, the court became the court of old; the courtyards echoed to the tread of royal feet, to the subdued laughter of court ladies and attendants.

Old Buddha's Return

LIFE SIZE WHITE JADE BUDDHA, OLD
BUDDHA'S FAVORITE, AT THE WINTER
PALACE, PEKING

PART OF THE FAMOUS COLONNADE, SUMMER PALACE, PEKING, A FAVORITE STROLLING PLACE OF THE OLD BUDDHA

Old Buddha's Return

Old Buddha, fleeing from her capital city, had not lost nearly so much as she herself believed. She believed she fled in disgrace, while actually her flight made a laughingstock of the foreigners who could not follow her into the fastnesses. While she did not laugh at their helplessness to mete out vengeance upon her, she might well have done so; for her court, during those two long years of exile, never once disintegrated, though badly decimated because of desertions—always desertions, however, of menials.

But the menials came back and were accepted, assigned once more to the old duties.

In a short time, it would have been difficult to tell that the court had ever been absent from the Forbidden City. Old Buddha's carpenters, stone masons and artisans were busy day and night, repairing, rebuilding, putting things to rights, and none was more interested in the progress than Old Buddha.

Save Li Lien Ying, perhaps, who handled the contracts for building and managed to squeeze another fortune for himself out of the prices mutually agreed upon by himself and the carpenters, stone masons and artisans in question.

So the Forbidden City and the Summer and Winter Palaces were reborn.

On several points, however, Old Buddha was adamant.

Though Li Lien Ying, in his usual insinuating manner, hinted that it might be well to repair certain stone walks within the Summer Palace, Old Buddha would never permit such repairs to be made—for the repairs called for obliterating the wheel marks of the foreign guns, and Old Buddha wished them to remain there forever, to remind her of the mistake she had made, and of her undying hatred of the foreigners.

A shell had gone through one corner of a building in Pei Hai, which is in the Winter Palace, and this was never repaired, for the same reason.

These reminders of the foreigners, and of Old Buddha's hatred for the foreigners, and all they represented, may still be seen in the Summer Palace and Pei Hai, for Old Buddha held out against Li Lien Ying's hints that these things should be repaired, until her death, and after her there was none who cared, one way or the other.

Shortly after the return of Old Buddha, foreign representatives submitted to her a list—a sort of "black list"—giving the names of those responsible for the Boxer Uprising, and demanding that those persons he fittingly punished. Old Buddha, though it was a bitter pill for the proud old sovereign to swallow, acceded to the demands—and the bitterness was alleviated somewhat when she saw that the name of Prince Tuan, whom she blamed, after the fact, for the whole thing, was borne conspicuously on the list referred to. Because he was a member of the Royal Clan, Prince Tuan did not suffer decapitation as so many others did, nor did he face a firing squad. His punishment was banishment forever. According to the law, all his family must be exiled with him.

This gave Old Buddha her chance to get rid of the Crown Prince without admitting her own lack of wisdom in selecting him.

Word went forth that the appointment of Ta-A-Ko as Heir Apparent had been rescinded because of the sins of the father, and because of the demands of the "foreign barbarians"—and because Old Buddha was glad of any opportunity to be rid of him, though she said nothing of this—and that Ta-A-Ko was to be sent into exile with his father.

Even then Old Buddha could not entirely concede the fact that the Crown Prince of her choice was the very worst she could have selected. She made it known that she believed Ta-A-Ko in no way responsible for the sins of Prince Tuan; and though she verbally banished him, and made a decree to that effect, it was common knowledge that Ta-A-Ko never left Peking, and that he was able to cause a great deal more trouble before he was finally subdued.

So much for Ta-A-Ko, the Crown Prince, first Crown Prince since the decree of Chia Ching, important only because it gives a side light on the stubborn character of Old Buddha, who could not be budged from her position, once she had made a decision, unless forced so to do by very force of circumstances.

It was this very stubbornness which, though it gave historians a right to call Old Buddha "great," caused no little of her trouble and heartache.

Old Buddha's Return

HER MAJESTY TZU HSI IN A SEDAN CHAIR CARRIED BY COURT EUNUCHS. LI LIEN YING ON EXTREME RIGHT

In the present instance it was caused by her intense hatred of Kwang Hsu, and her desire to further humiliate him—mostly because he had been a thorn in her side since the days of Tzu An, and because so many acts of his appeared in her eyes as direct slights to herself.

Thus we prove Old Buddha human, and a woman, once more—for she allowed her overweening vanity to control her when reason failed to convince her that many of her acts were wrong, capable of bringing untold woe to the hearts of her subjects.

Old Buddha was back. Her situation was difficult. All China, every member of every foreign legation, knew why she had fled, most blamed her for all the horror which had transpired; yet hers was the task of regaining her lost prestige.

She was not the kind to cringe, eat humble pie or make excuses. Her method of gaining the desired end was simple.

She resumed her place on the throne of China exactly as though nothing had happened since she had last occupied it, sent invitations to foreign ministers and their wives to attend her court functions, held morning audience as usual with her own ministers, to whom she had, for the past two years, transmitted her orders by messengers sent through the vast regions inland.

She behaved exactly as though she had done nothing unusual, and her poise was such that even her enemies began to wonder if, indeed, she had done anything unusual.

She carried it off easily, because of the sheer force of the most remarkable personality to be found in the history of the Middle Kingdom.

XL. A CHILD IS BORN

Three centuries ago, a frightened Emperor went and hanged himself. To this day they say that the silken girdle which he fastened about his neck to take his life swings gently in the wind that moans over historic Coal Hill, in Peking's Forbidden City. At the gates of the beleaguered city the son of a Manchu Emperor strove for ingress, hastening by request to aid the Emperor who was fated to be the last of the Mings. The son of an Emperor won his way into the city, just too late—for the last of the Mings, believing everything lost, and life no longer worth the living, had destroyed himself with rescue at his very doors. He had not known. He never knew, for when they found him the great Ming Dynasty had ended.

The son of the Manchu Emperor, too late to aid the Emperor who had sent forth his cry for aid, went into the Forbidden City to become Emperor in the suicide's stead; and the Manchu Dynasty began. There followed him many great ones from the Manchu royal family, for the Manchus remained in power almost three hundred years.

The greatest of them all was Tzu Hsi.

Tzu Hsi is dead now, these many years; and the queue of allegiance to the Manchus is no longer worn, save by those who are ignorant of what has befallen China, by those who regard the old allegiance as hallowed, to whom the new freedom is not welcome because it gives their simple, trusting souls no divinely appointed ruler before whose ornate throne they may worship, and glory in their servitude. Throughout China, the queue, as an emblem, has disappeared; and when, here and there, appears a solitary man who remains true to Tzu Hsi, though she is dead, that man is smiled upon in pity. He does not know, they tell themselves, that the Manchus are no more. To him, say they, Old Buddha has not died. She has merely gone away for a time, because China is not a happy country. Some day she will return, and those who remain true will be rewarded, as were the men who made full use of their talents in the famous parable.

The True Story of the Empress Dowager

The scoffers may smile at the queues which now and then are seen. But the scoffers do not know or sympathize. After all it is only the work-bowed heads of the coolies who remain true.

Away back in the long ago, the daughter of a Manchu General loved a simple Commander of the Imperial Guard. The Daughter's "milk name" was "The Orchid"; the name of the Guard Commander was Yung Lu. They loved each other, these two, in a way that only those who deeply love can understand, and the father of The Orchid approved his daughter's choice. There was happiness in the heart of The Orchid, happiness in the heart of Yung Lu. Some day they would be married. Yet, had they married, all the course of recent Chinese history would have been changed—and Pu Yi, the Pathetic Emperor, would never have been.

But deep in her heart, The Orchid nurtured great ambitions, unrecognized by her perhaps, ambitions which were to lead her to the pinnacle of power, make her name great through all the world, fill her life with sadness and heartache, separate her from Yung Lu, whom she loved, who loved her, by the width of that invisible insurmountable wall which separates royalty and commoner; ambitions which were to bring her in the end to a deathbed of sadness where, while yet she lived, those whom she had trusted all their days deserted her, sending her to her grave with the knowledge that, after all, her life had been a failure because love and faith had been lacking.

But this strong-willed woman, Tzu Hsi, the Empress Dowager, did the best she knew. She made Yung Lu her Grand Councillor and all her life he was near her, worshiped her, was faithful to her in word and deed, served her as only a strong man who loves may serve. Yet all those years, while each knew that the other still loved, Yung Lu might not even so much as take the hand of the erstwhile Orchid, nor touch the hem of her imperial robe. Tzu Hsi showered Yung Lu and Yung Lu's family with honors and riches; but Tzu Hsi and Yung Lu knew that all these possessions were empty of value beside the one thing in life that each wanted, and might not have.

There was never a lover so faithful as Yung Lu, never a lover who had less to hope for in his love—and Tzu Hsi knew,

A Child Is Born

sympathized, and repaid him in the only way possible. She could not know, of course, that her last payment upon her incalculable debt was the unkindest of payments—that by naming the son of Yung Lu's daughter to succeed her, she created an Emperor of pathos, who was to rule his Empire in sorrow and heartache, and to know no peace or happiness all his days.

A child was born to the daughter of Yung Lu, whom the Empress Dowager had loved. How much she loved him, only the Empress Dowager knew. This writer was at her side when word came that Yung Lu had passed away. For a moment she closed her eyes, and the hands on her lap clenched until the knuckles whitened with strain. There was pain in her face; but when she had conquered herself, by an effort of will such as only the proud Tzu Hsi might exercise, the face which peered out on a suddenly darkened world was the face of a graven image, from which the sunlight of a strange companionship had vanished.

The funeral, because of the calm commands of Tzu Hsi, will long be remembered in Peking, which has witnessed the funerals of so many great ones.

To the daughter of the man who had been faithful was born a son. Announcement, after the Chinese custom, went forth to all the family's friends—eggs, colored red to indicate the birth of a man child.

The little newcomer might not leave his room for a month, but knowledge of his arrival was imparted to the Empress Dowager, who gave him the name by which he is known throughout China. The name she gave him was Pu Yi, and, of all who knew of his arrival, none could foresee, least of all she who had named him, that he was destined to be the last of the Manchus, that his way was to be beset by thorns, that his life should be the life of one who might have been great had fate decreed in his favor. One wonders, had Tzu Hsi been gifted with prevision.

The fact was all that any knew: that a child had been born; that he had been named Pu Yi by Her Majesty.

XLI. TZU HSI IS PREOCCUPIED

The court of Tzu Hsi was a court of splendor all the days of Old Buddha. There were many ministers and court officials, many visitors who came in rich gowns and robes, many eunuchs who were officials of one class or another and whose dress brought color and striking effects to Her Majesty's court. Old Buddha liked beauty, beauty of face, beauty of dress, and striking manners; and her aged eyes were quick to note defects. Her subjects knew this, and forbore to offend, well knowing that Her Majesty would be quick to condemn. Old Buddha herself was wise in many ways, Chinese ways; and rigid rules of etiquette and of conduct were maintained always.

It was a constant spectacle, beautiful and awe inspiring, to be present at any court ceremony, and even the court in repose was like a frieze that was endless, ever changing; shifting figures, a perpetual rearrangement of perspective.

I was present when little Pu Yi, the Pathetic Emperor, was brought to Tzu Hsi by his mother, when he was perhaps two months of age. The little chap was wrapped in the swaddling clothes of custom, a huge ungainly bundle whose color scheme was red. Ignorant of the future, unmindful of the significance of this presentation, he stayed quiet in his mother's arms, his black eyes staring at whatever attracts the eyes of children, his wizened little face a masterpiece of helplessness.

The mother, proud of her offspring, brought the baby to Tzu Hsi. All who came to the Old Buddha were compelled by custom to kowtow; but the mother could not kowtow with the baby in her arms. She gave him into the keeping of a small eunuch until she should have performed this necessary ceremony, with all the humility of the loyal subject. When the small eunuch received the baby he bent his head above the awkward bundle, touched the wizened little cheeks with an explorative forefinger, and smiled into eyes which expressed no understanding of what they saw.

All eunuchs, for some strange, though perhaps not incomprehensible reason, love babies; and the eunuchs of the court of Tzu Hsi, of whom there were always a huge number, gathered about the little mite to examine, to touch, and to make comment in

Tzu Hsi Is Preoccupied

whispers. Did the eunuchs know, I wonder? Did they somehow realize that here was an important little personage? Did they recognize in this mite of humanity the last of the Manchu Dynasty? Did they foresee the sorrow and heartache that were to be his? Perhaps. Eunuchs have strange understanding of many things because—well, because, perhaps, they themselves were so often in need of understanding they never received.

The mother of the child performed her kowtows. Even now I can see her there, this mother of a future Emperor whose Empire was to end in chaos, bowing and bending before the woman who was one day, and that day not far distant, to place an evil crown upon the head of a helpless child. To me, as I look back, the mother of Pu Yi was a tragic figure, too. She was proud of her baby, as all mothers, if they be natural mothers, must be proud. It was a great thing for the child to be received at court. It conferred honor, distinction—and the little one did not know. The mother knew. Perhaps she was even thinking that this was the last visit, as well as the first, of Pu Yi at court, and that one day, when he had grown old enough to understand, she would tell him, and prove him his right to be proud of the honor. Perhaps the Empress Dowager would remember the baby, years later, and other honors might be his.

So she took the baby from the arms of the eunuch and, holding him across one ample arm, made him perform his kowtows, too; so that the baby, his eyes half closed, his wizened face uncomprehending, bowed and bent across his mother's arm, like a mechanical doll, to do Old Buddha honor.

Old Buddha, glancing at him carelessly, looked away, nor noticed the baby again. Her indifference to this, the grandson of Yung Lu, was noticeable, as though it had been studied indifference. But was it? I was with Her Majesty when Yung Lu died, as I have related. I know that she loved Yung Lu, for she made me her confidante on occasion, and there can be no mistake. It is useless to speculate upon her indifference to Pu Yi; but I have never ceased to wonder.

To me that indifference, in retrospect, is oddly symbolical. Did she intend, even then, to pay Yung Lu a little of her debt by naming this little one to succeed her? Did she realize that the end of the Dynasty was approaching, just beyond the horizon, and thus plan to avenge herself anew upon Kwang Hsu, half-brother to Prince Chun, by making this boy the Emperor who should abdicate his heritage in fear, before the threat of revolutionary bullets? It does not seem possible, yet when one knew Her Majesty as I grew to know her, one felt that little was hidden from her, even though that little lay afar off in the future, when her own name would be anathema to all good Chinese who desired to relieve themselves of the Manchu yoke—in order to bend their necks to other yokes that might prove even heavier.

It is so difficult to put oneself in the place of Tzu Hsi. For me there is no forgetting, ever, that presentation at court. Tzu Hsi, whose day was coming very soon, might almost have been numbered by hours, erect on the throne she had held for her own for almost half a century. There were lines on her old face, for Yung Lu was no more, and Tzu Hsi never was the same after his passing—a little of her, perhaps more than even she herself knew, had gone to the grave with her favorite. Some say that a bit of her mind was missing after that fateful announcement of the death of her favorite.

The mother of the child made her kowtows, wondering perhaps, while she performed them, if the small eunuch held the baby carefully. The small eunuch himself, smiling into the wizened face, and the child, understanding nothing, not sucking a dirty thumb, perhaps, because his swaddling clothes held his tiny hands bound stiffly at his sides. The eunuchs gathered around, with the stern Li Lien Ying, the famous eunuch who many said was not a eunuch, at the shoulder of Her Majesty, where he had stood so many times before to give counsel to Tzu Hsi, who trusted him. Later he betrayed that trust with callous brutality—but that is another story. I was there, too—and it seems like a dream, for I could not see what lay ahead of this Pu Yi, the Boy Emperor of tomorrow. I did not even understand that this presentation was a momentous one, and that I witnessed tragic history in the making.

But I noted the indifference of the Empress Dowager, and it gave me cause to wonder.

The baby, animated by the hands of his mother, awkward in his heavy quiltings, kowtowed senselessly before Her Majesty, who

Tzu Hsi Is Preoccupied

did not seem to see him. Did the mother sense the weird atmosphere? Did she, for even a single moment, see into the future, and vision what it held for her son? I do not think so.

For when she left the presence of Her Majesty, the daughter of Yung Lu was smiling her happiness, as though she and her son had been favored beyond all mortals.

When she left there was changed activity in the court. Eunuchs ran hither and yon on routine business, serving maids continued their labors where their labors took them, Li Lien Ying stepped from behind the shoulder of Her Majesty, and gave swift efficient directions to his underlings, Tzu Hsi herself turned to her court ladies and talked of other things.

Scarcely free of the room of the presentation, little Pu Yi was already forgotten, as though he really didn't matter.

Perhaps he *didn't* matter.

The tragedy of it all is this: that Pu Yi had nothing to say in shaping his destiny. He was a puppet in the hands of inexorable fate, whose instrument was Tzu Hsi, the Dowager Empress.

Old Buddha, I wonder if you knew!

Tzu Hsi, you were the most tragic figure at that presentation!

XLII. THREE YEARS OF RESPITE

For three years there was happiness in the life of Pu Yi, but since they were the first years of his life he does not perhaps recall them. They must have been happy for all that, as the lives of normal children are happy, and his only sorrow in those years must be in the fact that he cannot remember. For three years after his first presentation he lived the life of a normal Manchu child, in the home of his parents. There were doting *amahs* about him always. There was never anything for which he might not wish and have his wish fulfilled. He was a Prince's son, and a Prince's son wanted for nothing. There were always many servants about him, for the home of a Prince was a court in miniature. He played as little children play, once he was released from the bondage of his stuffy swaddling clothes. His hair was done up in little pigtails, and his olive-tinted cheeks appeared as Buddha-like as those of any other Oriental baby.

The Manchus, however, began early the education of their children. They were never allowed to grow as they listed, but were trained as delicate flowers and vines are trained, against the time when they would have need of their knowledge; and their training began almost in the cradle. Pu Yi, for example, though this period is somewhat outside my ken, started to school at about the age of two as do all Manchu children. The school, of course, was not a school in the usual meaning of the word in western countries, for Pu Yi had a tutor, and even at the age of two he was beginning to learn to make Chinese characters, that picture writing which even the adult westerner finds so incomprehensible, so difficult to learn. It can thus be seen that, while knowledge of Chinese characters is not second nature, not instinctive—as people who discover that even rickshaw coolies know many characters may perhaps suspect—it is *almost* second nature, since it is imbibed with the milk from the breast of the mother.

No educated Manchu can remember when his or her education began. And good manners are taught always. The men are taught how to behave, how to walk with decorum, how to meet other men, how, in short, to be Manchu gentlemen; and with their eyes to the future the parents of Manchu men-children begin this training at

Three Years Of Respite

the stage where the children of other races of people spend their time playing in the sand. This must not be taken to mean that there is no playtime for Manchu children, for even to the Manchu all work and no play makes for dull wits.

The Manchu girl is taught to become a good hostess, to know what to do if there seems a possibility that her career will be made at court. She becomes, if she belongs to the nobility, a feminine diplomat. One never knows, you know, to what heights a Manchu lady of the nobility may ascend. Tzu Hsi was the daughter of a Manchu general. She became Secondary Wife of Hsien Feng, and died as Empress Dowager who ruled over four hundred millions of people. All this, of course, before the fateful year of 1911, when the world turned topsy turvy for the Manchus.

But for the three years before the death of Tzu Hsi there were no clouds on the horizon for the Manchu Dynasty. There had been a little cloud in 1900, but the strong will of Tzu Hsi had dispelled it, and it seemed, before the coronation of the Boy Emperor, that the Manchu Dynasty might last forever. Tzu Hsi had unbounded faith in the Dynasty. She believed, or tried to make herself believe, that she would live forever, or that if she did die, her spirit would live on, watching over the Middle Kingdom, guiding its destinies. Probably there were wise men and women who saw the cloud gathering, hut even to them it was no larger than a man's hand. There was nothing in those fateful years before 1911 to indicate that Pu Yi had been born into misfortune, and that the three years of respite were passing all too swiftly.

To the child every day was a new experience, every minute was precious, worthy of being lived to the utmost of a child's capacity. Even his schooling must have been joyous, for all of it was new, and children are born into the world with a curiosity that seems never to be satisfied. To Pu Yi of those three years the sun was; always shining, the songs of birds were music new, strange, and captivating——else Pu Yi had not been a child.

But all the time, behind the curtain which masks the future, that hand-sized cloud was growing, and Pu Yi was moving, at a baby's toddle, through those three years to meet his destiny. When the three years began he was but a child in swaddling clothes; when they were finished he was an Emperor, a creature to be revered the length and breadth of China, yet was too young to comprehend his own importance. He was a figurehead at the end of those three years, but he was an Emperor. I wonder if outlanders can comprehend that statement? Westerners have their gods to worship, their heroes to eulogize. The Chinese—of before 1911—had their Emperor. Even today, here and there in China, are humble folk, those same folk who wear the queue of that aged allegiance, who, if you tell them there is no longer an Emperor, will point to the sun if it he day, to the star-bedecked sky if it be night, and make reply:

"There is no Emperor in China? How absurd! Make me believe such nonsense? Never! Else the sun would not be shining, and the stars of night would fall from their places!"

I fancy, I who am a Manchu, whose people were Manchus for uncounted generations, whose people came to Peking with the first Manchu Emperor—they were of the "Iron Hat" titular class, and their titles were hereditary—that I can see the future Boy Emperor in his home. There was another boy, brother to Pu Yi, in the household of Prince Chun, and to each were assigned *amahs* and serving maids, "boys" and companions. The nursery of Pu Yi and his brother must have been a busy place— where there was always laughter. The common belief that there is no joy in the life of the Oriental, that he never smiles, that his face is perpetually expressionless, is a fallacy. Show me the boy who never smiles or shrieks when something pleases or displeases him! No, Pu Yi was happy—for three brief years—while the cloud which was to overshadow all the years that followed was rolling up, becoming larger and larger, on the horizon of his future.

During this time things were happening at the court. Kwang Hsu, that tragic Emperor who was not an Emperor, save in name, being forever overshadowed by that greatest of China's rulers, Tzu Hsi, was approaching his grave in the cold arms of a slow and deadly illness—concerning which I have written in another place. Tzu Hsi, since that time when he had plotted against his life—for which she would have had him decapitated had he been less than Emperor—had hated Kwang Hsu. Little things, trifling things, occurred to her mind by which she could annoy Kwang Hsu. He was little more than a prisoner in his own palace. An Emperor without an Empire, a nonentity with a name and a body—but not a soul to call his own.

Tzu Hsi herself was aging, when she had thought never to STOW old, to live forever; and odd fancies troubled her after the death of Yung Lu. In distant provinces, perhaps, strong men were already plotting against the time when the Manchus would be overthrown—

These things, which we may merely touch upon here, helped to make larger the cloud that hovered over the destiny of Pu Yi.

But of all this Pu Yi knew nothing.

XLIII. THE DEATH OF KUANG HSU

And now comes the part of this chronicle which I would fain delete, were it not for the fact that I have set myself a task of telling- the truth as I have discovered it. Many stories have been told about the death of Kwang Hsu. I propose now to tell the true one.

Old Buddha, as we have so often seen, bitterly hated Kwang Hsu. She trusted Li Lien Ying as she trusted no other living person, not even excepting Yung Lu. She listened to the advice of Li Lien Ying—and the Pearl Concubine was thrown down a well and a rock dropped upon her head. She listened to Li Lien Ying perpetually, down the years, and made him rich. There is no doubt that Li was faithful to her up to a certain point—that point being exactly where he considered himself still faithful to his own interests.

Old Buddha listened to Li. He was power, grim, ruthless, sinister, behind the throne of Old Buddha, and, preposterous as it may seem, the chief eunuch dreamed of one day being Emperor of China!

This very wish of Li Lien Ying, fostered in his heart of hearts since the year when he had first become Chief Eunuch, probably had much to do with the death of Kwang Hsu, though I make no attempt to minimize the fault of Old Buddha—whom I loved.

Kwang Hsu, on Ying Tai, as related in another place, had begun a diary, in which he related day to day happenings, set down his innermost thoughts. Certain excerpts from this diary came to the attention of Li Lien Ying, and those excerpts were, the gist of them, as follows:

"I am ill, but I feel in my heart that I shall outlive the Old Buddha. In that case, it is decreed that, immediately she is dead, Yuan Shih Kai, the arch-traitor, be decapitated. It is also decreed that, immediately upon the death of Her Majesty, Li Lien Ying be put to death in the same manner."

Now the possible decapitation of Yuan Shih Kai in no wise startled Li Lien Ying. But his own name in the decree, which lacked only date and seal—to be affixed after the death of the Old

The Death of Kwang Hsu

Buddha, who now was well along in years—did startle him somewhat.

Kwang Hsu had been practically a prisoner in his own palace since the *coup d'etat*. He had served first on Ying Tai, and later, when Old Buddha went to the Summer Palace, he was removed to that place, where he was placed in a room in which an inner wall had been built, making of that place a prison house, too. He had been practically a prisoner during the voluntary exile in Shi An.

He was still a prisoner whom Old Buddha, and her eunuch-spies, watched with the eyes of preying hawks.

Li Lien Ying, hearing of this diary, and gleaning his bit of information as to what it, in part at least, contained, straightway carried a tale to Old Buddha. She received the information quietly and her face was like a thunder cloud.

"His Majesty," said the smirking eunuch, "seems to believe that he will outlive the Old Buddha. One wonders if he has reason so to believe! One recalls, with regret, the one time before when he conspired against the life of Her Majesty, and tried to inveigle Yuan Shih Kai into the conspiracy to do away with Your Majesty."

"You think, Li Lien Ying," said Her Majesty, "that this hints at another attempt on his part to take my life?" Li Lien Ying, if I knew him—and none knew him better!—allowed just the proper shade of sadness to show on his ugly face, and made just exactly the right reply to this question.

"What do you suggest?" said the Old Buddha.

"It would be beneficial to all concerned were His Majesty Kwang Hsu to die before Old Buddha."

It was never the policy of the famous eunuch to make direct suggestions. He was the type which believes in veiled hints—not too heavily veiled—and since his hints, down through the years he served at the back of Old Buddha, stood him in such good stead, there might have been something worth learning in his policy, after all.

So Old Buddha, waiting for Li Lien Ying to make the suggestion which he had already made indirectly, waited in vain. Then she took the bit in her teeth and gave the orders for which Li Lien Ying was waiting.

"His Majesty is desperately ill. He has always been ill. He always will be ill. It is in my mind that those to whom we have entrusted the task of preparing his medicine have perhaps been careless, which may account for the fact that he mends so slowly. Hereafter, Li, you will have charge of ministering to Kwang Hsu."

Li Lien Ying needed no more. He at once took charge of the ailing monarch, of his diet and of his medicinal care.

Shortly thereafter Kwang Hsu took to his bed. The care of Li Lien Ying appeared detrimental to him, rather than beneficial; and Kwang Hsu, powerless to do anything about it, knew that he was slowly but surely being poisoned.

Kwang Hsu was sinking so fast that gossip seized upon his strange malady as something very much out of the ordinary, and in order to turn suspicion away from herself, Old Buddha thought it best to call upon Kwang Hsu, to ask after his health.

"It grieves me beyond words," she told him simply, "that you are so ill. I cannot understand why it is your health does not mend, but grows steadily worse."

To which Kwang Hsu replied—well knowing that the cause of his ill health, in the shape of his murderess, stood over him, looking down into his face, unable to mask an expression of satisfaction in the knowledge that Kwang Hsu was dying:

"Your Majesty, I cannot understand it myself, however, Li Lien Ying has always hated me. Li Lien Ying gives me my medicine, and I am becoming steadily worse, as you say."

Old Buddha, still covering herself, though she in no wise hoodwinked Kwang Hsu, sent for the Chief Eunuch.

"What have you been giving His Majesty?" she demanded angrily. "He is becoming more ill as the days pass. It must be your fault! Perhaps you have made errors in mixing his medicines."

And Li Lien Ying, never for a moment allowing a hint of criticism of himself, replied to Old Buddha:

"I did exactly as I was told by Your Majesty. No one thing was done by me save as a result of the Old Buddha's express commands!"

It is odd, if I may be permitted a digression here, that I should recall in this connection a dream which Kwang Hsu had while I myself was at the court of Old Buddha. His Majesty told me this

The Death of Kwang Hsu

dream, and asked me if I did not think it a warning of his approaching doom. In his dream he saw a strange character, like but unlike the Chinese character for "shou" or "long life." It was no character that Kwang Hsu knew, no character that I knew, and there were strange additions too. Kwang Hsu outlined this dream-character on paper for me to examine. Besides the central character already inadequately described, there were clouds above the character, a strange animal to the left of the character, facing it, while a jagged flash of lightning struck at the character from the right.

But to continue. Old Buddha knew, of course, that Kwang Hsu was dying, and tried to place the blame for his death at the door of Li Lien Ying, who would accept none of it—yet Old Buddha did not relieve Li Lien Ying of the duty of caring for the dying monarch, whose life had been so unhappy and difficult.

A eunuch named Chang Teh, who now lives in Tientsin, told me of the death of Kwang Hsu, which took place sometime after I left the court. Chang Teh informed me that the death-chamber was a place of horror.

Li Lien Ying was there, solicitous for the ease and comfort of the dying Kwang Hsu, hovering above him like a bird of ill omen, commiserating with him with his lips, grinning derisively at him with his eyes, but standing there refusing to leave until Kwang Hsu should have gone to whatever reward was his. But though he told Kwang Hsu he was sure that the Emperor would soon be up and around with his health regained, at Old Buddha's orders he caused him to be clothed, hours before his death, while he was still conscious, in the clothing in which he would go to his final resting place!

A place of abysmal terror, the death chamber of Kwang Hsu. The dying monarch, knowing he could blame Li Lien Ying directly for his approaching death, compelled to look up constantly at the savage neuter who but waited, and rather impatiently, for him to die; knowing that somewhere outside that chamber Old Buddha waited, too.

The sister of the Pearl Concubine, that fat sister whom Kwang Hsu had always disliked, came to his bedside before the end. But Kwang Hsu, since she reminded him of the Pearl Concubine, how she had gone very much the same way as he himself was going, refused to look at her.

To his bedside came also the Young Empress, that unhappy colorless wife of his who had been forced upon him by Old Buddha, and whom he had always disliked most intensely—and Kwang Hsu closed his eyes, turned his tortured face to the wall.

Kwang Hsu died in torment.

I dwell upon this terrible incident solely because it has much to do with the appointment of Hsuan Tung— sometimes called Pu Yi, known to the world as the Boy Emperor"—to succeed Kwang Hsu. It was a sort of omen of disaster.

Examining the facts carefully, eager as I am to do Old Buddha full justice, I can find no least excuse for the murder of Kwang Hsu, nor for Old Buddha's almost lifelong mistreatment of him.

But of this thing I am sure: I was with Old Buddha when word was brought to her of the death of Yung Lu, as I relate in another place, and I know that she was never the same after his passing. Something of her soul, of her stout old heart, went to the grave with her staunch favorite—and something of her mind, too. She was very old now, not only because of her years, but because of the countless hardships which she had endured, and probably was often beset by imaginary dangers which warped her judgment, caused her to imagine things which were not true, caused her to believe the whole world in league against her—and to place the blame at the door of Kwang Hsu, who had dared to defy her before the *coup d'etat*.

This is the only excuse I can find for her, and perhaps it is a poor one. In any case, I feel it is time the truth were known however much I may be condemned for telling it—for I am constantly recalling that Old Buddha once said to me:

"I wish you to know the truth about me in order that someday, when you return to that other world which is really yours, you may tell that world the truth—the truth which I have so carefully hidden from the world, especially the world of the foreign barbarians!"

It is difficult for the westerner to grasp the Oriental viewpoint, but I do not recall so much the death of Kwang Hsu, do not recall so much the many horrors perpetrated by Old Buddha, do not so much recall the Boxer Uprising—though my own family was in

The Death of Kwang Hsu

jeopardy in this, being *"er mao tzu"*—as I recall the fact that I knew Her Majesty as a kind old lady, who loved me, and whom I loved—intensely human despite the weight of her many and arduous responsibilities. She was the right person in the right place.

Were she on the throne of China today—

But surmise is futile.

Warning of her own approaching death caused her to make that appointment of an Emperor who was to be the last of a Dynasty, and I dwell at length upon pitiful Pu Yi for that reason.

XLIV. THE OMINOUS PARALLEL

In the latter 60's, when Tzu Hsi was at the very height of her powers, when she held her four hundred millions in the hollow of her capable hands, she firmly believed she would sit forever upon the throne of the Manchus. Because, however, there would not be an Empress Dowager except when there was a minor upon the throne, whose will should be subservient to that of the Queen Mother, Tzu Hsi had named to succeed her the boy Kwang Hsu, and a more unfortunate ruler—save perhaps Pu Yi —never ascended the throne of China or any other country.

She had sent for Kwang Hsu at midnight, and all the omens were against his success, though the Empress Dowager, always a strong believer in the efficacy of signs and portents, picked the date and the hour herself, as she invariably picked the hour and the date for everything which she undertook. It is remarkable, to those who do not understand the Chinese, and what to other people appears to be silly superstition, how a woman who possessed such capabilities, who could rule so long and so successfully a country so vast as China, could be so gullible in the matter of divinations, portents and omens. Yet never a morning dawned that Tzu Hsi did not consult her book of good-and-evil fortune to ascertain whether or not the day was lucky, and whether or not whatever she planned would prosper on that date. Only China really understands these things, for, to the Chinese, divination —or that which we understand as divination—plays an unbelievably important part in the everyday life of the people.

Tzu Hsi, who knew that since the death of her own son her people expected her to name another to succeed him, named Kwang Hsu, who was then a boy of perhaps four years of age. She chose a boy because it would be many years before he could reach the age to rule and she would rule in his stead as Queen Mother.

But she could not make such an appointment, could issue no such decree, until she had consulted the signs which indicated good or bad luck in connection with such an appointment, and she went to the book which dealt with such matters—that book which was as much her Bible as the Old Testament is the law book of the Hebrews.

She wished to know what day and what hour would be lucky for this appointment—

And sent at midnight for Kwang Hsu, to make him Emperor of China!

Details are lacking in connection with the midnight coronation, nor are they germane to this story, except in so far as they show the fateful parallel. Kwang Hsu, the most unfortunate of Emperors, was called to his throne at midnight, and became the Emperor who was an Emperor in name, the figurehead ruler of an Empire which already had a ruler whose will was absolute—Tzu Hsi, the Empress Dowager. Kwang Hsu lived out his reign in sorrow and perpetual unhappiness. About his life weird stories have been told. How many of them were true there is no way of knowing. Kwang Hsu was a strange man, that I know, for I enjoyed the friendship of Kwang Hsu, as far as anyone was able to enjoy the friendship of so strange and unusual a man. Kwang Hsu was a boy whom no one understood, who was reared in the care of eunuchs, the very least of whom regarded him as a nonentity. As a man he was ignored, though he was Emperor. The Empress Dowager disregarded him in her autocratic administration of the affairs of the Empire. She began by disliking Kwang Hsu, the boy, and ended by slaying the man—and between the man and the boy stretched years of misery, misunderstanding, distrust, and hatred. Few people even know, unless they are students of history, that there was an Emperor during the reign of the late Empress Dowager, and that decrees were issued in his name, though he knew nothing of those decrees until, perhaps, long after they had been issued, if at all.

Tzu Hsi, who could not perhaps have explained her aversion to Kwang Hsu, missed no opportunity to treat him spitefully. There were always little ways she could make him feel his unimportance, and she never neglected such an opportunity; and in the latter days of his reign, during the times when custom required him to partake of food from the table of the Queen Mother, he invariably took the first opportunity to dispel the contents of his stomach because he mistrusted the motives of Tzu Hsi, and had no desire, evilly as life had treated him, to pass from it through poisoning. To Kwang Hsu life at court was a never ending horror.

I can well remember Kwang Hsu. He was a weakling, that is true, else he might have accomplished many good things for China. He had brains, but he feared to use them. When the Empress Dowager disposed, Kwang Hsu walked in fear and trembling. He was cowed from the moment he first appreciated the powerful personality of Tzu Hsi, and never was able to conquer his fear of this woman who could be so baleful. His life was a perpetual nightmare. Napoleon on Elba suffered less than Kwang Hsu in his own palace, for even on Elba Napoleon dared to be himself. Kwang Hsu was only a name, though he stands in history as next to the last of the Ching, or Manchu, Emperors.

I can still see the stately, somehow effeminate figure, moving here and there in the palace grounds, interested in nothing, watched over by eunuchs who reported his least activity to Her Majesty, spied upon and maligned by Li Lien Ying, who was his evil genius as far as it lay in the power of any eunuch to be the evil genius of folk at court, in order that that same Li Lien Ying might cement his favor with Her Majesty.

No more unhappy Emperor ever ruled an Empire.

And herein lies the ominous parallel: Tzu Hsi picked the hour and date of the coronation, and sent for Kwang Hsu to make him Emperor of China; Tzu Hsi picked the hour and the date of the coronation of Pu Yi, the last of the Manchus, the Boy Emperor.

And each went forth at midnight to face his evil destiny.

XLV. VIA DOLOROSA

Kwang Hsu, the second of the ill-fated Boy Emperors, Tzu Hsi's own son being the first, died in agony. His deathbed was a place of horror. Tzu Hsi, that enigmatical woman who could be so gentle and so cruel, was at his deathbed, and watched him die. She commiserated with him, and ordered the Imperial Robe to be placed upon his body while yet he lived and understood—understood that his hours were numbered, that this robe was destined to be that in which he should take his last long sleep. Tzu Hsi becomes many times a monster at the deathbed of Kwang Hsu. Kwang Hsu had been poisoned at the "suggestion" of Her Majesty, and the insidious poison was working its terrible will upon the body of this man whom Tzu Hsi had always hated. Tzu Hsi saw the effects of it, for when Kwang Hsu had passed, his abdomen—but let it pass. There is enough of tragedy in the story of Pu Yi, and the tragedy of Kwang Hsu, save as it affects the story of Pu Yi, has no place here.

But the Empress Dowager, wrinkled now with age, soured by hatred that had lasted almost forty years, smiled down upon Kwang Hsu in his bed, expressed her sorrow at his passing—well knowing that her own will had been the cause of that passing, well knowing that Kwang Hsu himself knew that his murderess stood at his bedside, looking calmly down upon his sufferings. Tzu Hsi showed no signs of relenting, did nothing to stay the ravages of the drug, showed no emotion, and when the body of Kwang Hsu, hideous in death, had ceased its convulsive struggles, she strode from the now silent, horror-impregnated chamber of death—

And sent post haste for Pu Yi to set him in the place of Kwang Hsu!

So we too pass from the death chamber of an ill-fated Emperor, and go to the silent home of Prince Chun, where all the lights are out and the household lies asleep, to await with these unconscious ones the arrival of the decree; when all the lights come on again, servants and amahs are wakened and flushed with excitement—and a boy is rudely aroused from the dreamland of happy boyhood, to be told that he is to be placed in a position of untold responsibility, where all China must henceforth do him homage.

Pu Yi awakes, rubs his eyes, and cries because he is sleepy. He does not wish to be an Emperor. He wishes to sleep instead, and regain his dream which, however unhappy it may have been, could never have been as unhappy as the reality which he was compelled against his childish will to face.

"Come, son," said the father, Prince Chun. "Her Majesty has decreed. We must make haste! The Old Lady will wax impatient. Kwang Hsu is dead, and the throne of the Middle Kingdom lacks an Emperor!"

But Pu Yi only wept. What, to him, were power and empire?

Tzu Hsi, however, had spoken, and nothing might be changed, not even by a miracle.

Pu Yi was lifted from his bed by his *amah*, an ancient servant who had served in this same capacity to Prince Chun himself, when Prince Chun had been a child; and though he wept and kicked, they dressed him and made him ready. A lamb to the slaughter—

Pu Yi wept, as I have said, and all the servants muttered. His weeping was an evil omen, they said—and Chinese servants know much of evil omens. They are not clever, they are uneducated, but they are susceptible to intangible, to others incomprehensible, psychical influence. In their heart of hearts they knew, these humble servants who loved Pu Yi, that a sacrifice of a human soul was being offered up—to what? That they could not answer. They only knew what their hearts told them, because their brains were not clever. Foresight, prevision, made them wise—and so they muttered dolefully among themselves as Pu Yi, being made ready, wept and protested. The long, solemn faces of the court eunuchs who had been sent by Her Majesty to help make ready this third Boy Emperor who had been called since Tzu Hsi herself had taken the reins of power, must have made the humble servants, who feared them, think of birds of prey. They were so quiet, so purposeful, so long of face —and Pu Yi, moreover, was weeping.

No wonder they muttered. No wonder they rolled their eyes in fear. No wonder they studied the faces of the eunuchs, seeking for some sign—any sign—that might be construed as hopeful.

Then Pu Yi was escorted from his home, to which he might never return, because he was going away to become Emperor; with the eunuchs about him as bodyguard, with the faithful old *amah* trailing the procession and muttering, shaking her head, with Prince Chun himself cast in the role of Abraham, in the vanguard to deliver up his Isaac to the god of custom.

Even the Heavens declared themselves displeased with this thing which Tzu Hsi had ordered must come to pass. But even the Heavens might not dissuade Tzu Hsi from her course. A premonition perhaps, had Tzu Hsi; for coming events, they say, cast their shadows before—and Tzu Hsi herself would be on her deathbed within hours. There was no slightest hint of this—since she was stricken suddenly—but something must have whispered to Tzu Hsi that her own time was short. So she sent for Pu Yi, and Prince Chun brought to her his eldest son, who had known three years of happiness and of life.

Wind howled and shrieked through the narrow streets of Peking, as though invisible, insane devils danced and, shaking their invisible arms and bodies, made a mock of the midnight procession which wended its way toward the Forbidden City. The wind, ceasing its howling in the lulls, moaned softly, making the marchers think of earthbound souls in torment—as though all these who, down the years, had died in Peking, had come forth to condole with those who were delivering up the boy Pu Yi.

The lights which guided the feet of the procession swayed and danced in the wind, and the marchers bowed their heads to save their faces from the blasts, which seemed determined to drive the procession back whence it came, seeking to divert the offering. Peking dust, that searching stuff which we are told comes on the wings of the wind from Gobi, swirled and cavorted about the slogging feet of the eunuchs, the chair-bearers, the servants, and whistled and whispered around the corners and under the sedan chairs. Like a cloud that blanketed everything, that was the sport of all the winds that blew, but that was never dispersed, the Peking dust almost hid even the moon, which looked like a silver ball with all its natural luster dimmed—to those who believed in the evil of evil omens.

The servants muttered. The eunuchs whispered softly among themselves, their solemn and somewhat brutish faces invisible, save when the dancing lights etched strange expressions on their yellow cheeks.

Pu Yi, too young to know, could not repress his weeping; but the wind bore the sound away, and the dust of Peking muffled it for any who might have heard. The moon rode serenely on, despite the dust which almost hid her face, despite the shrieking and howling of the wind.

The *amah* bearing Pu Yi, wrapped his clothing more closely about him, to protect him from the bitter cold.

So they came to the closed gates of the Forbidden City, of which gates there are three. The center gate is the highest of arch, for the use of the Emperor only; but when he entered Pu Yi was not the Emperor. He entered one of the gates designed for the less than imperial, and the Forbidden City swallowed him. The gate of the Emperor remained closed. It was not for him; but when, if ever, he should return—

They sent word to the Empress Dowager, the Queen Mother, who ordered the eunuchs to make everything ready, to command the attendance of the Imperial Clan, and came herself to make sure that her wishes were carried out.

In the deserted streets of Peking, outside the walls of the Forbidden City, the wind howled and shrieked, the dust of Peking eddied and swirled through every nook and cranny. The night was dark and noisy with mockery—

Pu Yi wept and would not be comforted, and his *amah* was silent with foreboding.

In a matter of minutes Pu Yi would be the nominal ruler of hundreds of millions. In a matter of days the Empress Dowager would be no more, and the last of the Manchus would sit upon a throne that already was tottering.

XLVI. THE CORONATION—AND THE FATEFUL WORDS

Little Pu Yi, so shortly to be the ruler of four hundred million, was smothered in thickness after thickness of clothing. Other clothing, the habiliments of royalty, had been prepared against his arrival in the Forbidden City, for the Empress Dowager, having made her decision, had given orders to the imperial tailors, and Pu Yi was decked at once in the robes of office.

I was not present at this coronation, but there lives today in Tientsin, Chang Teh who, after the death of the Empress Dowager and the betrayal of her confidence by Li Lien Ying, took the place of Li Lien Ying as Chief Eunuch. This creature was present at the coronation, and just a few weeks ago I talked to him of this midnight travesty. What I have to say, then, is based upon my conversation with him, and my knowledge, which was intimate, of Her Majesty Tzu Hsi.

From the moment Pu Yi entered the hall where the coronation took place there was a weird sort of tension in the air; there was none of the suppressed excitement, the pleasurable anticipation which had always attended a coronation—the beginning of the reign of a man who might remake the history of China. There was something in the very atmosphere to which everyone present— and especially the eunuchs, whose feelings were uncanny in such things for some weird reason—reacted after his or her own way. Pu Yi was sleepy and did not wish to don the clothing of his new office, and wept when he was compelled to assume the imperial dress. His *amah* muttered to herself, as she had muttered incessantly since the departure from the home of Prince Chun. Prince Chun was nervous and ill at ease. Even the Empress Dowager, usually the most emotionless of women, was so nervous that she could not occupy her throne, but must needs leave it at intervals to stride, almost manlike, to and fro in the hall of the coronation, her hands opening and closing at her sides, her eyes darting, birdlike, here and there as though she listened to voices no one else could hear.

The Imperial Clan, members of the royal family, stared into the faces of one another, their eyes asking questions which perhaps even the questioners did not understand, nor knew they asked. There was no loud talking. The tension was nerve-racking. Pu Yi wept and fought against the sacrifice, because he had no desire to be Emperor. The eunuchs felt that this coronation was not a real coronation, but a ghastly jest—though perhaps not one of them could have put thoughts into words. They, too, looked into each other's faces—these eunuchs who had witnessed so many things at court, so many things concerning which there is no written record available to the eyes of man. Many of the eunuchs were old—so old that they had witnessed the life of the Empress Dowager almost since the passing of Hsien Feng—and they knew that this coronation was wrong.

To them this ceremony was a mockery, a terrible thing, a thing they would remember with something akin to terror, all their days. The eunuch who now lives at Tientsin—who by the way is worth many millions of *taels* because of emoluments which were his at court—tells me that he knew this coronation was the last he would ever witness, that it was the last coronation of a Manchu, at least within the life span of anyone present at the coronation of Pu Yi. He knew, moreover, and cannot explain how he knew, that the days of Tzu Hsi, who still would rule because Pu Yi was but a child, were numbered. He felt, when he looked at her, noting her nervous pacing up and down, that he looked upon the person of a human being who would soon be dead.

It is strange beyond comprehension how eunuchs know these things. I do not pretend to understand it. The eunuchs themselves do not know. They are ignorant, for the most part, being endowed with instinct and superstition in place of intelligence; but that they sense many things which affect normal beings not at all, I am quite sure. Nor am I able even to give you a hint into this strange fact, for to the outlander a eunuch is a monstrosity, which is quite true. People who know nothing of courts where there are eunuchs cannot possibly understand, and even people at those courts do not understand. It is just one of those incomprehensible things that are.

But though the boy Pu Yi kicked and fought against the ascension, they placed the emblem of authority upon his head, seated him upon the throne, and bowed down, making their kowtows, to do him honor. Even his father kowtowed, for now the

The Coronation and the Fateful Words

son was Emperor, the father only a Prince. The ceremony was almost completed, and it had been difficult, because Pu Yi had hated the whole proceedings, from beginning to end, from the awakening in his father's house to the reception of the crown. It had been his father whose will had compassed the ceremony at all, for the father had kept repeating, as he urged Pu Yi, now known as Hsuan Tung, to act less the boy and more the Emperor, those words which they who attended the ceremony believe now to have prophesied the fall of the Manchus.

"It will all soon be over, son!"

It will all soon be over!

And it was. Three years later the boy who had ascended the throne left it at night—as though to fulfill his father's prophecy.

But then no one knew—anything—save that a new Emperor had been crowned and that the emblem of supreme authority rested upon the head of a mere child.

A few days later, with the Empress Dowager breathing her last, the Chinese Empire turned topsy turvy, and the cloud on the horizon of the Boy Emperor's destiny swept into view, growing as it came, until all the world saw it and understood its meaning—all the world, that is, save Pu Yi, who, though naturally the most interested, cared the least what might befall.

XLVII THE PASSING OF TZU HSI

After the death of Kwang Hsu the Empress Dowager walked in fear and trembling. Ugly whispers went here and there in the Forbidden City, and some of these whispers reached the world outside, and their content was discussed in diplomatic circles everywhere in Peking. Diplomatic Peking, all the world for the matter of that, had known of the hatred of Tzu Hsi for Kwang Hsu; for the tale of the forced abdication, or what amounted to abdication, of Kwang Hsu in 1898 was public property.

The world knew nothing, save such as it could gleam from illusive rumors, coming from none knew where, started by none knew whom, of the love of Yung Lu and Tzu Hsi; but that Tzu Hsi was never the same after his passing everybody at court was well aware. Tzu Hsi, who had ruled her four hundred millions for half a century was losing her grip. Her nerve, hitherto as strong as that of any Manchu ruler of the past, had broken.

Enter that baleful personality, that brutish power behind the throne—Li Lien Ying, "cobbler's wax" Li—to hasten the dissolution of a mighty power by a worse- than-Judas-like betrayal. Li Lien Ying, that Chief Eunuch who was more famous, greater in many ways, than An Teh Hai, whom he succeeded. Li Lien Ying, the fiend incarnate, who possessed neither heart nor soul if we may judge him by what he did.

Li Lien Ying heard the whispers, if whispers there were which seems probable, since the "diplomats" were often unduly interested in affairs at court, affairs which concerned them not at all, whether or not they personally approved and took them to the already sorely tried Tzu Hsi.

"The Legations are whispering among themselves, Your Majesty," he said. "They are wondering about Kwang Hsu, what manner of death he died."

Tzu Hsi heard, and something snapped within her brain. She turned to Li, staring at the ugly face of the eunuch in abject fear. Her lips moved as she strove to speak the fears to which she was prey—trying to give those fears a name, trying to find in his face some indication that what he said was not true, though there never lived a eunuch who dared to jest with Old Buddha. But with

The Passing of Tzu Hsi

whatever words she might have spoken dying upon her lips, Tzu Hsi swayed—and fell as an aged tree falls.

Sorely stricken was Tzu Hsi. She was borne to the bed which she never left again, and from which she gave certain last orders in badly articulated words—badly articulated because she had almost lost her voice through the sudden paralysis that had closed icy fingers about her stout old heart. Li Lien Ying must have smiled to himself at the success of his words. Li Lien Ying must have foreseen the end of the Dynasty which had made him many, many times a millionaire, and he was thus eager to make an end and secure for himself whatever he could from the wreckage. Tzu Hsi was losing her grip. There was little more she could do for her favorite eunuch, and Li Lien Ying knew it.

Tzu Hsi took to her bed.

Tzu Hsi, just before her passing, sent for "cobbler's wax" Li. It is believed that she wished to warn him of the end and that, with her passing, he would be beset by enemies. He had no friend at court, save only Tzu Hsi herself, and had wanted no other. And Tzu Hsi was passing. The eunuch of Tientsin, who became Chief Eunuch to Pu Yi, or rather to the new Empress Dowager, known during the latter years of Tzu Hsi as the Young Empress, assures me that Old Buddha wished to give a last warning to Li Lien Ying, wished before the end, to do something for the creature she had trusted. But Li Lien Ying, knowing that Tzu Hsi was now without power, refused to go to her on her deathbed, and the words, he spoke in his refusal were the words of that hypocrite all the court knew the famous eunuch to be.

"I worshiped Her Majesty during her lifetime, and it is as she was that I wish to remember her. I cannot bear to gaze upon her last suffering. I cannot go!"

What Tzu Hsi thought will never be known, for she died without speaking after the word came—

And the pall of death, ever funereal, ever terrible to those to whom life is precious, settled over the Forbidden City. Eunuchs walked in silence, with bowed heads— all save Li Lien Ying who, when they went to tell him, could not be found. He was never seen again inside the Forbidden City. This monster, whose head on a paling in a public place would have delighted all China, died a natural death years later in Peking, still with his talon like hands clasped about the millions Tzu Hsi's bounty, and his own grasping dishonesty, had placed within his clutches. One wonders what thoughts were Li's in his last hours; but he told those thoughts to no one, because he had no man, nor woman, to call friend.

Serving maids moved on tiptoe in the Forbidden City after the death of Old Buddha, whose voice had so long been heard from the seat of the mighty. Folk who feared her in life, now that she was dead, caught themselves stealing startled glances right and left as they walked, or went about their labors, half expecting to hear that voice again and to witness the approach of the stately old lady whose voice would be heard no more—whose spirit, they firmly believed, would hover forever over the country which had known her so well.

The Tientsin eunuch was at her bedside when she passed, and from him I got a picture of a subdued chamber where few lights were, where words that were spoken were whispered, where candles flickered softly in such breezes as there were, where the wrinkled face of Her Majesty, calm now in the greater majesty of death, awaited the day when she would be carried forth to her last resting place in Hsi Ling. That she had known life, that her life had been lived to the full, was evident in her tired old face. Such sorrow as she had known had been swept from those wan cheeks. She had forgotten the betrayal of the eunuch who had played Judas when she needed him.

A raised bed in a chamber which none save the Imperial Clan dare visit. Flickering candles which wrought odd shadows on the walls, and on the cheeks of Her Majesty. In fancy I can see her there, and the picture is very plain, for I knew her, remember, and loved her. To others she may have been cruel. To me she was a kind old lady who needed understanding, but who never got it because she was too proud to disclose that part of her I knew reposed behind the imperial mask of custom.

In a way, I suppose, she died happy, for during her life there was never a wish denied her. What she wanted she received. What was denied her she took if she desired.

She knew the end was coming. She had sent for Pu Yi. Pu Yi had been made Emperor.

And when she breathed her last it was with the knowledge that the Emperor of her choosing sat upon the throne of the Manchus.

True to herself to the very last, this greatest of the Manchus went toward the Door by which there is no return, and fear of what might he beyond it was not in her.

For Pu Yi her passing was the beginning of the end.

XLVIII. THE COURT OF UNHAPPINESS

And so Pu Yi became Emperor, one of the most unhappy Emperors of the Manchu Dynasty, with the possible exception of Kwang Hsu. The lady who was known as the Young Empress, wife to the dead Kwang Hsu, became Empress Dowager after the passing of Tzu Hsi. Prince Chun, father of Pu Yi, became Prince Regent, and was the virtual ruler of China. The life of the Young Empress had been so unhappy during the life of Tzu Hsi— partly because she feared Tzu Hsi all her days, partly because her husband, Kwang Hsu, would have none of her—that after she became Empress Dowager she would have nothing to do with affairs of state but turned her attention to pleasurable things which had hitherto been denied her. During her regime theatres prospered in the Forbidden City and the Summer Palace, and the time of the Empress Dowager was a period of indifference to matters of state.

The Young Empress was the niece of Tzu Hsi, and was appointed by her to be Empress Dowager because of the family connection, in order that a relative of Tzu Hsi should continue in power. Tzu Hsi, perhaps, felt that even after her death it would be a great thing for her family to hold the reins of the ruler. It would seem, then, that the Empress Dowager, the successor to Tzu Hsi, would have had the most to say in the training of

Pu Yi in the way he should go—but with sometimes characteristic lack of foresight, Tzu Hsi had managed to so tangle things that there was constant discord, and perpetual unhappiness for Pu Yi. Kwang Hsu's concubine —sister of the Pearl Concubine—also arrogated to herself certain responsibilities in the matter of the boy Pu Yi. To add to these conflicts, while she had named the Young Empress to be Empress Dowager after her own passing, Tzu Hsi had also made Pu Yi the adopted son of her own dead son, Tung Chih. Two of Tung Chih's concubines were still living after the death of Tzu Hsi, and these two concubines likewise assumed responsibility in the affairs of Pu Yi. Pu Yi was therefore ruled by four women— no pleasant thing for a boy of three or four to experience! The Young Empress, now Empress Dowager, might tell Pu Yi that he was permitted by custom to do this and so, while one or both of the two concubines of Tung Chih

The Court Of Unhappiness

might a moment afterward inform him that his instructions from the Empress Dowager were all wrong and that the way he should conduct himself, was this way or that— while the fourth woman who believed herself divinely appointed to guide the faltering footsteps of Pu Yi felt absolutely certain that the other three were ruining the career of the Boy Emperor.

Was Pu Yi happy? Impossible! Pu Yi, moreover, just because he was Emperor, was not exempt from the arduous studies to which the well-born Chinese and Manchu children were heir. No outlander can comprehend the rigor of a Chinese scholastic course. Take my own case as an example: I began to learn Chinese classics at the age of four, a year later than is usual with Manchu children. When you realize that it takes nineteen years of most exacting study to pass the examination in Chinese classics—few foreigners ever master them—you can understand something of what lay before Pu Yi. He had several tutors. To begin with, he was given a certain example to follow. I don't know what particular Emperor of the past was set up as an example for Pu Yi, It might have been Chien Lung, or Hsien Feng, but whichever, if either, it was, Pu Yi was always deterred in whatever he might have undertaken on his own account by some warning from one or the other of his tutors.

"Chien Lung would never have thought of doing that!" Or "Hsien Feng would never have done this, Your Majesty!"

Pu Yi might be Chien Lung or Hsien Feng in practice; he might never be just the boy, Pu Yi. Certainly he must have found this business of aping an Emperor dead, gone —but not forgotten— trying indeed. He most certainly must have grown to hate the name of his dead preceptor, but if lie did lie kept his hatred secret, in order to keep his tutors quiet. Tutors, moreover, of Manchu or Chinese children were never allowed to praise their students. No matter how well those children might acquit themselves, the best they could hope for from their tutors was something like this:

HER MAJESTY TZU HSI ASSISTED DOWN PEONY HILL BY COURT EUNUCHS, THE AUTHOR ON RIGHT

The Court Of Unhappiness

TUNG LING, THE LAST RESTING PLACE OF THE OLD BUDDHA

"Yes, that was fairly well done; but Your Majesty should be able to do so much better. Hsien Feng was far wiser, much more clever, at your age!"

For Pu Yi, as you will recall, there was, besides his tutors, an added trial—four of them to be exact—in the- four women who wished to rule him, and these four took up the cue where the tutors dropped it. Verily, Pu Yi must have dreamed nightmares in which the figures of dead and gone Emperors, carping tutors, and the indefatigable four women, must have been chaotically blended into an organization built up for the sole purpose of proving to him that his soul wasn't and never could be his own. His nightmare figures must have perched on the foot of his bed, and pointed accusing fingers at him even while he slept.

Besides the four women there was also the father, Prince Chun, who was Prince Regent, and by the very nature of things, because of the custom which dictated the conduct of the Prince Regent toward the Emperor, Prince Chun must also have had a hand in removing from the life of Pu Yi such happiness as might possibly have remained to him after his tutors, the four ambitious women, and his dead preceptors had finished with him for the day.

A court of perpetual unhappiness. That the unhappiness at the court should affect the subjects of the Boy Emperor was a foregone conclusion, for the court was the pulse of the nation. I spent almost three years at the court myself, and I am quite sure that not one person there was happy. I say this advisedly, and from an intimate knowledge of the people who lived the life. I enjoyed court life, for a time at least, because I was a mere child, with all the curiosity of a child, and was not a little proud of the honors which became mine at an age when young ladies in other countries were in school, with nothing save their studies to worry them. That I left court before unhappiness settled upon my own life was a fortunate circumstance. It helped me to retain a few of my illusions. But where others at court were concerned—!

Kwang Hsu was unhappy "because he hated and feared the Empress Dowager, and was a prisoner, empty of all hope, in his own palace. The Young Empress was unhappy because Kwang Hsu, her royal husband, took never a bit of notice of her. She was wife in name only, and could never be more. Even on his deathbed,

The Court Of Unhappiness

Kwang Hsu refused to look at the Young Empress. Kwang Hsu's concubine, she who after his death laid claim to voice in the affairs of Pu Yi, was unhappy because her lord and master hated her. The court ladies were unhappy because they were literally slaves to the whims of Tzu Hsi, who was the most exacting of women. If they displeased her she made them feel the weight of her anger, and even when they pleased her they realized that her pleasure was ephemeral, and that a moment later they might offend her to their own undoing. The eunuchs, from the highest to the lowest, were unhappy because all the emoluments which were theirs could not buy them the normal pleasures to which mankind is heir. Li Lien Ying, the most famous of them all, knew himself the power behind the throne; but his greatest unhappiness in life lay in the fact that he could never realize his maddest ambition—which was to rule China as her Emperor! A mad ambition, true enough, but there was no limit to the aspirations of "cobbler's wax" Li, and because realization might never come, Li Lien Ying was unhappy.

But perhaps the unhappiest of all in the Manchu court was Her Majesty herself, Tzu Hsi, who, though she ruled China for half a century, could never have that which must have nested nearest her heart—her lover Yung Lu, that most faithful of men, that great lover who was great in his perpetual renunciation, whose greatest ambition, since he might not have Tzu Hsi, was to serve her. That he was thus allowed to serve may have given him a modicum of happiness, yet that he could have been entirely happy seems beyond the bounds of reason.

They were slaves to custom, these people who "enjoyed" the court life of China, and even the Empress Dowager could not do exactly as she wished—mostly because her pride forbade doing things for which she might be criticized.

This unhappiness, which had been born with the Dynasty, which would not die with it because the royal family would live on after the Fall, this unhappiness which had grown through the ages, feeding upon itself, was the dubious heritage of the boy Pu Yi.

Let folk who envy those who sit in high places consider this man, the last of the Manchus, ere they desire themselves to aspire to a place of power and prominence—for possession of such grandeur is not worth the price.

And Pu Yi himself, a private citizen of China, now living in Tientsin, would be the first to raise his voice in affirmation if he spoke as he believed!

But even now, when there is no longer a throne in China, the old shibboleths would perhaps hold mute the tongue of the Boy Emperor—for he is still an Emperor, though he rules no Empire, and not easily is age-old custom disregarded.

XLIX. PU YI PASSES

But the cloud which had been gathering for uncounted years had grown to widely visible proportions. No one, save perhaps the court itself, could mistake the fact that the Manchu Dynasty was doomed. Inside the court, which was a little world in itself, and to which news from beyond the walls came as news from a foreign country, no credence was placed in persistent rumors of rebellion. Of all the folk at court only Prince Ching, the Grand Councillor, really made sure that the end was not far off. But when he tried to tell his fellows his words were derisively received. Highly placed Manchu officials, always in the midst of lavish entertainments given for their friends, pooh-poohed the tales of insurrections, laughed at the reported success of the rebellion. They could not be convinced.

City after city fell into the hands of the revolutionists. City after city was evacuated by the Manchu soldiery. Officials who for years had pretended friendliness to the Manchus went over to the revolution. Sun Yat-sen preached his sermons of violence, and the Manchu dragon withdrew day by day the deeper into himself. The Manchus contested every foot of the way. Not lightly would they relinquish their hold upon a country which, for two hundred and sixty-seven years, they had held in the hollow of their hands.

But as time passed, with the flame of rebellion growing with all the speed of a forest fire, sweeping all opposition from its path, the time came when the Manchus were compelled to face the truth. Manchu blood stained the dusty streets of a hundred cities, as the alien rulers of China fought to maintain foothold, and paid for their temerity at the point of revolutionary bayonets, or gave their lives to the bullets of the Republican fanatics. By scores, hundreds, and thousands, they fell before the resistless tide of the rebellion. Manchu women were ravished by barefoot soldiery—soldiery which had never, a few months before, dared to raise its eyes so high, soldiery to whom Manchu women had been little less than divine, absolutely unattainable for love or price. Wells were clogged with the bodies of Manchu suicides.

Even the Empress Dowager, known as the Young Empress during the regime of Tzu Hsi, tried to commit suicide, believing herself responsible for the catastrophe, and unable to stand the disgrace of being the ruler during the downfall. She was prevented from taking this drastic step—and lived to die broken-hearted two years after the fall had passed into history as one of the most astounding things that had ever happened in the history of China. China a Republic? Impossible! Yet the fact remained. Since the dawn of history China had worshiped at the feet of Emperors, Empresses, Empress Dowagers—and she could no more change so easily now than a leopard could change its spots! Yet change she did—and even on her deathbed it is probable that the last Empress Dowager half believed she had dreamed the catastrophe.

Eunuchs who had served Pu Yi and his people faithfully fled from the sinking ship. The court began to crumble. It would have taken the hand of a Tzu Hsi to save the Manchu Dynasty from the wreckage—and even she perhaps might only have prolonged the inevitable. She had left the court in a tangle, and the tangle could not he unsnarled in time. There had been ample time to foresee what was coming. Kwang Hsu had seen it coming, and had striven for reform as best he could. But what could be done by a prisoner Emperor, whose law was the word of an Empress Dowager who believed solely in her divine right to do exactly as she pleased? Had the *coup d'etat* failed there might have been another ending to the Revolution, for Kwang Hsu was a man of parts. He might have done great things for China, had he been permitted to do so. But he conspired against Tzu Hsi and was deposed by her—and ever afterward was a figurehead.

It is useless to guess what might have transpired had things been otherwise than they actually were. For the fact remains that the Manchus fell.

And on February 12, 1912, the Empress Dowager, in the name of herself and the Emperor—the boy Pu Yi— signed the decree of abdication.

With the fateful words of the decree Pu Yi ceased to be the ruler of an Empire, and became a citizen of that Empire—an Emperor without a throne.

And as the curtain fell, and the Republic came in, Pu Yi, the Boy Emperor, still a mere child, passed from the stage to return no more—the last and most pathetic of the Manchus.

L. CONCLUSION

Today in China there are aged folk who wear the queue of an ancient and hallowed allegiance. To these pitiful ones Old Buddha still lives. She has only gone for a time, hut she knows cdl things that transpire in China. Her spirit, against her inevitable return, hovers forever over the Forbidden City, and though centuries come and go, though the Forbidden City fall into ruins, and the Great Wall crumble stone by stone, Old Buddha keeps watch and ward over the Middle Kingdom.

She is there, on the ghost of the throne she once occupied, and her eyes are sad as she looks down upon the chaos which today is China, as she sees ambitious coolies enthroned on the seats of the mighty who have fallen, as she listens to the monotonous footfalls of grey-clad soldiers who ceaselessly march and countermarch across the vast domain which once was hers.

As she sits on this aerial throne of hers there is nothing she can do. She may only hope against hope for resurrection or reincarnation, and eat her suffering heart out with remorse. If she might live her life over again she might live it differently, but we may never know. We may only surmise. Old Buddha was stubborn. She was China's greatest woman.

I thoroughly believe that Old Buddha does watch over the country she once ruled, for that she would so watch, after death had claimed her, she herself most firmly believed.

The sadness in this whimsy lies in the fact that she may only watch, and wait, earthbound; but that she may never return in the flesh to relieve the least of China's sufferings.

For those who believe in these fancies, who feel that life somehow cheated Old Buddha of those things which the world of men, and of women, hold so dear, there is consolation in the fact—perhaps—that Yung Lu, the faithful slave and vassal of Her Majesty, waits with her there, somewhere behind Death's impenetrable Curtain—and that the lovers have been united at last, for all eternity!

THE END

www.ingramcontent.com/pod-product-compliance
Lightning Source LLC
Chambersburg PA
CBHW071559080526
44588CB00010B/960